MW01087724

Global Policymaking

This book analyzes the politics of global governance by looking at how global policymaking actually works. It provides a comprehensive theoretical and methodological framework which is systematically applied to the study of three global policies drawn from recent UN activities: the adoption of the Sustainable Development Goals in 2015, the institutionalization of the Human Rights Council from 2005 onward, and the ongoing promotion of the protection of civilians in peace operations. By unpacking the practices and the values that have prevailed in these three cases, the authors demonstrate how global policymaking forms a patchwork pervaded by improvisation and social conflict. They also show how global governance embodies a particular vision of the common good at the expense of alternative perspectives. The book will appeal to students and scholars of global governance, international organizations, and global policy studies.

VINCENT POULIOT specializes in the study of global governance, specifically the politics of multilateral diplomacy, changing and hybrid practices, and global history. He has authored or coedited six books with Cambridge University Press, including *International Pecking Orders* (2016), *Diplomacy and the Making of World Politics* (2015), and *International Practices* (2011).

JEAN-PHILIPPE THÉRIEN'S work focuses on international organizations and global governance. He has published widely on the United Nations, North–South relations, global ideologies, and the inter-American system. He is the coauthor of *Left and Right in Global Politics* (Cambridge University Press, 2008) and the coeditor of *Summits and Regional Governance* (2016).

Cambridge Studies in International Relations: 162

Global Policymaking

EDITORS

Evelyn Goh
Christian Reus-Smit
Nicholas J. Wheeler

Cambridge Studies in International Relations is a joint initiative of Cambridge
University Press and the British International Studies Association (BISA). The
series aims to publish the best new scholarship in international studies, irre-
spective of subject matter, methodological approach or theoretical perspective.
The series seeks to bring the latest theoretical work in International Relations
to bear on the most important problems and issues in global politics.

Other titles in the series are listed at the back of the book.

Global Policymaking

The Patchwork of Global Governance

VINCENT POULIOT
McGill University

JEAN-PHILIPPE THÉRIEN
Université de Montréal

CAMBRIDGE
UNIVERSITY PRESS

Shaftesbury Road, Cambridge CB2 8EA, United Kingdom

One Liberty Plaza, 20th Floor, New York, NY 10006, USA

477 Williamstown Road, Port Melbourne, VIC 3207, Australia

314–321, 3rd Floor, Plot 3, Splendor Forum, Jasola District Centre, New Delhi – 110025, India

103 Penang Road, #05-06/07, Visioncrest Commercial, Singapore 238467

Cambridge University Press is part of Cambridge University Press & Assessment, a department of the University of Cambridge.

We share the University's mission to contribute to society through the pursuit of education, learning and research at the highest international levels of excellence.

www.cambridge.org
Information on this title: www.cambridge.org/9781009344951

DOI: 10.1017/9781009344999

First published 2023

A catalogue record for this publication is available from the British Library

A Cataloging-in-Publication data record for this book is available from the Library of Congress

ISBN 978-1-009-34495-1 Hardback
ISBN 978-1-009-34496-8 Paperback

Cambridge University Press & Assessment has no responsibility for the persistence or accuracy of URLs for external or third-party internet websites referred to in this publication and does not guarantee that any content on such websites is, or will remain, accurate or appropriate.

Contents

Figures

Tables

Preface

Global governance is paradoxical. It impacts everyone, everywhere, and all the time, yet nobody really knows where to look for it, or how to "grasp" it. Puzzled by this evanescence, we have written a book that seeks to open new avenues for research by asking a surprisingly simple question: How does global governance actually work?

Our combined decades of investigating global governance have left us with the same feeling that the six blind men have in the famous Indian tale when discovering an elephant by touch. Innumerable scholars have approached global governance in terms of, alternatively, actors, institutions, power, regimes, networks, practices, norms, ideas, modes, and so on. While each of these angles has obvious analytical value, they provide only a partial take on the broader phenomenon at work. As the blind men do, many an observer ends up mistaking the elephant of global governance for its limber trunk (is it a snake?), pointed tusk (a spear?), large leg (a cow?), giant ear (a carpet?), or coarse tail (a rope?). While the quest for a silver bullet would obviously be vain, we have striven to find and develop the most encompassing grasp of global governance politics possible – intrinsically imperfect as it may remain.

We claim that the best view on global governance is provided by the concept of global policymaking. We argue that global policymaking is the engine, or core, of global governance, and that focusing on *policymaking* is the most heuristic road to elucidate the *politics* of global governance.

Our approach is founded on the relentless extension of global policies in all spheres of human activity. As contemporary textbooks of international relations explain, global policymakers include international organizations such as the United Nations, the International Monetary Fund, and the World Trade Organization as well as global corporations such as Meta Platforms (Facebook) and Huawei, and large nongovernmental organizations such as OXFAM and Amnesty International. But more fundamentally, it should be added that global policies have to do with war and peace, trade, human rights, health, and the environment among other existential issues. Every time you use your cellphone or surf the Internet, you are subject to a global telecommunications policy.

Not surprisingly, social scientists recognize the importance of global policies more and more. According to Google Scholar, between 2000 and 2020, references to "global policy" have increased more than tenfold. Given that the focus on global policymaking is here to stay, it is time for global governance students to pay more attention to it.

Convinced that global governance is an unscripted process whose future remains open, we argue that global policies can be understood as patchworks. To describe these patchworks, we use the French term "bricolage," which emphasizes the haphazard nature of global policymaking. As the book develops in detail, the bricolage of global policies rests on a complex mix of material and ideological components that we account for as practices and values.

We have tried to strike a balance between the theoretical, empirical, and methodological dimensions of our work. Theoretically, the book offers a critical reflection on the notions of global governance and global policy. Empirically, it documents three in-depth case studies that illustrate the crucial role of the United Nations as a global policymaking site in the fields of development, human rights, and security. And methodologically, the book seeks to be as pedagogical and systematic as possible in its demonstration, so that students and actors of global governance may apply our portable framework to as many cases of global policymaking as there exist. We sincerely hope that this threefold theoretical, empirical, and methodological effort will meet the different needs of scholars and (future) practitioners.

Over the years, this book project has benefited from the advice of many colleagues and friends. We are especially grateful to Michael Barnett, Laurie Beaudonnet, Christian Bueger, Alain Noël, Denis Saint-Martin, Jan Aart Scholte, Jens Steffek, Jennifer Welsh, and Michael Zürn. Between 2016 and 2021, our work was presented at several meetings of the International Studies Association and the Academic Council of the United Nations System, as well as at seminars at the University of Copenhagen and the University of Munich. The feedback we received on each of these occasions was extremely helpful in clarifying our argument and our own thinking.

Writing a book is a collective journey. Along the way, we benefited from the help of remarkably talented research assistants, namely, Simon Bertrand, Junru Bian, Émile Boucher, Alice Chessé, Nina Jaffe-Geffner, Zaheed Kara, Félix Larose-Tarabulsy, Brendon Novel, and Lou Pingeot. For their educated feedback, pointed questions, and constructive criticisms, we also thank the few dozen students who took the McGill honours seminar built around this research project as we were conducting it. Graduate students who attended the seminar on international organizations at the Université de Montréal similarly helped sharpen our views on global governance. Copyeditor Ryan Perks provided invaluable advice to make our prose more fluid. And the Social Sciences and Humanities Research Council of Canada offered us generous financial support for which we are deeply appreciative.

Earlier versions of our work have appeared in *Global Policy* and *International Studies Review* (Chapter 2) as well as in *Review of International Political Economy* (Chapter 3). We thank the editors and reviewers of these journals for their very helpful feedback. We also thank their publishers for giving us the permission to use some of that material. Finally, we are grateful to the anonymous reviewers of Cambridge University Press, who provided thorough and constructive comments on our manuscript, as well as to John Haslam for his unflagging support.

Our greatest thanks go to our families, especially our children Colin, Laurent, and Mathilde, who have helped us find the stamina to bring this book project to its end.

Most of the thinking that went into this book occurred to us while sitting together at one of the many picnic tables spread around beautiful Parc Lafontaine in Montréal. We dedicate the outcome of these sunny afternoons to the local bands of squirrels for their amazing intelligence in mapping their own world.

Abbreviations

CARICOM	Caribbean Community
CBDR	common but differentiated responsibilities
CHR	Commission on Human Rights
C34	Special Committee on Peacekeeping Operations
DFS	Department of Field Support
DPKO	Department of Peacekeeping Operations
DPO	Department of Peace Operations
DRC	Democratic Republic of the Congo
ECOSOC	Economic and Social Council
E10	the ten elected members of the Security Council
FIB	Force Intervention Brigade
GAVI	Global Alliance for Vaccines and Immunization
HIPPO	High-Level Panel on Peace Operations
HLP	High-Level Panel of Eminent Persons on the Post-2015 Development Agenda
HRC	Human Rights Council
IAEG-SDGs	Inter-Agency Expert Group on SDG Indicators
ICRC	International Committee of the Red Cross
IEAG	Independent Expert Advisory Group on a Data Revolution for Sustainable Development
IGN	Intergovernmental Negotiations on the Post-2015 Development Agenda
IGO	intergovernmental organization
ILO	International Labour Organization
IMF	International Monetary Fund

IO	international organization
IR	international relations
LDCs	least developed countries
MDGs	Millennium Development Goals
MSF	Médecins Sans Frontières
NGO	nongovernmental organization
OCHA	Office for the Coordination of Humanitarian Affairs
OECD	Organisation for Economic Co-operation and Development
OHCHR	Office of the United Nations High Commissioner for Human Rights
OIOS	Office of Internal Oversight Services
OWG	General Assembly Open Working Group
PoC	Protection of Civilians doctrine
PPP	public–private partnerships
P3	France–UK–US group within the Security Council
P5	the five permanent members of the Security Council
R2P	Responsibility to Protect
SDGs	Sustainable Development Goals
SDSN	Sustainable Development Solutions Network
SIDS	Small Island Developing States
TCC	troop-contributing countries
TST	Technical Support Team
UfC	Uniting for Consensus
UN	United Nations
UNDG	United Nations Development Group
UNDP	United Nations Development Program
UPR	universal periodic review
WTO	World Trade Organization

Introduction
The Politics of Global Governance

Global governance remains a mystery because so much about global society itself eludes our grasp. Everywhere we can see the impact of things global, foreign, far away. How does it all work, how do all the pieces fit together? How is public power exercised, where are the levers, who are the authorities, how do they relate to one another?[1]

In today's world, few aspects of our lives escape the purview of global governance. Whether one thinks of the COVID-19 pandemic, stark socioeconomic inequalities within and between countries, accelerating climate change, massive population movements, economic crises spilling over borders, multiplying technical standards for the circulation of goods and services, or the development of human rights and labor norms, the number of issues that are of direct concern to private citizens worldwide, and yet get handled to a significant extent at the global level, grows almost by the day. The late John Ruggie, using Easton's famous definition of politics, sums up this political transformation as follows: "The arena in which 'the authoritative allocation of values in societies' now takes place increasingly reaches beyond the confines of national boundaries."[2]

This book seeks to understand how the expanding global governance process actually works. In recent years, research on global governance has become something of a cottage industry within the wider discipline of International Relations (IR), to the point that the concept now imposes itself as "one of the central orienting themes in the practice and study of international affairs."[3] Conventional wisdom suggests that, as new problems of a transboundary nature surface, politics ought to scale up as well, "beyond the state," so to speak, to include a whole new cast of transnational private actors. And yet, from a political perspective, we must bear in mind that this development is

---

[1] Kennedy 2008, 827.　　[2] Ruggie 2004, 521.　　[3] Barnett and Duvall 2005, 1.

1

neither natural nor inevitable, and that history is not, in and of itself, "efficient."[4] In this context, reducing the ongoing expansion of global governance to a functional response would be quite shortsighted. As Avant et al. put it, "knowing global needs is rarely enough to explain how and why a particular governance outcome was chosen."[5]

In contrast to a sizeable portion of existing literature, we set out from the premise that global governance results from a collective "muddling through,"[6] involves normative cleavages and power struggles, and plays out on a staunchly unequal playing field. The concern for efficiency in the delivery of so-called global public goods certainly matters, as many rationalist theories would have it, but the global governing process is nevertheless fraught with politics, the logics of which largely depart from the process's institutional design. In the background, it also needs to be recognized that the governance of global change is inextricably bound up with the legacies of Western hegemony, capitalist modes of production, inequality, and hierarchical rule. Making sense of these politics thus requires that we accept, from the get-go, that global governance is neither good nor bad, but highly significant and salient in its effects. It is yet another political development in the history of humankind – perhaps the most pressing one for coming generations – and grasping its politics is therefore all the more urgent.

The phenomenon of global governance is not exactly new, even though the term itself was coined only relatively recently. Born in the mid-1990s at the frontier of policymaking[7] and academia,[8] it describes a set of political processes that have arguably been on the move for at least 200 years. To be sure, social scientists did not create global governance; politicians, diplomats, industrialists, bankers, and activists did. A bit like the processes of globalization, which started long before scholars named them as such, the idea of governing the world – what Mazower calls "the mystique of global governance"[9] – has a relatively established pedigree. Already in the nineteenth century, heads of states and princes of all stripes were coming together to manage their joint affairs through the Concert of Europe.[10] The simultaneous rise and spread of industrial capitalism led to the creation of a variety of

---

[4] March and Olsen 1998.   [5] Avant, Finnemore, and Sell 2010b, 1.
[6] Lindblom 1959.   [7] Commission on Global Governance 1995.
[8] Rosenau and Czempiel 1992; Murphy 1994.   [9] Mazower 2012, 415.
[10] Mitzen 2013.

functional organizations whose successors are still with us today.[11] The management of empires and their legacies then led to a new global governance push, as winners of the First World War created a League of Nations whose spirit, institutions, and political valence have in part weathered the passage of time.[12] As the twentieth century progressed, "to an ever increasing degree, all sorts of actors learn[ed] to define themselves and their interests … [in terms of] the global cultural and organizational structures in which they [were] embedded."[13] Overall, while global governance has had "ebbs and flows" over the past two centuries,[14] the long-term trend is one in which "certain political issues and functions are displaced from the national or imperial, and into the international, realm."[15]

The evolution of global governance over the *longue durée* has led to a fascinating phenomenon, one that we capture in this book under the rubric of *global policymaking*. This process, by which a variety of actors come together to address issues of a planetary scope despite their profound disagreements and power inequalities, is incredibly complex, intricate, and messy. Our book seeks to provide an analytical framework, a methodology, and a set of illustrative cases to assist scholars in understanding the politics of global governance. We revisit the conventional wisdom that conceives of global policymaking as the delivery of global public goods,[16] and instead argue that the process is best construed as a *bricolage*, or patchwork, of competing value claims and politically charged governing practices. The best way to capture the politics of global governance, we contend, is to focus on the "making of" global policies. After all, as Lindblom so aptly put it, "one can look at all of government and politics as a policy-making process."[17]

While the first two chapters develop this analytical framework and methodology, the following three apply them to a set of contemporary case studies. We use the United Nations (UN) as our main policy-making "site," since it sits at the confluence of so many global governance dynamics (more on this below). Drawn from the fields of development, human rights, and security, our three global case studies concern the adoption of the UN's Sustainable Development Goals

---

[11] Murphy 1994; also Steffek and Holthaus 2018.
[12] Mazower 2009; Pedersen 2015.   [13] Boli and Thomas 1999, 4.
[14] Grigorescu 2020.   [15] Pedersen 2015, 4–5. See also Steffek 2021.
[16] E.g. Weiss 2000; Stone and Ladi 2015.   [17] Lindblom 1980, 5.

(SDGs) in 2015, the institutionalization of the Human Rights Council (HRC) from 2005 onward, and the ongoing promotion of a Protection of Civilians (PoC) doctrine in UN peace operations. We unpack these three policymaking processes in order to show how they result from persistent value cleavages and rest on more or less exclusionary governance practices. The final chapter and conclusion then draw comparative insights, and point toward longer-term trends and ongoing debates in global governance.

But first, we aim to do three things in the remainder of this introduction. To begin, we discuss a set of key approaches by which scholars have studied global governance in recent decades. Institutionally, we are told, global governance works through "regime complexes" that are increasingly "fragmented." Heterogeneous actors are "orchestrated" via new forms of association and collaboration. Concurrently, "informal governance" is on the rise and a new spirit of "experimentalism" dominates global policymaking. All the while, issues of legitimacy, including patterns of authority and contestation, are taking center stage. After reviewing these different research programs, we briefly present our own alternative – that of global policymaking – and show how this approach helps bring together disparate insights, systematically capture the political nature of global governance, and make sense of current trends within a larger historical context. Finally, we introduce our case studies and discuss the relevance of the UN as a prime site of global policymaking in the early twenty-first century.

1 Global Governance Studies Today

How can we make sense of the dynamics of contemporary global governance? The booming field of global governance studies probably counts thousands of articles, chapters, and books that have sought to address this question in one way or another in recent decades. It would be foolish to think that we could mount a full review of this literature in a few paragraphs. Instead, we organize our discussion around four key research programs that, we contend, have dominated the field for the past ten to twenty years. Overall, we find in this work many useful insights on which to build; yet we also observe a number of critical blind spots. We end up locating our own alternative, which is centered on the concept of global policymaking, at the intersection of the "problem-solving" theories that currently prevail in the field of IR and those more "critical" theories that have been so instrumental in reinserting politics into the frame.[18] From the former, we retain an analytical interest in how global governance actually works; in tune with the latter, we highlight the role played by politics, power, and historicity in the making of global governance.

By implication, our use of the global governance concept is analytical rather than ideological.[19] We are fully aware that the term "global governance" is also used to describe a (neoliberal) political project generally associated with managing the transboundary consequences of global capitalism.[20] For some, this ideological connection is a sufficient reason to let the concept "die without too much fuss."[21] We respectfully disagree and instead argue, with others, that global governance is a theoretical device that "helps us identify and describe transformation processes in world politics."[22] As Hofferberth puts it, "as an analytical perspective, global governance allows us to see things we would otherwise miss"[23] – first and foremost the growing variety of actors on the global stage and their changing political relationships. Recall that from a purely pragmatic perspective, concepts are neither true nor false; the question, rather, is whether or not they are useful.

It seems to us quite possible to take the politics of global governance as our analytical object without ipso facto endorsing the neoliberal political project that undergirds much of its contemporary dynamics. The concept can help group seemingly disparate empirical phenomena under categories that reveal new insights into global politics.[24] In a nutshell, global governance makes it possible to describe the reconfiguration of social interactions on the world stage that has been taking shape – with some recent acceleration – over the past two centuries.[25] While we refrain in these pages from offering policy advice, we provide analytical tools for interested parties around the world to critically reflect on (and possibly pursue) their varied political endeavors. And the stakes are very high, as Murphy lucidly reminds us, since "preventing genocide and the avoidable cascading violence of regional war,

---

[18] Cox 1981. On global governance, see among others Cox 1992; Cox and Sinclair 1996; Hewson and Sinclair 1999; and Lederer and Müller 2005.
[19] Weiss and Wilkinson 2022, 4.
[20] Ferguson 1990; Smouts 1998; Murphy 2000; Brand 2005; Soederberg 2006.
[21] Mazower 2014, 220.   [22] Dingwerth and Pattberg 2006, 196.
[23] Hofferberth 2015, 610.   [24] Dingwerth and Pattberg 2006.
[25] Sending and Neumann 2006; Avant, Finnemore, and Sell 2010b.

finding ways efficiently to provide essential international goods that
markets will never provide, and challenging globalization's sudden
reversal of the twentieth-century's democratic gains, are some of the
most compelling reasons for trying to understand the nebulous global
polity and the governance it provides."[26] Critical as we may be of
existing structures, we nonetheless think it important to bear in mind
Sinclair's question: "Can we imagine a world without [any form of]
global governance?"[27]

The notion of global governance, then, seems inescapable when it
comes to describing significant political developments worldwide. In
an agenda-setting article, Ruggie speaks of "the beginnings of a fundamental reconstitution of the global public domain—away from one
that equated the 'public' in international politics with states and the
interstate realm" to one in which states and nonstate actors interact in
the same "institutionalized arena."[28] Other scholars describe a "global
administrative space,"[29] a "new [transgovernmental] world order,"[30]
a shift to "transnational neopluralism,"[31] or the rise of an "international rule" characterized by a "systematised body of practices
aimed at 'the maintenance of order' and 'the protection of life.'"[32]
Building on these observations, we argue that this "global agora" for
policymaking, as Diane Stone puts it, has become a political realm in
its own right, enmeshed as it is with other levels and sites of policymaking.[33] Instead of conceiving of global governance as "the sum-total
of all interactions"[34] in a "multi-level" system,[35] then, we locate global
policymaking on an analytically separate (if ontologically entangled)
plane.

It is true that the concept of global governance has proven "notoriously slippery."[36] Yet, as is often the case in intellectual endeavors, the
plurality of approaches and definitions is actually quite productive.[37] In
order to locate our contribution to this debate, we will review four key
research programs in contemporary global governance studies: (1)
regime complexes and fragmentation; (2) orchestration; (3) informal
governance and experimentalism; and (4) legitimacy, authority, and
contestation. While we find much to commend in each of these bodies

---

[26] Murphy 2000, 792.   [27] Sinclair 2012, 180.   [28] Ruggie 2004, 500.
[29] Krisch and Kingsbury 2006.   [30] Slaughter 1997.   [31] Cerny 2010.
[32] Orford 2011, 1.   [33] Stone 2008.   [34] Rosenau 1995.   [35] Zürn 2012.
[36] Weiss and Wilkinson 2014, 220; also Finkelstein 1995.
[37] Hofferberth 2015.

of literature, we also feel the need to gather these scattered insights under one overarching framework – global policymaking – that is specifically geared at capturing the political nature of global governance.

1.1 Regime Complexes and Fragmentation

A key theme in contemporary global governance studies is that of regime complexity, which "refers to the presence of nested, partially overlapping, and parallel international regimes that are not hierarchically ordered."[38] Focused on rules and institutions, this research program documents a number of dysfunctional consequences of regime complexity, including "fragmentation,"[39] "forum-shopping," "regime-shifting," and "strategic inconsistency."[40] These patterns are understood as being induced by competing institutions that are rationally devised by states to foster their individual interests. Often associated with a decline in global governance,[41] fragmentation is thought to lead to new intervention practices[42] and accountability challenges.[43] Some scholars go as far as to suggest that fragmentation signals the dawn of "postgovernance."[44]

The regime complex research program is part of a broader literature that construes global governance as a "complex system."[45] There is at least some overlap here with long-standing discussions of "complex interdependence"[46] and "complex multilateralism."[47] The fragmentation of regime complexes captures a key organizational development in the twenty-first century, one that cuts across a variety of subfields ranging from the environment to trade to health.[48] Its dispersed nature notwithstanding, the contemporary institutional setup of global governance reflects more than rational designs and calculations.

---

[38] Alter and Meunier 2009, 13. See also Raustiala and Victor 2004; Keohane and Victor 2011; Alter and Raustiala 2018; Eilstrup-Sangiovanni and Westerwinter 2022.

[39] Greenhill and Lupu 2017; Kim 2019.

[40] Alter and Meunier 2009; Morse and Keohane 2014.

[41] Zürn 2018, 13. For a more optimistic view, see Faude and Große-Kreul 2020.

[42] Margulis 2021.   [43] Widerberg and Pattberg 2017.

[44] Hofferberth and Lambach 2020.

[45] Orsini et al. 2019. For a different take, see Srivastava 2013.

[46] Keohane and Nye 1977; Farrell and Newman 2016.   [47] O'Brien et al. 2000.

[48] See e.g. Hanrieder 2015a.

As Hurrell correctly notes, "liberal interest-driven accounts of the problems of global governance all too often disguise or evade the deep conflict over values, underlying purposes, and ways of seeing the world."[49] Put differently, if we are to make sense of complexity and fragmentation, we must expand our political analysis beyond the clash of interests and rationalities.

1.2 Orchestration

When it comes to identifying the set of actors that have come to populate the global stage, the concept of orchestration has proven particularly salient.[50] According to Abbott et al., "IGOs [intergovernmental organizations] engage in orchestration when they enlist intermediary actors on a voluntary basis, by providing them with ideational and material support, to address target actors in pursuit of IGO governance goals."[51] The concept describes a particular arrangement of ties among global governors, which is allegedly on the rise in the twenty-first century and which is said to add "new modes of governance in the global system."[52] Compared to more traditional forms of governance such as intergovernmentalism, orchestration stands out to the extent that it is "both indirect (because the IGO acts through intermediaries) and soft (because the IGO lacks control over intermediaries)."[53] In the "governance triangle"[54] composed of states, nongovernmental organizations (NGOs), and firms, relationships based on authority and delegation take on new layers of complexity and "organizational progeny,"[55] as "multistakeholder partnerships" are formed around common problems.[56]

The notion of orchestration helps specify the "organizational ecology"[57] or "organizational fields"[58] that characterize contemporary global governance. It is particularly useful to understand the role of

---

[49] Hurrell 2007, 10.   [50] Abbott and Snidal 2010.   [51] Abbott et al. 2015, 3.
[52] Koenig-Archibugi and Zürn 2006. See also Barnett, Pevehouse, and Raustiala 2022b.
[53] Barnett, Pevehouse, and Raustiala 2022b.
[54] Abbott and Snidal 2009. See Ruhlman 2015.   [55] Johnson 2014.
[56] Andonova 2010; Andonova 2017; Raymond and DeNardis 2015. See also Ottaway 2001; Pattberg 2007; Bexell and Mörth 2010; Green 2014; Bäckstrand and Kuyper 2017; and Hickmann et al. 2021.
[57] Abbott, Green, and Keohane 2016; Lake 2021.
[58] Hanrieder 2015b; also Kauppi and Madsen 2014.

international organizations (IOs) in what is sometimes referred to as the new "polycentrism" of world politics.[59] Without a doubt, the concept advances our understanding of IO agency beyond bureaucratic politics[60] and transnational access[61] so as to encompass the convoluted policymaking process involving diverse actors.[62] Global governors "divide labor, delegate, compete and cooperate with one another."[63] That being said, and similar to the regime complex research program, the orchestration literature appears rather thin on politics. We are told, for instance, that orchestrators use "inducements" to obtain "voluntary" compliance from other actors.[64] Yet, politics generally involves power struggles and coercive modes of action. What is more, orchestration works only when "interests are sufficiently aligned to overcome these conflicts."[65] Functional as it may be under some circumstances, orchestration takes on a different meaning in the context of conflict-ridden initiatives and a deeply unequal global playing field.

1.3 Informal Governance and Experimentalism

A fast-growing body of literature suggests the increasing importance of informal governance on the world stage, in the form of either informal international organizations[66] or, alternatively, shadow politics operating at the margins of formal procedures.[67] According to Roger, "informal organizations are a pervasive feature of today's global political landscape."[68] Presaged by the growth of "soft law"[69] and "informal international lawmaking,"[70] this development is characterized by "emergent flexibility,"[71] "liquid authority,"[72] and a new spirit of "experimentation."[73] According to de Burca et al., "Experimentalist Governance describes a set of practices involving open participation by a variety of entities (public and private), lack of formal hierarchy

---

[59] Scholte 2002. See also Koinova et al. 2021.   [60] Barnett and Finnemore 2004.
[61] Tallberg et al. 2013; Anderl, Daphi, and Deitelhoff 2021.
[62] Also Reinalda and Verbeek 2004.
[63] Avant, Finnemore, and Sell 2010b, 2; also Ohanyan 2015.
[64] Abbott et al. 2015, 4.   [65] Ibid., 4, 18.
[66] Vabulas and Snidal 2013; Abbott and Faude 2021; Westerwinter, Abbott, and Biersteker 2021.
[67] Stone 2011; Pouliot 2016.   [68] Roger 2020, 8.
[69] Abbott and Snidal 2000.   [70] Pauwelyn, Wessel, and Wouters 2012.
[71] Búzás and Graham 2020.   [72] Krisch 2017.   [73] Hoffmann 2011.

within governance arrangements, and extensive deliberation throughout the process of decision making and implementation."[74]

The research on informal governance draws attention to a very
important change in global politics.[75] Scripted as it is, policymaking
takes place against a backdrop of practices and rules that have evolved
incrementally and often without official sanction.[76] However, in most
cases, this framework remains steeped in a functionalist logic
according to which informalization is seen as a rational response to
the nature of global problems, to a growing multilateral stalemate, or
to the preferences of certain dominant actors.[77] While these logics
certainly obtain, they tell only one part of the story, and they miss
the more political aspects of the process. Revealingly, it is admitted
that "Experimentalist Governance is likely to be impractical or
unworkable where key actors are unwilling or reluctant to cooperate."[78] Yet, instead of limiting our scope to conditions of harmony, it
would seem more realistic to embrace the pervasiveness of conflict in
global affairs.

In fact, a trait common to all three research programs reviewed so
far – regime complexes, orchestration, and informal governance – is
the tendency to emphasize rational choice and design at the expense of
politics.[79] Indeed, the major patterns described by these programs are
usually theorized as "an optimal response to the functional and strategic problems that an institution seeks to solve."[80] The problem with
such a liberal view is not only that it tends "to mask the presence of
power"[81] but also that it often "leaves conflict and contestation uncon-
sidered."[82] Such "managerial logic" assumes that "global problems
are tractable and solutions feasible if actors will only come and work
together to solve them. Drawing too heavily on this logic deprives
global governance and the problems it is concerned with of their
political character."[83] The fourth and final research program that we
discuss seeks to address this weakness.

---

[74] De Burca, Keohane, and Sabel 2012, 738.   [75] Westerwinter 2021.
[76] Pouliot and Thérien 2018a.   [77] Stone 2011; Hale and Held et al. 2017.
[78] De Burca, Keohane, and Sabel 2012, 784.   [79] Mattli and Woods 2009.
[80] Voeten 2019, 149.   [81] Barnett and Duvall 2005, 4.
[82] Hofferberth 2015, 616; also Hurd 2020.
[83] Hofferberth 2015, 616; also Hurrell 2007.

1.4 Legitimacy, Authority, and Contestation

Over the past decade or so, the concept of legitimacy has become a staple of global governance studies.[84] The many contributors to this analytical frame start from the observation that global rule is often contested.[85] Global governors must therefore resort to different forms of legitimation, including expanded participation, technocratic arguments, or impartiality posturing. According to some scholars, the "authority-legitimacy link"[86] implies that the more influential global governors become, the more contestation they are likely to face, which in turn places higher demands on them for legitimation. Others explain growing contestation through "a far-reaching rise of democratic legitimation in global governance."[87] As a form of justification, legitimation targets a variety of audiences, ranging from elites to larger populations.[88] In the background, contestation in the form of "politicization" and "counter-institutionalization" is growing as "reflexive authority" – based on the provision of services – takes hold on the global stage.[89]

The legitimacy literature advances our understanding of the political nature of global governance by emphasizing debate, conflict, and normativity. It draws attention to the narrative work performed by global governors, whether in terms of democracy or efficiency, aimed at obtaining compliance. It also maps the "loosely coupled" and "functionally differentiated spheres of authority" that comprise global governance today.[90] Yet in our view, the rampant focus on compliance comes at a steep price, thereby turning legitimacy into a political technology. As Hurd correctly points out, here "legitimation is conceived as separate from, or an alternative to, politics."[91] Contestation is deemed a problem (because it constitutes a deficit of legitimacy), an attribution that glosses over the fact that, ultimately, "legitimation is a

---

[84] Hurd 1999; Steffek 2003; Zürn 2004; Dingwerth 2005; Buchanan and Keohane 2006; Koppell 2010; Bernstein 2011; Brassett and Tsingou 2011; Bexell 2014; Steffek 2015; Tallberg, Backstrand, and Scholte 2018; Zürn 2018; Schmidtke 2019; Tallberg and Zürn 2019; Kreuder-Sonnen 2020; Oguz Gok and Mehmetcik 2022.

[85] Wiener 2014; Deitelhoff and Zimmermann 2018.   [86] Zürn 2018.

[87] Dingwerth, Schmidtke, and Weise 2020, 714.

[88] Dingwerth et al. 2019b; Verhaegen, Scholte, and Tallberg 2021.

[89] Zürn 2018; also Zürn, Binder, and Ecker-Ehrhardt 2012.   [90] Zürn 2018.

[91] Hurd 2019, 721.

tool of social control."[92] If we are to capture the politics of global governance, then, we need a concept of legitimacy (and, relatedly, of authority and contestation) that treats debate and conflict as the normal condition of politics – not as something to be managed or even suppressed.

To sum up, we draw three conclusions from our review of the prevailing currents in global governance studies over the past two decades. First, recent scholarship tends to be a bit presentist in focusing on the latest trends in global governance, whether experimentalism, politicization, multistakeholder partnerships, or forum-shopping. Critical as these developments may be to any attempt to make sense of our times, our alternative – framed as global policymaking – has a longer historical pedigree and helps us to identify continuities on top of novelties. Second, the rich insights to be gleaned from global governance studies are often confined to various intellectual silos, as if they were separate dynamics instead of deeply connected, as we intend to show. As a concept, global policymaking helps us bring together processes of fragmentation, orchestration, experimentation, and legitimation. Third and most importantly, the recent literature on global governance seems thin when it comes to politics, often relying on a functionalist logic while also taking for granted the notion of compliance as a normative good and, inversely, conflict as a pathology to be managed. By contrast, instead of "stigmatizing politics,"[93] the lens we develop in this book emphasizes social conflict, value cleavages, and power dynamics as inherent conditions of global policymaking.

2 Global Policymaking

One of the most significant developments in political science over the past few decades is the tendency among students of policy studies to pay growing attention to world politics, while scholars of global governance are more and more interested in policy studies. Increasingly, the former see globalization as a powerful driver of policy, while the latter consider policy scholarship as a major source of inspiration and an intellectual bridge to a broader community of social scientists. The emergence of global policy as a distinct field of research is the main outcome of the cross-fertilization between global

---

[92] Ibid., 719.   [93] Louis and Maertens 2021, 187.

governance and policy studies.[94] Our book is a contribution to this new domain of academic research as it argues that global policymaking is a most useful notion for grasping the politics of global governance. More specifically, we contend that the study of global policymaking makes it possible to highlight the political processes through which global governance takes shape.

In Diane Stone's apt recollection, the field of policy studies has long been "a prisoner of the word state."[95] With the globalization of economic, security, environmental, and communications issues, however, the field has broadened considerably. This expansion and the consequent rise of global policy studies are the result of two social processes that gathered speed during the latter part of the twentieth century. First, states have delegated an increasing share of their authority to international and local organizations, both public and private. Second, a range of transnational organizations have gained unprecedented influence in the structuring of a wide variety of social activities. The first process can be illustrated by the expansion of the roles of the World Trade Organization (WTO) and the International Monetary Fund (IMF), or by the proliferation of multistakeholder partnerships. The second process has been spurred most notably by the growing role played by multinational corporations and NGOs. A major effect of this twofold shift has been the "deterritorialization"[96] of politics, whereby an increasing number of policies now extend to more than one nation-state. Such was the historical context that gave birth to the dual ideas of global governance and global policy.

Today, the field of global policy studies remains a work in progress, and the very definition of global policy continues to be a matter of debate. In this book, we conceive of global policies as world-spanning courses of action on issues deemed to be of common concern, and we identify these according to three specific criteria. First, a policy deserves to be called "global" when its sphere of applicability extends to a significant portion of the world. Second, for a global policy to be recognized, it needs to be expressed in terms of collective interests; as such, it can emanate from governments as well as from private actors. And third, a social fact fits our conception of policy when it refers to a

---

[94] Soroos 1986; Reinicke 1998; Stone and Ladi 2015; Klassen, Cepiku, and Lah 2017; Stone and Moloney 2019; Stone 2020; Porto de Oliveira 2022.
[95] Stone 2008, 19; emphasis added. [96] Scholte 2005, 17.

program of action designed to promote certain political ideas. In what follows, we will utilize this definition of global policy in the service of a critical approach to world politics in which social conflicts and power relations will be given pride of place.

Our analytical framework is rooted in a questioning of the concept of "global public goods," which tends to dominate thinking on global policies.[97] Indeed, a majority of scholars and political actors would seem to fuse global policies with the objective of producing global public goods such as an open trade system, a clean environment, or a peaceful world order. In recent years, for example, the World Bank and the United Nations Development Program (UNDP) – two international institutions that have traditionally held contrasting views on development – have come to share a similar discourse on the importance of global public goods. For advocates of the idea, global public goods are described as simply the best way to manage globalization. Their implementation seems all the more urgent in that they seem to offer the ideal solution to "global public bads" such as recessions, pollution, or terrorism.

Yet, the problem with the catchall concept of global public goods is that it obscures fundamental political controversies. Who has the legitimacy to identify global public goods? Who can establish an order of priority among them? And who should decide on a fair distribution of burdens in their provision? These deeply divisive questions are largely brushed under the rug by proponents of global public goods, even though, in our view, they should be at the heart of the analysis. Not everyone on the global stage wants the same thing. Rather than being thought of as an obstacle to global policymaking, the lack of consensus among actors – what is often referred to in the media as the international community's lack of political will – should be seen as an inherent characteristic of global governance. To elucidate this lack of consensus, we propose to deconstruct the process by which global policies are made.

As a starting point, we argue that global policymaking can best be viewed as a form of social "bricolage." Drawn from the writings of anthropologist Claude Lévi-Strauss,[98] the notion of bricolage – the

---

[97] Kaul, Grunberg, and Stern 1999; Weiss 2000; Barrett 2007; Stone and Ladi 2015; Kaul 2019; Stone 2020.

[98] Lévi-Strauss 1966 [1962].

closest translation would be "handiwork" – has inspired numerous
recent studies across the social sciences.[99] Given our own objectives,
bricolage provides a particularly useful metaphor because it highlights
the patchwork and improvised nature of global governance. We argue
that bricolage is an enduring feature of global policymaking (cutting
across time and issues), even though the precise degree of improvisation varies from one policy to the next, based among other things on
prior formalization. We further maintain that the bricolage of global
policies is made up of an amalgam of practices and values – two
concepts that help connect the material and the ideological underpinnings of global governance. It is worth stressing that our approach in
no way denies the centrality of power and interest in global policymaking; instead, we study these irreducible social factors indirectly,
through the public normative clashes and political patterns of action
that structure them.

Our attention to practices as collective ways of doing allows us to
highlight the forces that shape the social configuration of the global
arena.[100] Among its key advantages, such an approach means that we
can focus on the informal political processes that are just as significant
as codified procedures. In addition, practices open a window onto the
social stratification against which global policymaking is enacted.[101]
Just as they generate new social ties and diversify the array of actors,
practices also reinforce existing power structures. Put differently, the
study of practices is instructive in that it brings out the inclusionary
and exclusionary dynamics that inform cooperation and global
policymaking.

To apprehend the ideological dimension of global policies, we also
emphasize how debates over values shape global policymaking and
global governance.[102] A particularly prominent feature of these
debates is that the values that frame them are generally defended by
recourse to their purported universality. Also striking is the fact that,

---

[99] Kincheloe 2001; Baker and Nelson 2005; Carstensen 2011; Cleaver 2012;
Carstensen 2016; Kalyanpur and Newman 2017.

[100] Adler and Pouliot 2011; Bueger and Gadinger 2014; Pouliot and Thérien
2018a.

[101] Pouliot 2016. See also Towns 2012; Zarakol 2017; Fehl and Freistein 2020;
Kimber 2020; Viola 2020.

[102] Falk, Kim, and Mendlovitz 1991; Bernstein 2001; Steffek 2006; Hurrell 2007;
Pouliot and Thérien 2018b.

when they negotiate global policies, global actors typically hold different normative views on three basic questions: What is the problem? What are the ends to be achieved? By what means are those ends to be reached? The value cleavages reflected in the different answers to these three questions reveal various ambiguous arrangements that we call polysemous compromises.[103] Having arrived at an ostensible consensus on any given issue, global policymakers have the possibility to interpret the end result of a given policymaking process as they wish. In sum, as they are constructed from a haphazard and nonteleological combination of practices and values, global policies take the form of large-scale patchworks.

Instead of looking at the what or the why of global governance, then, this book is much more interested in the how. In this respect, our analysis is resolutely process-oriented. Rather than using the language of policy "inputs" and "outputs," we follow Lindblom's perceptive view according to which policymaking is "an extremely complex process without beginning or end and whose boundaries remain most uncertain."[104] This heterodox approach aligns with our own epistemology, which straddles the much-touted division between problem-solving and critical theories by reconstructing, as empirically as possible, the patterns of exclusion and the roads not taken that preside over global policymaking. Our methodology is inductive and interpretive, aimed at analytically informed "thick descriptions" of the sausage-making of global governance. In the end, as will be shown, focusing on how the bricolage of global policies takes shape through the articulation of practices and values sheds a wholly innovative light on the politics of global governance.

3 Global Policymaking at the United Nations

For practical reasons, it is not possible to capture the intricacies of global policymaking without zooming in on specific sites and issues. Our research starts from the belief that the UN provides a particularly suitable focal point for studying the bricolage of practices and values by which global policies are formed. First, the UN is *primus inter pares* in the sense that it is the sole international organization with a

---

[103] On the polysemy of international institutions, see Costa-Buranelli 2015.
[104] Lindblom 1980, 5.

universal membership and a global mandate. Second, the UN Charter is the closest approximation we have of a global constitution.[105] Far from a world government, the organization nonetheless positions itself as the political steward of the world. And third, the UN constitutes the most important political locus on the global stage around which various actors converge in order to speak and act. As Béland and Orenstein argue, in contemporary public policy, IOs have become crucial "sites of contestation,"[106] and the UN is probably the most central one of these organizations. In short, by looking at the UN, we are able to access a singular window onto the "big picture" of global policymaking and global governance.[107] Building on this last observation, the book analyzes three public policies formulated within the framework of the UN. These three policies are the adoption of the SDGs in 2015, the creation of the HRC in 2005, and the ongoing promotion of PoC in peace operations.

Critics may point out that the UN offers no more than a fragmentary perspective on the universe of contemporary global policies. In recent years, countless commentators have denounced what they see as the increasing irrelevance of the UN and its bureaucracy. Indeed, the current crisis of international cooperation is frequently blamed on the legendary pathologies of the UN. On these grounds, putting the spotlight on the global policies emanating from the UN may seem like a pretty bad scholarly decision. Favoring a different approach, some may think it more in line with the current zeitgeist to investigate private actors' policy entrepreneurship in the management of all sorts of global economic, environmental, technical, or humanitarian issues. Although we would of course warmly welcome studies of this kind, we believe that large IOs continue to serve as the prime political platforms for today's global governance, convening as they do not only states but also a slew of other actors, from NGOs to corporations. And despite all its shortcomings, there is no political institution comparable to the UN in terms of its ability to form "an essential arena" for global policymaking.[108] As is often said, "If the UN did not exist, we would have to reinvent it."[109]

---

[105] Doyle 2012.   [106] Béland and Orenstein 2013, 126.

[107] Claude 1964; Coate and Puchala 1990; Diehl 2005; Kennedy 2006; Weiss and Thakur 2010; Thérien 2015; Wiseman 2015; Weiss and Daws 2018.

[108] Weiss 2013, 52. See also Reinicke et al. 2000; and Thakur and Weiss 2009.

[109] Weiss 2018, 1.

Beyond these elements of contextualization, several reasons justify our focus on the SDGs, the HRC, and PoC. First, these three policies cover the fields of development, human rights, and security, and thus provide a fairly panoramic view of UN activities and global policymaking writ large. Former UN Secretary-General Kofi Annan identified the pillars of global governance when he framed the organization's overarching mission in terms of "perfect[ing] the triangle of development, freedom and peace."[110] Upon taking his oath of office in 2016, Secretary-General António Gutteres painted a similar image when he stated that "[h]umanitarian response, sustainable development and sustaining peace are three sides of the same triangle."[111] By focusing on the SDGs, the HRC, and PoC, our research touches upon all sides of the UN triangle, thus offering a comprehensive view of global policymaking.

Second, our three case studies constitute key turning points in the recent evolution of the world order. In their own respective ways, the creation of the SDGs, the HRC, and PoC have redefined the values and practices of global politics at a significant level. The SDGs are indeed the most ambitious policy initiative in the history of international development.[112] The creation of the HRC represents the most important reform of human rights governance since 1946.[113] And over the past two decades, PoC has emerged as the political objective most often invoked to justify peace operations.[114] In sum, the public policies examined in this book all have a very high political salience and are likely to shape the course of global governance for a long time to come.

Third, the UN policies studied here allow us to explore the interaction between what has come to be called the "three UNs." As many experts suggest, today's UN is a trifaceted forum that includes not only member states and the international civil service but also a galaxy of nonstate actors.[115] As it happens, the adoption of the SDGs, the creation of the HRC, and PoC provide strong examples of the dynamics of cooperation and conflict that structure relationships between the three UNs. For sure, states remained the main drivers of the policymaking process in all three cases, but their domination was far from

---

[110] UN General Assembly 2005d, para. 12.   [111] UN Secretary-General 2016.
[112] Dodds, Donoghue, and Leiva Roesch 2016; Kamau, Chasek, and O'Connor 2018.
[113] Ramcharan 2011; Freedman 2013.   [114] Willmot et al. 2016; Foley 2017.
[115] Jolly, Emmerij, and Weiss 2009; Carayannis and Weiss 2021.

absolute. As our analysis will make clear, UN officials, civil society groups, representatives of the private sector, think tanks, and experts have contributed significant practical and normative inputs to the bricolage that resulted in the policies that we examine throughout the book.

Fourth, our three case studies instantiate the institutional designs and modes of governance behind a broad spectrum of global policies. The SDGs, the HRC, and PoC, respectively, respond to distinct logics of goal-setting, institution-building, and norm promotion.[116] The three policies are also based on different time frames. The SDGs are part of an international accord that was adopted en bloc, at a specific time and place. The HRC is an institution whose operational parameters have been defined incrementally, based on a timetable fixed in advance through a formal agreement. As for PoC, this, too, has evolved incrementally, but in an ad hoc manner, without reference to any predetermined timetable. In short, our three case studies enable us to account for the various forms that global public policies can take today.

One last point needs to be clarified in order to avoid disappointment among our readers. Our case studies could perhaps frustrate the expectations of some development, human rights, and security experts, who might find them overly focused on process at the expense of substance. Indeed, it is impossible to account for the full complexity of the SDGs, the HRC, or PoC – and the rich literature that relates to all three issues – in a single book. It is therefore important to stress from the outset that our primary objective is to compare a set of global policies rather than to provide an exhaustive analysis of each one. In our view, the key point is that our case studies will help demonstrate the value of unpacking global public policies as sets of practices and values.

4 Overview

This book has three parts. The first part (Chapters 1 and 2) explains the foundations of our theoretical framework. The second part (Chapters 3, 4, and 5) applies this framework to our case studies: the adoption of the SDGs, the creation of the HRC, and the development of a PoC doctrine in peace operations. The third part (Chapter 6) then draws an analytical

---

[116] Kanie et al. 2017, 8. See also Barnett, Pevehouse, and Raustiala 2022b.

comparison between our three cases. Finally, the conclusion situates our work within the macropolitics of global governance.

Starting with the first part, Chapter 1 demonstrates the heuristic potential of the concept of global policymaking. We begin by recalling the origins of the notion of global policy and then explain our own definition of the term. From there, we show that the dominant approach in the study of global policies, which is framed in terms of global public goods, fails to capture the politics of global policymaking because of its rationalist assumptions. As an alternative to the global public goods perspective, we argue that global policymaking should be looked at as a form of political bricolage. Chapter 2 then methodically exposes how the bricolage of global policymaking takes shape. In short, we claim that global policies can be best understood as improvised configurations of practices and values. On one hand, the analysis of practices makes it possible to emphasize the dynamics of inclusion and exclusion in global policymaking. On the other, the unpacking of debates over values helps bring to light the ways in which global policies represent polysemous compromises that paper over normative cleavages. Above all, the added value of our attention to practices and values rests with its capacity to account for both the material and the ideological dimensions of global policymaking.

The second part includes three empirical chapters dealing with the making of the SDGs, the HRC, and PoC. Each of the three stories that we tell exposes a political bricolage of practices and values. Focused on the SDGs, Chapter 3 demonstrates how this unprecedented global planning exercise was carried out without a blueprint, and how it ended without any consensus on the very meaning of its core notion, sustainable development. Chapter 4 shows that the continual fits and starts that have punctuated the evolution of the HRC never succeeded in resolving the very problem – politicization – that had justified its creation in the first place. Finally, Chapter 5 describes the ad hoc emergence of PoC as a key concern of the Security Council in the midst of deep political divisions over the status of the traditional peacekeeping principles of consent and nonuse of force.

Turning to the third part, Chapter 6 offers a comparison of our three cases and identifies ten key features that characterize most contemporary global policies: the clash of sovereignties, the growing focus on individuals, the universalization of aspirations, the promotion of a holistic narrative, the orchestrating role of international organizations, the pursuit of inclusion, increasing codification, the emphasis on expertise, the resilience of the North–South divide, and Western hegemony. In addition to showing how these different trends shaped the bricolage of the SDGs, the HRC, and the PoC doctrine, we suggest that they inform global policymaking in general.

Finally, the conclusion broadens the discussion to reflect on how global policies are embedded in the broader practices and values of global governance. Extending the study of the three global policies examined in the book, our discussion concludes with a call for a better understanding of world politics based on a rapprochement between critical theory and problem-solving theory.

1 | Global Policymaking

From Public Goods to Bricolage

In recent years, a fruitful dialogue has started between the fields of policy studies and global governance. Among the manifold results of this dialogue, the most important one is undoubtedly the broad recognition that "global policy studies and new scholarship on transnational administration are becoming key elements towards understanding the diversity of global governance."[1] Drawing analytical traction from this observation, we argue that investigating global policymaking is the most fruitful way of gaining access to the black box of global governance. After all, argues historian Mazower, "Today there is more global policymaking, in more varied forms, than ever before."[2]

This chapter explores the concept of global policymaking from a variety of angles. We begin by reviewing the development of global policymaking as a distinct field of research. We then define the concept of global policy and posit its methodological and epistemological implications. The third part contrasts two approaches to global policymaking – that of global public goods, inherited from economics, and that of bricolage, which takes its cue from sociology and anthropology. We side in favor of the latter, as we believe that it better captures the roles played by politics, contingency, and process in global governance. Overall, the chapter seeks to flesh out Hurrell's key insight that "global governance cannot be reduced to the provision of international public goods or the resolution of well-understood collective action problems."[3]

1 Global Policymaking: An Overview

Policy science, as it was termed by Harold Lasswell, was born as a state-centric field of knowledge.[4] The actors, processes, and issues that

---

[1] Stone and Moloney 2019, 3.   [2] Mazower 2012, xvii.   [3] Hurrell 2007, 10.
[4] Lasswell 1968.

22

it examines are traditionally defined within the framework of the sovereign nation-state. With the exception of a few scholars who identified themselves with the subfield of comparative policy studies, little attention was initially paid to the international environment of policymaking. In short, "methodological nationalism" has long been a basic characteristic of policy studies.[5]

The state-centric attitude of policy studies began to change with the rise of interdependence and globalization. Exploring the impact of these two megatrends on states' policy preferences, several researchers describe and explain the processes of public policy diffusion, policy convergence, and policy transfer.[6] Taken together, this stream of research helps us understand the "internationalization" of public policies.[7] According to Doern, Pal, and Tomlin, public policy internationalizes "when at least one aspect of domestic policy begins to depend on or be affected by forces beyond the borders of the state."[8] While acknowledging that the literature on the internationalization of policies grants an unprecedented role to external variables, the primary objective remains accounting for national policies.

In parallel with the proliferation of analyses of the internationalization of public policies, a distinct current of research draws attention to the "globalization" of such policies. This current developed in order to make sense of two systemic transformations in world politics that accelerated at the end of the twentieth century. First, a growing number of policies now cover multiple national territories. Second, far from being limited to states, policymaking is an activity in which IGOs, NGOs, transnational corporations, and experts play an increasing role. While admitting that there may be some overlap between the internationalization and globalization of public policies (think of the IMF's structural adjustment programs, for instance), many scholars underline the need to differentiate the two processes.[9] These historical developments, which correspond with the mutations of modernity, suggest that global policies appeared long before the terms

[5] Stone 2020, 6.
[6] Bennett 1991; Dobbin, Simmons, and Garrett 2007; Marsh and Sharman 2009; Nay 2012; Evans 2019; Gilardi and Wasserfallen 2019.
[7] Unger and van Waarden 1995; Keohane and Milner 1996; Coleman and Perl 1999; Howlett and Ramesh 2002.
[8] Doern, Pal, and Tomlin 1996, 3–4.   [9] Porto de Oliveira 2022.

"globalization" and "global governance" became fashionable.[10] Old policies such as the establishment of an international date line (1884), the creation of the Permanent Court of Arbitration (1899), or the codification of international rules for fighting epidemics (1903), to mention just a few examples, share many characteristics with today's global policies.

Soroos was probably the first author to rigorously examine the notion of global policy in his pathbreaking 1986 book *Beyond Sovereignty: The Challenge of Global Policy*.[11] Conceiving of global policies as "the product of the international community as a whole,"[12] Soroos demonstrated "the applicability of the policy approach to the study of world politics."[13] Building on this insight, other authors have highlighted the rise of global policy networks and transnational policy communities.[14] The overarching intuition informing these pioneering writings is that changes in the fields of trade, security, communications, and the environment have given birth to new forms of "global management."[15] In the process, policies became less and less applicable to "territorially delineated national communities governed by ... states."[16]

Still "at its very early stages,"[17] global policy studies have quickly spread thanks to the creation of new journals such as *Global Governance* (founded in 1995), *Global Social Policy* (2001), *Global Policy* (2010), *Global Summitry* (2015), the *International Review of Public Policy* (2019), and *Global Public Policy and Governance* (2021), as well as the publication of handbooks on the subject.[18] Many issue-specific works have also illustrated the analytical potential of the global policy approach by exploring themes such as global trade policy,[19] global refugee policy,[20] global education policy,[21] global environmental policy,[22] global social policy,[23] global development policy,[24] and global health policy.[25] Finally, the creation of courses and graduate programs devoted to the study of global policies has

---

[10] Murphy 1994; Pouliot and Thérien 2015; Yates and Murphy 2019.
[11] Soroos 1986. See also Jacobson 1979; Nagel 1991.   [12] Soroos 1986, 19.
[13] Ibid., 374.   [14] Reinicke 1998; Slaughter 2004; Stone 2008; Gaus 2019.
[15] Reinicke 1998; Reinicke et al. 2000.   [16] Coleman 2012, 673.
[17] Ibid., 685.   [18] Klassen, Cepiku, and Lah 2017; Stone and Moloney 2019.
[19] Klasen 2020.   [20] Miller 2014.   [21] Ball 1998; Mundy 2010.
[22] Eccleston and March 2014.
[23] Deacon 2007; Yeates and Holden 2009; Yeates 2014.   [24] Sondarjee 2021b.
[25] Brown, Yamey, and Wamala 2014.

helped strengthen the status of global policy as an important subject of academic interest.[26]

Reflection on global policies has also been nourished by the development of several adjacent concepts, in particular those of "transnational administration" and "global administrative law." Transnational administration scholarship has expanded on long-standing concerns for the role of international public bureaucracies in policymaking.[27] Transnational administration consists of "the regulation, management, and implementation of global policies of a public nature by both private and public actors operating beyond the boundaries and jurisdictions of the state."[28] As such, transnational administration looks at how policy networks, public–private partnerships (PPPs), and private regimes operate at the global level.[29] For its part, global administrative law seeks to understand how globalization is impacting transgovernmental regulation and administration.[30] Its proponents attend to "the mechanisms, principles, practices, and supporting social understandings that promote or otherwise affect the accountability of global administrative bodies."[31] A major contribution of global administrative law is to offer a legal perspective on the normative dimension of global governance.[32]

Overall, there exists a broad consensus that, even in the absence of any form of world government, global policies already cover a large set of areas.[33] These policies have addressed a wide range of synchronous, transboundary, and/or collective property issues. Moreover, although there are many similarities between public policymaking at the domestic and global levels, critical differences are well recognized. Besides their fluidity and fragmentation, global policies are characterized most notably by their lack of implementation capacity.[34] In addition, it is increasingly agreed that states are often no more than *primus inter*

---

[26] Moloney and Stone 2019.
[27] Reinalda and Verbeek 2004; Knill and Bauer 2017; Lundgren, Squatrito, and Tallberg 2018; Christensen and Yesilkagit 2019.
[28] Stone and Ladi 2015, 840. See also Tao 2019.
[29] Moloney and Stone 2019; Ronit 2019; Wessal and Wescott 2019.
[30] Shapiro 2001; Kingsbury, Krisch, and Stewart 2005, 16; Anthony et al. 2011; Kuo 2019.
[31] Kingsbury, Krisch, and Stewart 2005, 17.   [32] Ibid., 61; Kuo 2019, 341.
[33] Stone and Moloney 2019.   [34] Soroos 1986; Stone 2008; Zürn 2012.

pares among global policymakers.[35] By shedding light on different channels of global authority and communication – whether public, private, or a mix of both – global policy studies have broadened the scope of the global public sphere.[36]

As an emerging research program, global policy studies is facing a number of theoretical and methodological debates, starting with the very definition of global policy. One issue has to do with the spatial scope of global policies. For some authors, global policies can be restricted to "a few countries."[37] For others, a policy can be considered global only when "representatives of each of the principal types of states and geographical regions [are] involved."[38] Between these two positions, we might imagine several political configurations. This divergence of views is not trivial because, in addition to having an impact on the number of policies that could be considered global, it also raises the question of whether and to what extent "the globe" is an appropriate unit of analysis in political science. Another issue, arguably more fundamental, is that the dominant definition of global policy, which refers to the delivery of global public goods, involves implicit normative choices.[39] In fact, no one can say exactly what public goods consist of, for the simple reason that public goods are political constructs rather than natural categories (more on this in Section 3.1). Revealingly, beyond such abstract formulations as the promotion of world peace or the strengthening of international law, global politics provide a daily reminder that negotiating the production of public goods rarely arouses unanimity. For better or worse, the quest for legitimacy in the effort to determine what is "good" for the entire world can hardly escape the vicissitudes of politics.

At the methodological level, the study of global policies continues to confront a fundamental ambiguity. Of course, most observers agree that global policymaking is a messy process; according to Diane Stone, for instance, "there is no consistent pattern in global policy processes" – rather, "disorder and unpredictability are the norm."[40] And

---

[35] Gordenker and Weiss 1995; Keck and Sikkink 1998; Martens 2005; Pattberg 2007; Weiss, Carayannis, and Jolly 2009; Bexell and Mörth 2010; Ougaard and Leander 2010; Willetts 2011; Green 2014.

[36] Ruggie 2004; Steffek, Kissling, and Nanz 2008; Volkmer 2014.

[37] Stone 2020, 13.   [38] Soroos 1986, 20.

[39] Stone and Ladi 2015, 840; Kaul 2019; Moloney and Stone 2019, 107.

[40] Stone 2008, 29.

yet we also lack recourse to some analytical instrument specifically designed to account for the role of continuous improvisation in global policymaking. In fact, scholars of global policy studies find it difficult to break away from the rationalist framework archetypically embodied in the policy cycle model.[41] Granted, most scholars agree that, far from being a mirror of reality, the policy cycle is nothing more than a heuristic tool by which to better understand global policies. Nevertheless, the problem-solving assumptions of the policy cycle model – starting with the misleading belief that "global problems" and "global solutions" could be identified in a neutral and objective way that sidesteps politics – are rarely questioned.

In our view, these theoretical and methodological challenges are neither surprising nor insurmountable. After all, global policy studies remain a young and evolving field of study. Choosing to see the glass as half full, we contend that the global policymaking lens offers an innovative complement to traditional approaches based on rules, interests, norms, actors, and ideas, and can therefore help us to better understand the politics of global governance. Without succumbing to the illusion that global policy studies will give rise to a form of normal science organized around a unified paradigm, we argue that, by giving more importance to conflicts, debates, and power relations, global policymaking scholarship has the potential to become increasingly relevant and useful, both analytically and socially.

2 Defining Global Policy

To take full advantage of the global policy framework, we should first define what a global policy is. In this regard, it should be remembered that the literature on public policies is notoriously reluctant to define its key concept in an overly strict fashion. According to a widely used conception, "public policy is whatever governments choose to do or not to do."[42] As flexible and heuristic as this approach may be, it is clearly underspecified. For our part, we define global policies as world-spanning courses of action over issues of common concern.[43] Let us tease out the three conceptual components of this definition in turn.

---

[41] Soroos 1986, 87; also Stone 2008, 26–8.
[42] Dye 1998, 2. See also Klassen, Cepiku, and Lah 2017, 1.
[43] For alternative definitions, see Stone and Ladi 2015, 840; Thakur and Weiss 2009, 19.

First, we deem a policy to be global when its sphere of applicability spans national and regional borders and extends to a significant portion of the world.[44] This is in contrast to domestic policy – however internationalized – and regional policy, whose bearings are limited to a given state or region. To be sure, the implementation of global policies hinges on country-level action, in the same way that national policies are often set in motion by subnational actors such as municipalities. Moreover, global policies are not enacted uniformly by all national jurisdictions involved. Global policymakers are, indeed, "deeply interconnected with, and frequently controlled by, political actors and administrative agents working within national contexts and across levels of governance."[45] However, both the formulation of and decision-making processes around global policies involve actors whose authority claims are not limited to a particular state, but emerge out of a new "global public domain"[46] supported by "international public administrations."[47]

Second, global policies need to be "recognized by the community in which they are carried out as being of common concern."[48] Contrary to conventional policy studies, we do not limit our definition of public action to that undertaken by state actors. States are involved in many facets of global governance, but certainly not in all of them and as such governments have no monopoly over the management of world affairs. Using the politically contingent criterion of "common concern" allows for the possibility that policymaking can be undertaken even in the absence of widely recognized public actors such as states or their delegated agents (namely, IOs). By all accounts, international credit rating or Internet regulation are issues of common concern even though their functioning largely depends on nonstate actors. As Deborah Stone explains, what matters most is that what may be called "the public interest" is itself an object of struggle: "There is virtually never full agreement on the public interest . . . . Let it be an empty box, but no matter; in the polis, people expend a lot of energy trying to fill up that box."[49]

---

[44] In a related vein, Coleman writes that "policy becomes *global* when it draws input, advice and participants from *anywhere* in the world in its formulation. Similarly, once policy is agreed upon, that policy has the *potential* to be *implemented* in any place or all places in the planet" (Coleman 2019, 223–4, emphasis original).

[45] Stone and Moloney 2019, 7.   [46] Ruggie 2004; also Zürn 2018.

[47] Knill and Bauer 2017.   [48] Best and Gheciu 2014a, 32.

[49] Stone 2012, 13. On the "public interest" see also Steffek 2015.

Finally, a policy describes a declared program of action designed to achieve certain political goals.[50] As was discussed earlier, policies are not limited to the activities of governments. In line with our conception of what is public, we consider that IOs, NGOs, and transnational corporations formulate and implement policies on a daily basis. In addition, it is not necessary for a policy to be fully agreed-upon, or even implemented, for it to count as such. Inconclusive or shelved programs of action often present as much analytical interest as those that are completed. What is crucial, though, is that policies, global or otherwise, are by essence both practical and normative. For this reason, we propose to analyze global policies in terms of the practices and the value debates that give them structure. As will be explained below, a focus on the diversity of practices and values that inform global policies ultimately helps us to better highlight the patchwork nature as well as the political character of global governance.

It is important to note that our approach to global policy is more restrictive than the common view, according to which global policy is merely policy "beyond the nation-state."[51] For some authors, internationalization, regionalization, and diffusion are all markers of the globalization of public policies. We favor a stricter definition, acknowledging that it is probably impossible to determine where the universe of global policies begins and ends in any categorical sense. How many countries must be involved for a policy to be considered "global"? Do all joint responses of the global (international) community to common problems count as global policies? Can a declaration of principles be considered a comprehensive policy?[52] It is difficult if not impossible to offer definitive answers to such questions, and it is probably best to leave them open.

Furthermore, in keeping with established scholarship in policy studies, the level of aggregation at which scholars should approach global policies should match the research question at hand. For instance, in a macrohistorical study, it would make sense to conceive of the UN's PPPs as one single policy. For their part, students of international development might prefer to focus on the Global Alliance for Vaccines and Immunization (GAVI) – a specific PPP involving the

---

[50] In an application to the UN, Thakur and Weiss define policy as "the statement of principles and actions that an organization is likely to pursue in the event of particular contingencies" (Thakur and Weiss 2009, 19).
[51] See Petiteville and Smith 2006.   [52] Donnelly 1990, 221–2.

UN – as their unit of analysis. For health policy analysts, meanwhile, GAVI's vaccine-delivery program in West Africa may be the appropriate level of study. In brief, global public policies may be empirically identified at different scales, depending on the analytical problem one wants to examine.

Of course, the concept of global policy entails certain epistemological assumptions. Quite naturally, the basic debates that divide policy studies analysts reverberate in the study of global policymaking. As such, it should be remembered that the field of policy studies opposes conventional and critical approaches, depending on the vision of knowledge adopted by any given scholar.[53] The conventional approach defends a positivist conception of knowledge according to which rationality and the common good can be defined in an objective manner. In other words, by grounding itself in evidence and ostensibly neutral information, effective policymaking could transcend politics. Driven by a bias in favor of science and expertise, the conventional policy approach minimizes the importance of the historical and cultural context in the search for universal solutions. This quest for universalism emerges most notably from the belief that there is a rational path to development, or that the market provides the optimal form of division of labor.

In a different way, the critical approach of policy studies "adopts an interpretive, culturally and historically constructivist understanding of knowledge and its creation."[54] Contesting the positivism of the conventional approach, scholars looking at the subject through a critical lens therefore reject the separation of facts and values and admit the existence of a plurality of rationalities. In addition, the critical approach is particularly sensitive to the fact that the production of the knowledge on which policies are based is inseparable from power structures. In this regard, Deborah Stone points out that policymaking is "a constant struggle over the criteria for classification, the boundaries of categories, and the definition of ideals that guide the way people behave."[55] The critical approach is therefore particularly concerned with the dynamics of social exclusion and inequality that characterize policymaking. Mistrustful of technocracy and its managerial

---

[53] Fischer 2003; Hajer 2003; Jessop 2010; Shore, Wright, and Però 2011; Stone 2012; Fischer et al. 2015b.
[54] Fischer et al. 2015a, 2.   [55] Stone 2012, 13.

approach, it values public deliberation with respect to the ends as well as the means of governance. Critical scholars are also skeptical of one-size-fits-all policies based on universalist principles. This skepticism is particularly evident in the highlighting of the diversity of development trajectories and in the systematic search for alternative modes of social organization.

While recognizing that the dialogue between the conventional and critical approaches to public policies is necessary and useful, this book intends to show that the critical perspective has much to offer in the analysis of global policymaking. Among other things, a critical approach could play a central role in the development of a "global politics paradigm" that stresses hierarchy over anarchy in global governance.[56] Focusing on the conflictual and political nature of policymaking, the notion of global policy advanced in these pages has the potential to shed new light on the practical and ideological foundations of global governance.

3 From Global Public Goods to Bricolage

Global policymaking is most often associated with the provision of global public goods, such as clean water, poverty reduction, basic education and health care, or peace and security. As Weiss put it a generation ago, "the logical link between the patterns of governance at the national and global levels lies in solving the collective action puzzle to provide public goods."[57] Widespread as it is, though, this approach tends to analytically assume away both the objective of global policymaking (the production of public goods) and the method through which it is achieved (voluntary cooperation through institutional incentives). Alternatively, we emphasize the "making of" global policy and global governance in order to answer a fundamental question: How are world-spanning collective courses of action over issues of common concern actually generated? By paying closer attention to process, we show that the key challenges of global governance do not primarily consist in the search for more efficient solutions to technical problems. Global policymaking is instead best viewed as a bricolage of value conflicts and social practices. Such an approach helps capture the political and patchwork nature of global governance.

---

[56] Zürn 2018, 21.   [57] Weiss 2000, 807.

3.1 *Global Public Goods*

A majority of scholars and practitioners consider "the delivery of public goods"[58] the main objective of global policies. For instance, one renowned expert writes that any "fitting global policy" should first and foremost put the provision of global public goods "at the centre of policy analysis and policymaking."[59] Coined in the 1950s by economist Paul Samuelson, the concept of public goods stands in contrast to private goods, which are excludable (it is mine, not yours) and marked by rivalry (your consumption affects mine). Samuelson argued that the market cannot adequately produce public goods because in such cases, the usual rational incentives do not operate properly. Samuelson's thesis proved to be convincing enough that the notion of public goods soon became a theoretical pillar of political economy.

In 1999, a trio of UNDP economists first put the global public goods concept on the map.[60] The term was soon picked up by the World Bank, the Organisation for Economic Co-operation and Development (OECD), the UN, and several foreign ministries and national aid agencies, including those of Sweden and France. In a 2006 report, the International Task Force on Global Public Goods, cochaired by former Mexican President Ernesto Zedillo and former Ivorian Minister of Planning and Development Tidjane Thiam, argued that "global public goods affect almost all states, and many or all states must be involved in their provision."[61] Today, the notion of global public goods is a standard reference among global actors – public but also private ones, including the Gates, Rockefeller, and Soros Foundations.[62] According to an increasingly shared rhetoric, the creation and funding of public goods finds its ultimate justification in the need "to regulate the adverse effects of global public bads."[63]

Scholars and analysts have quickly jumped aboard the global public goods bandwagon. For Ruggie, the new "global public domain" is "concerned with the production of public goods."[64] Weiss concurs, positing that "in many ways global governance is about the challenge of providing global public goods whose benefits are 'non-excludable'

---

[58] Stone and Ladi 2015, 840.   [59] Kaul 2019, 264.
[60] Kaul, Grunberg, and Stern 1999.
[61] International Task Force on Global Public Goods (ITFGPG) 2006, 15.
[62] Carbone 2007, 179.   [63] Stone 2019, 378.   [64] Ruggie 2004, 500.

and 'non-rival.'"[65] As these two authoritative endorsements suggest, the notion has become a kind of buzzword in academic circles, especially among economists,[66] but also political scientists[67] and legal scholars.[68] Overall, it seems fair to say that in the early decades of the twenty-first century, the concept of global public goods pervades the making as well as the analysis of global governance and global policymaking.

Following a widely shared narrative, globalization has seen a "growing number of national public goods … [go] global."[69] Various observers note that the domestic economic logic also applies to global public goods: the market cannot supply these in sufficient amounts because of the absence of rational incentives. The problem of market failure is compounded at the global level because of so-called anarchy – that is, the absence of a central, formal authority with state-like capacities. "If the power of compulsion were given to an international authority," argues Barrett, "if a world government were established, then global public goods could be supplied by the same means employed domestically."[70] Yet, insofar as there is no superseding world executive, global governance essentially means building the proper institutional incentives so as to organize "voluntary" cooperation.[71]

According to the advocates of this approach, the most effective way to supply global public goods is to build multistakeholder partnerships that help close the gap between jurisdiction, participation, and resources.[72] In contrast to top-down, formal legal authority, partnerships are based on the economic rationale of comparative advantage. These voluntary associations tend to be issue-driven and focused on the resolution of a set of common problems. As such, consensus building, inclusive participation, and the open sourcing of knowledge are privileged management techniques "specifically designed for experimentation, inclusiveness, and peer review."[73] The Montreal Protocol to Protect the Ozone Layer and the Global Fund to Fight

---

[65] Weiss 2013, 40.
[66] E.g. Gerrard, Ferroni, and Mody 2001; Ferroni and Mody 2002; Kaul et al. 2003c; Barrett 2007.
[67] Constantin 2002; Bjola and Kornprobst 2013; Stone 2020.
[68] Maskus and Reichman 2005; Bodansky 2012; Nollkaemper 2012.
[69] Kaul and Mendoza 2003, 96; also Ferroni and Mody 2002, 2.
[70] Barrett 2007, 17.
[71] International Task Force on Global Public Goods (ITFGPG) 2006, 21.
[72] Kaul, Grunberg, and Stern 1999.   [73] Avant 2016, 332.

AIDS, Tuberculosis and Malaria are often cited as successful examples of multistakeholder partnerships.

The concept of global public goods has two important advantages. First, it highlights the fact that in a globalizing world, the issues that confront humanity have fundamentally changed. Second, the concept captures commonalities across contemporary problems, such as the tendency toward free riding. This notion of "transitivity"[74] may favor knowledge accumulation – for instance, through the exchange of so-called best practices when it comes to incentivizing cooperation. Both advantages explain why the idea of global public goods has become so popular in the last couple of decades.

For global actors in search of legitimacy, the public goods concept thus provides a convenient argument for their existence and their growing scope of action. IOs, for example, position themselves as key "convenors"[75] in the provision of global public goods. Politically speaking, the concept also justifies public intervention in the absence of reliable market mechanisms. This helps explain why a development agency such as the UNDP has become a champion for the provision of public goods. Facing stiff competition from the World Bank and other emulators of the dominant neoliberal discourse, who have long blamed state (in)action for underdevelopment, the UNDP and other organizations find in the concept "a rhetorical means of convincing orthodox representatives to extend to the level of the international economy that which has long been accepted at a national level."[76] In other words, construing global governance as the production of global public goods carves a kind of "third way" – "a soft alternative to neoliberal development"[77] that connects certain social-democratic sensitivities with the neoliberal orthodoxy of our time. This convergence helps explain why political actors of all stripes – from the governments of rich countries to development agencies and a number of NGOs – now embrace the global public goods concept in their discourse.[78]

Yet, conceiving of global governance as the supply of global public goods also entails a number of blind spots. In fact, the notion of global public goods, which has rightfully been qualified as "abstract,"[79] tends to obscure the politics behind global governance processes. More

[74] Barrett 2007, 2.   [75] Ferroni and Mody 2002, 4.   [76] Coussy 2005, 185.
[77] Carbone 2007, 185.   [78] See also Long and Woolley 2009.
[79] Stone 2019, 378.

specifically, it depoliticizes debates over two fundamental questions: What does the human collective want? And how do we get there?

First, by focusing on technical problem-solving, the focus on global public goods downplays the widespread contestation over the object-ives and solutions that should be pursued at the global level.[80] As Bodansky explains, people can disagree "about whether something is a global public good or a global public bad – and, hence, whether international law should seek to promote it or prohibit it."[81] For this reason, the very act of naming global public goods is far from politically innocent. Consider, for example, the "priorities" for action identified by the International Task Force on Global Public Goods: preventing the emergence and spread of infectious disease, tackling climate change, enhancing international financial stability, strengthening the international trading system, achieving peace and security, and generating knowledge.[82] These ostensible goods, for all their apparent universality, are arguably quite contestable. Some, such as "enhancing international financial stability" or "strengthening the international trading system," are inherently conservative and ideo-logically biased.[83] At the very least, they express a certain perspective that should not obscure the many alternative courses of political action that some actors may prefer. Other "priority global public goods" listed by the Task Force, such as "tackling climate change" or "achiev-ing peace and security," are banal and trite to the point of wishful thinking. As Long and Wooley put it, "the analysis provided in the public goods literature can at best identify a collective action problem; it does not supply a solution."[84]

Some advocates do recognize that global public goods are "social constructs."[85] Yet, they typically add that "lack of consensus on process issues often holds back policy consensus and action."[86] They further argue that "many such differences occur for conceptual and technical reasons, not political ones."[87] The bottom line, simply put, is that if only people could agree, then we could resolve our problems. As the Task Force explained, the notion of global public goods is meant to show that "the global interest and the national interest can not only be reconciled

[80] Moon, Røttingen, and Frenk 2017.   [81] Bodansky 2012, 656.
[82] International Task Force on Global Public Goods (ITFGPG) 2006.
[83] Long and Woolley 2009, 118.   [84] Ibid.   [85] Kaul and Mendoza 2003, 80.
[86] Kaul et al. 2003b, 4.   [87] Ibid., 6.

but are mutually reinforcing."[88] As a result, disagreement and contention are often portrayed as the key obstacles to global governance.

While it is true that global actors are often divided, from a political perspective, this should come as no surprise. Furthermore, from a pluralistic point of view, calling for the submergence of difference in order to deliver public goods makes for a questionable proposition. The notion that the whole world should agree on a single solution to shared problems certainly betrays a certain detachment from reality. Even in rich countries, rampant undersupply of particular public goods such as health care or education serves as a reminder of the collective political choices involved.

The second major difficulty posed by the global public goods framework has to do with how we get there – that is, with the process by which global public goods may be properly supplied. Remember that for proponents of this approach, "[t]he market cannot price these goods efficiently."[89] They further stress that the domestic solution to such market failure, enforcement, does not apply at the global level because of anarchy. We are left instead with voluntary cooperation, which operates on the basis of self-interest and incentives. Admittedly, though, between a world government on the one hand and strictly incentive-based, voluntary cooperation on the other lies a vast span of political action that is barely scratched by the literature on global public goods. And while some authors emphasize the importance of "political decision making" and its "limited publicness,"[90] the primary focus of this literature is generally on the output of global governance rather than on its input. Little attention is paid to how and by whom resource allocation should be decided.[91] Downplaying such political issues, the International Task Force, to take one example, left the follow-up to its proposals for a vaguely defined "informal forum" made up of the states "that are the most responsible, capable and representative."[92]

Assuming that discontent mostly stems from "the ways that global public goods are – or are not – provided,"[93] proponents of the public goods approach prefer to emphasize evidence-based solutions over

---

[88] International Task Force on Global Public Goods (ITFGPG) 2006, 17.
[89] Kaul and Mendoza 2003, 80.   [90] Kaul et al. 2003a, 21–4.
[91] Bodansky 2012.
[92] International Task Force on Global Public Goods (ITFGPG) 2006, 74.
[93] Kaul et al. 2003b, 4.

legitimacy, and substance over process. In other words, the notion of global public goods risks glossing over the power relations and inequalities that pervade the rules and practices structuring global governance. Because it emphasizes voluntary cooperation through institutional incentives, one has to presume a straightforward, efficiency-driven decision-making and production process. Upon closer scrutiny, though, global policymaking seems much messier than that. "Partnerships," "multistakeholder initiatives," and "best practices," which figure among the primary tools championed by the advocates of global public goods, hinge on a dialectics of inclusion and exclusion that creates a deeply uneven playing field. As a result, concludes Viola, "IOs are better understood as providing club goods rather than public goods."[94]

Of course, no one is against virtue. As political objectives, reducing poverty, protecting the environment, and providing education for all can hardly be treated as negative outcomes. But the global public goods story, to the extent that it unfurls a narrative in which social conflict is largely kept from view, sounds too good to be true. We argue instead that these processes should be interrogated for the way they reveal the presence of politics. Put differently, construing global policy-making as the mere production of global public goods obscures the depth of political choices and the social dynamics involved in the process. What is more, the primary solution proposed to undersupply – generating private incentives toward voluntary cooperation – is based on a set of ideological priors that are far from self-evident, *pace* neoliberal economics.

By emphasizing the technical side of problem-solving and the need for cost-effective solutions, the global public goods perspective ends up depoliticizing global governance. It systematically neglects the substantive disagreements, value struggles, and power dynamics that actually characterize global decision making. In Mazower's colorful words, "There is no fighting here, no blood, not even any really sharp clashes of opinion. In short, this is a rosy picture of a world governed [by management]."[95] Seeking to explore issues that have been neglected by the global public goods perspective, this book foregrounds the political debates that accompany the choosing of certain courses of action over others (value debates), as well as the patterned ways in which problems

---

[94] Viola 2020, 167.   [95] Mazower 2012, 416.

are posed, decisions are made, and collective action is set in motion on the global stage (governance practices). Both of these processes are central components of the alternative analytical framework that we propose in the following pages.

3.2 Global Bricolage

By contrast with proponents of the public goods perspective, a number of scholars emphasize the patchwork nature of global governance and global policymaking. Several authors stress the fragmentation of international authority and the cacophony of would-be global governors in order to point out how global governance departs from the idea of "a coherent whole."[96] In International Political Economy, for instance, proponents of the "new interdependence approach,"[97] as well as a variety of historical and discursive institutionalists,[98] directly confront the assumptions of rational design and its public goods version.

Following a similar line of reasoning, we start from the observation that the politics of global public policymaking rarely resemble the long march toward Pareto-optimality described by public goods theorists.[99] Instead, trial and error, the search for working compromises, the creative combination of old and new practices, and the prevalence of normative ambiguity point to a political dynamic that comes very close to Lévi-Strauss's notion of bricolage. This French word refers to the activity of a handyman – a bricoleur – who builds new artifacts from a variety of at-hand materials. Lévi-Strauss famously illustrated two modes of thinking by contrasting the engineer and the bricoleur. Whereas the engineer works with a blueprint, the distinctive feature of the bricoleur is "always to make do with 'whatever is at hand.'"[100] Her toolkit and set of materials are not only "heterogeneous" but also inherently finite – "the contingent result of all the occasions there have been to renew or enrich the stock or to maintain it with the remains of

---

[96] Hoffmann and Ba 2005, 9. See also Rosenau 1999, 293; Devin 2013, 10; Weiss and Wilkinson 2014, 208; Zürn 2018, 79.

[97] Farrell and Newman 2014; Farrell and Newman 2016.

[98] E.g. McNamara 1998; Blyth 2002; Best 2005; Jabko 2006; Seabrooke 2006; Schmidt 2008; Eagleton-Pierce 2013; Widmaier 2016.

[99] According to Voeten, "Rational functionalist theories posit that institutional design reflects an optimal response to the functional and strategic problems that an institution seeks to solve" (Voeten 2019, 149).

[100] Lévi-Strauss 1966 [1962], 17.

previous constructions or destructions."[101] Methodologically, the concept of bricolage echoes the insights of practice theory regarding the importance of know-how, craft, experience, and knack in making sense of agency and political action.[102]

Influential in a number of social science disciplines ranging from management to media studies, the concept of bricolage was introduced ~origins~ in political science and sociology by historical institutionalists.[103] For instance, Campbell argues that "actors often craft new institutional solutions by recombining elements in their repertoire through an innovative process of bricolage whereby new institutions differ from but resemble old ones."[104] The notion was brought into IR by practice theorists to describe the nature of political agency.[105] Mérand, for example, uses the concept to contrast the actual making of a European defense policy with the typical story of institutional design that scholars like to tell: "To build something, [diplomats] try materials that work and discard other materials that do not work, using their know-how to change the shape of the object incrementally."[106] Inspired by historical institutionalism and practice theory, Kalyanpur and Newman speak of "design by bricolage" to explain the evolution of the international financial architecture: "Change typically occurs through the grafting of modular components rather than the de nova invention of individual institutional features."[107] Applying the notion of bricolage to the field of development, Cleaver concludes that this is essentially how "actors innovate."[108]

In a nutshell, the concept of bricolage seeks to capture the improvisatory, haphazard, and combinatorial nature of global policymaking.[109] Of course, there is variation in the specific balance between improvisation and design from one policy area to the next. Bricolage is arguably more apparent in new global problems than in highly legalized policy domains. However, we contend that the basic logic of bricolage pervades global policymaking across time and issues. This book thus contributes to the burgeoning literature on bricolage by elaborating a framework for the study of a wide range of global policies.

---

[101] Ibid.   [102] Pouliot 2008. See also Lindblom 1959.
[103] Kincheloe 2001; Baker and Nelson 2005; Carstensen 2011.
[104] Campbell 2004, 69.   [105] Pouliot 2008, 281.   [106] Mérand 2008, 134.
[107] Kalyanpur and Newman 2017, 364.   [108] Cleaver 2012, 46.
[109] Pouliot 2020; Pouliot 2021.

What particular materials or resources do global actors actually combine when devising collective courses of action? While a variety of answers could be given to this question, we analyze global public policymaking in terms of the practices and the value debates that structure the process. Our approach builds on an old tradition inaugurated by Lasswell and Kaplan, who defined a policy as "a projected program of goal values and practices."[110] In other words, we seek to emphasize that policies – global or otherwise – are simultaneously practical and normative. This dual nature, by which action and norms coalesce, has been aptly captured by Goodin, Rein, and Moran, who call policy studies "a 'persuasion' that aspires to normatively committed intervention in the world of action."[111] In short, policies constitute joint undertakings based on certain social purposes. In order to unpack the Janus-faced character of public policy, we find inspiration in both the "practice turn" and the "discursive turn," each of which has marked the field of policy studies in recent years.[112] As conceptual tools, practices and value debates provide a parsimonious heuristic that can bring us further into the political bricolage of global governance.

Grasping global policymaking as a bricolage of practices and values advances our understanding of the patchwork nature of global governance in three key ways. First, the concept of bricolage reminds us that a significant chunk of global policymaking emerges from the bottom up, via a never-ending flow of evolving practices.[113] Indeed, global public policies consist of practical assemblages achieved through a complex mix of replication and experimentation.[114] Written rules may abound on the international stage, but they generally contain many gaps and ambiguities, forcing actors to be creative as they move forward. Through informal modes of governance,[115] global actors are often left to build on established ways of doing things by way of improvisation. As they operationalize and sometimes even contradict codified procedures, such practices provide a baseline for debating, negotiating, and deciding on global public policies. Crucially, global governance practices structure the policymaking process in ways that are far from

---

[110] Lasswell and Kaplan 1950.   [111] Goodin, Rein, and Moran 2008, 6.
[112] Fischer 2003; Freeman, Griggs, and Boaz 2011; Stone 2012; Adler-Nissen 2016.
[113] Lipsky 1980. See also Hanrieder 2014; and Búzás and Graham 2020.
[114] Pouliot and Thérien 2018a; Pouliot 2020; Pouliot 2021.   [115] Stone 2020.

politically neutral. The much-celebrated multistakeholder partnerships, for example, come with power dynamics that combine inclusionary and exclusionary tendencies in complex ways.

Second, the notion of bricolage draws attention to the fact that public policy is a "purposeful course of action"[116] of which political choices are an inherent feature. Fundamentally, not everyone on the world stage aspires to the same thing. Most often, global policies consist of normative patchworks that are equivocal, resting as they do on conflicting interpretations of the common good.[117] Throughout the policymaking process, actors debate and struggle as they use different repertoires of universal values. Our focus on these struggles sheds light on global power relations, by making it possible to define the contours of certain dominant worldviews and their alternatives. As it highlights the ideological clashes that characterize global policymaking, our analysis ultimately seeks to trade the management approach of global public goods for one centered on the notion of political struggle. In so doing, we aim to show that for every course of global policymaking actually taken, several alternatives are not.

Third, the bricolage perspective stresses the fact that the amalgam of practices and value struggles through which global public policies are shaped is rarely programmed beforehand. By envisioning global policymaking as an open-ended bricolage of practices and norms, our approach helps make sense of its complexity and contingency. Murphy suggests a useful metaphor to account for the improvised nature of global policymaking: "Like most gothic cathedrals," he writes, "the institutions of each of the successive world orders have been built sporadically over many dozens of years as the interest of the community to be served waxed and waned and as different sponsors and benefactors were found to realize one or another part of the originally imagined project."[118] This architectural metaphor is perfectly in line with our own approach. Above all, it suggests that while some historical forces may be irrepressible, there is no "inherent teleology" in the evolution of global governance.[119]

---

[116] Soroos 1986, 19–20.   [117] Pouliot and Thérien 2018b.
[118] Murphy 1994, 33.   [119] Hofferberth and Lambach 2020, 568.

Conclusion

Critics may ask: Why should we care? Why should we draw such a complex picture of global governance and global policymaking when the global public goods approach seems so much simpler and straightforward? While theoretical simplicity and parsimony are of course virtues to be cultivated, we argue that the three conceptual tools that inform our analytical framework – bricolage, practices, and value debates – capture the politics of global governance in a more exhaustive and penetrating way than their alternatives. First, the bricolage lens is a useful reminder that the "how" is as politically significant as the "what" when it comes to understanding collective decision making. Politics, after all, is primarily about process. Second, attention to practices allows us to emphasize the power relations involved in global policymaking. Politics is also a matter of inclusion and exclusion. And third, by focusing on value debates, we provide a broader understanding of historical trajectories and paths not taken. Politics is a struggle over steering the collective ship.

A basic insight of our analysis is that global policymaking is far more intricate than the mere supply of global public goods. It is also "more fluid and fragmented than might be found in [the] stable political systems of most OECD nations."[120] Stone and Moloney usefully delineate the complexities of global policymaking along three axes.[121] Horizontally, it involves a range of policy networks with unclear lines of authority. Vertically, global policymaking requires coordination across multiple levels, especially (though not only) when it comes to implementation. And diagonally, it spans the public–private divide, even to the point of resting on unilateral private initiatives. Taken together, these three dimensions describe "a global public sector or a discernible transnational administrative space"[122] whose policymaking processes are akin to a "maze."[123] We argue that trying to make sense of such a maze from the rationalist public goods perspective amounts to a major oversimplification of global governance.

Indeed, if the literature on global public goods were right, one should observe much more convergence on the objectives and means

---

[120] Stone 2020, 29.   [121] Stone and Moloney 2019, 13.   [122] Ibid.
[123] Stone 2020.

of global governance than what we see in the world today. While proponents of the concept acknowledge the politics involved in defining and prioritizing public goods, they also propose ready-made solutions and methods centered on the institutional incentivization of voluntary cooperation. Yet, a quick survey of everyday global governance suggests that actors often disagree not only on the nature of the problems that they are confronting but also on the destination they want to reach and the path they must take to get there. This flurry of politics cannot be properly captured by a concept that emphasizes technical problem-solving and rational decision making.

Similarly, the global public goods perspective would suggest a far more streamlined production process than what is actually on offer. It is true that advocates emphasize the distributional politics involved and the recurrent mismatch between decision makers and "consumers." But they also reduce the politics of participation and inclusion to the notion of "stakeholders," a contemporary buzzword that tends to brush aside some tough political questions: Who determines the stakes here? What are the boundaries of jurisdiction? Which actors should be involved in the process, and how?[124]

In a programmatic piece, Weiss and Wilkinson write that "[t]he crucial challenge in the near term is to push the study of global governance beyond the notion 'add actors and processes into the international organization mix and stir.'"[125] We believe that the concept of global policymaking provides the perfect intellectual device with which to do this. For one thing, it helps capture recent global trends (e.g., orchestration, fragmentation, experimentation, legitimation) in a longer historical perspective. As a heuristic, it also helps capture the extent to which global governance is a process of political struggle. As Chapter 2 develops, we operationalize these insights in the form of value analysis (which sheds light on struggle and alternatives) and practice analysis (illuminating power dynamics and exclusion).

---

[124] See Steffek 2010.   [125] Weiss and Wilkinson 2014, 213.

2 | *The Making of Global Policies*
Analytical Framework and Methodology

This chapter lays out an analytical framework and a step-by-step methodology for the study of global policymaking. Building on some of the concepts introduced in Chapter 1, we argue that the making of global policies is a sociopolitical process akin to bricolage because of its improvisatory, haphazard, and practical nature. While existing scholarship is correct in stressing that policymakers pursue their interests on the global stage, the overall result is definitely not one of Pareto-optimizing rational design. Instead, we argue that global policies form protean patchworks of governance practices and competing universal value claims. Governance practices can be defined as socially meaningful patterns of action that are constitutive of the policymaking process, including its shifting playing field. Values, which capture the ideological dimension of policymaking, refer to the normative beliefs that inform the definition of global problems and the formulation of solutions.

The chapter is organized into two sections, the first dealing with practices and the second with values. Both follow a similar structure. We begin by explaining the analytical potential of the concepts we propose. We use preliminary evidence to illustrate the value of our framework. We then offer methodological advice to assist in the empirical study and operationalization of governance practices and universal value debates. Full case studies follow in Chapters 3, 4, and 5.

1 Global Policymaking in Practice

Let us start with a thought experiment. Imagine that a transnational team of physicists and engineers gathered to invent a functioning teleportation device. At minimal cost, both people and goods could be moved instantly from one corner of the globe to another. We can easily envision how such a revolutionary discovery would impact global governance. As capital funds and cutting-edge start-ups rush to invest and take control of the technology, a group of leading nations would confer, in an informal summit, to coordinate their position. The UN would soon hold a special session of the General Assembly on the matter, setting up a panel of international experts to come up with analysis and policy recommendations. Nonstate actors would no doubt get involved too. Multinational corporations would form a network to lobby for friendly domestic regulations and ask the WTO for the continuation of free trade, while coalitions of human rights groups and development NGOs would call for the worldwide diffusion of the technology. Upon reading the expert report, the UN Secretary-General would convene a large multistakeholder conference in one of the world's major cities, where states would adopt, under the scrutiny of international media, global activists, and private corporations, a hard-fought and partly hollow declaration. The UN General Assembly would later establish a dedicated working group, which would take two more years to negotiate an International Convention on Teleportation. Once adopted, this convention would give rise to repeated conflicts in which national governments from the Global North and South, teleportation companies, and civil society organizations would disagree on how the new global regime should operate.

As far-fetched as our teleportation example may sound, this description of how global problems are addressed is much more realistic. The social infrastructure of global governance, which is relatively stable and predictable, is composed of typical governance practices – that is, of socially organized and meaningful patterns of activities that tend to recur over time as societies navigate the vicissitudes of political and social change. In other words, global governance is made of well-established ways of doing things that serve as the platform for politics beyond the state. In contrast to rules set out in multilateral treaties, charters, and resolutions, practices are often less formal and thus harder to grasp, yet they nonetheless constitute a critical component of the architecture of global governance. Indeed, as they operationalize, fill the gaps between, and sometimes even contradict codified procedures, practices constitute a baseline for debating, negotiating, and deciding on global public policies. As such, established ways of doing things help organize world politics to a degree that has yet to be fully captured by students of global governance.

Analyzing global governance in practice helps us draw a more comprehensive picture of, and clarify the politics involved in, global policymaking. A practice approach, moreover, makes it possible to emphasize the recurring, albeit largely unwritten, patterns that form the backbone of everyday global governance – that is, "how the everyday business of global governance works in practice."[1] While practice scholarship has surged recently in IR (including in global governance studies), the fact remains that this unit of analysis has historically received less systematic attention than norms, regimes, and institutions. This is somewhat curious given the fact that practices figure centrally in seminal definitions of our object. For example, Cox defines global governance as "the procedures and practices which exist at the world (or regional) level for the management of political, economic, and social affairs."[2] For his part, Ruggie explains that governance refers to "the workings of the system of authoritative rules, norms, institutions, and practices by means of which any collectivity manages its common affairs."[3] Unfortunately, these insights have not been properly developed in global governance studies so far.

Our framework seeks to redress this deficit by emphasizing the political implications of global policymaking practices. Specifically, we show that governance practices often generate complex and contradictory social effects. Consider the case of global conferences, to take but one example. It is indeed the case that the hosting of global conferences, which has become a standard way of doing things in world politics, has enabled a broader variety of participants to join in the global conversation – NGOs, business corporations, experts, cities, etc.[4] The 2012 Rio+20 Conference, for example, was attended by 18,000 participants from across civil society. At the same time, though, global conferencing entails dynamics of co-optation and domination, and these in turn institutionalize a boundary between insiders and outsiders, favor lowest common denominators, and reinforce certain inequalities such as the North–South cleavage. Activists exert external pressure from the outside in, call into question the legitimacy

---

[1] Broome and Seabrooke 2012, 3. See also Adler 1998; Leander 2010; Bicchi 2011; Adler-Nissen 2014; Autesserre 2014; Best 2014; Best and Gheciu 2014b; Bremberg 2015; Bueger 2015; McNamara 2015; Græger 2016; Hofius 2016; Glas 2017; Henke 2017; Barnett 2018; Haugevik 2018; Jabko and Sheingate 2018; Pingeot 2018; Adler-Nissen and Drieschova 2019; Bode and Karlsrud 2019; Gehring and Dörfler 2019; Laurence 2019; Nair 2019; Cornut and de Zamaróczy 2021; Knappe 2021; Louis and Maertens 2021; Sondarjee 2021a; Sondarjee 2021b.

[2] Cox 1997, xvi.   [3] Ruggie 2010, xv.   [4] Finnemore and Jurkovich 2014.

of the negotiation process, and denounce the resulting sham democracy and status quo bias.[5] Along this line, Death argues that "it is extremely unlikely that any major diplomatic event ... could take place without some form of disruptive protest."[6] Overall, then, the inclusionary rules of global conferences remain subject to a rather restrictive view of public order.

In sum, global governance practices are infused with power dynamics that often point in conflicting directions. By adopting a constitutive rather than a causal orientation, a practice perspective helps us better understand the competing forces at play in global policymaking and elucidate the politics of global governance.

1.1 A Practice Approach to Global Governance

Practice theory is a large and diverse movement in both social and IR theory, and there is much debate over what practices are, what they do, where they come from, how best to study them, etc.[7] At the risk of oversimplifying, practice theory may be construed less as a substantive theory than as a methodological approach. Its most important contribution to knowledge development is to specify a unit of analysis – namely, practices, which may be defined as socially meaningful and organized patterns of activities. While practices remain a fairly new topic in global governance studies, a handful of scholars have demonstrated the benefit of such a focus in accounting for phenomena like international interventions, transnational agencies, multilateral diplomacy, and global experts.[8] Collectively, these authors have shown how the patterned ways of doing things globally constitute key political drivers of world politics. So far, however, few analysts have examined global policymaking or global governance as an integrated set of meaningful practices.

How does one know a global governance practice when one sees it? Observing recurring patterns of action generally requires minimal

---

[5] della Porta et al. 2006.   [6] Death 2015, 593.

[7] Pouliot 2008; Hopf 2010; Adler and Pouliot 2011; Bueger and Gadinger 2014; Cornut 2015; Pouliot 2016; Bourbeau 2017; Hopf 2018; Lechner and Frost 2018; Adler 2019.

[8] E.g., Eagleton-Pierce 2013; Autesserre 2014; Best and Gheciu 2014b; McNamara 2015; Sending 2015; Pouliot 2016; Cornut 2017. See also fn. 1.

insider knowledge of the social realm under study.[9] Often, the researcher may rely on practitioners themselves in identifying policy-making practices: for example, multilateral diplomats know very well what "holding the pen" entails in a multilateral negotiation. Through interviews, memoirs, handbooks, meeting minutes, and similar practical accounts, policymaking patterns of action become visible and lend themselves to a kind of inventory. Sometimes, though, it is up to scholars to organize their empirical observations and label certain ways of doing things based on analytical objectives. Such a procedure helps describe a set of overlapping practices that would otherwise remain disparate at the level of action. It should also be clear that the level of aggregation at which one pitches practice analysis should align with the particular research question. Sometimes, it is more useful to take a granular view and throw the spotlight on everyday routines, while other circumstances call for scaling up to macropatterns.

A practice approach to global governance promises two key advantages. First, studying global governance in practice helps draw attention away from formal rules – treaties, written procedures, etc. – and toward informal patterns of action that often pass under the scholarly radar.[10] Without a doubt, the politics of global governance is still largely defined by its institutionalized structures and norms. That being said, when formal rules lack specificity or contradict each other, practitioners are left to experiment and improvise ways of doing things, and these tend to accumulate over time. We suggest that such informal practices are integral to the global public policymaking process – on par with textual norms or codified rules.[11] Interestingly, in public policy studies, such a claim is not particularly controversial.[12] Lipsky's pathbreaking work on "street-level bureaucrats," to take one seminal example, showed that "public policy is not best understood as made in legislatures ... [but rather] in the crowded offices and daily encounters" of practitioners.[13] The same observation can be said to apply at the global level, where informal routines abound.

Beyond formal acts like the UN General Assembly voting on a resolution, global policymaking includes practices as varied as casting

---

[9] See Pouliot 2007; Pouliot 2013; Pouliot 2014.
[10] Pouliot 2020; Pouliot 2021.
[11] See Soroos 1986; Thakur and Weiss 2009; Cooper and Pouliot 2015; Pouliot and Thérien 2015.
[12] Laws and Hajer 2006; Yanow 2015.   [13] Lipsky 1980, xii.

an abstention at the Security Council, organizing cocktail parties at national delegations, granting certain countries leadership positions in an IO, forming groups of friends among states, or launching advocacy coalitions with NGOs. Such socially meaningful and organized patterns of (often informal) activities are recurring forms of action on the world stage. As they evolve over time, they structure global governance and fill in the many gaps that characterize the corpus of legal rules and procedures. As Weiss notes, "[a] surprisingly large number of elements of predictability, stability, and order are present in the contemporary international system despite the absence of a central authority."[14] Importantly, at the political level, not only do practices bring people together in effecting collective moves but also they pit them against one another in a variety of struggles.

Best provides a useful illustration of the practice approach when she maps key practices in global financial governance and observes their transformation over time. She asks, "Why is it that everyone working at a development agency or government-funded NGO nowadays (at least in certain countries) knows how to prepare a results matrix when proposing or evaluating a program, whereas they had not even heard of the practice fifteen years ago?"[15] The same problems had hitherto been addressed in a myriad of different ways, which shows that the historical development of global governance practices is neither linear nor inevitable, as the functionalist logic would have it. Peacekeeping practices also offer a stark reminder of the political importance of established as well as emergent ways of governing the globe. As Autesserre explains in her landmark study, "mundane elements – such as the expatriates' social habits, standard security procedures and habitual approaches to collecting information on violence – strongly impact the effectiveness of intervention efforts."[16]

By fleshing out the politics of global practices, we arrive at the second advantage we want to highlight: a practice approach fosters the study of global governance by spotlighting the structuring effects of widespread practices, especially those related to dynamics of inclusion and exclusion. After all, "[n]o governor governs alone."[17] This is where politics and power dynamics enter the analytical picture.

---

[14] Weiss 2013, 39.   [15] Best 2014, 25.
[16] Autesserre 2014, 9. See also Pingeot 2018; Laurence 2019; Bargués 2020.
[17] Avant, Finnemore, and Sell 2010a, 2.

Practice theory makes the innovative wager that practices are not merely outcomes to be explained; they are also *explanans* – that is, active social forces in the making and remaking of the world.[18] Put differently, established ways of doing things are socially productive: they generate effects and make other phenomena possible. Governance practices frame the global public policymaking process by creating baselines against which to measure political debates and interactions. Prevailing practices materialize power relations in ways that parallel and sometimes escape codification. If we want to understand "who governs the globe,"[19] then, we need to account for the patterned ways in which global actors come to socialize.

Of course, the fact that global governance practices are Janus-faced, in the sense that they generate both inclusionary and exclusionary effects, should not come as a surprise.[20] After all, the core positional logic of politics is a struggle between social forces that prefer the status quo (the incumbents) and those that favor transformation (the challengers).[21] The same goes for global governance, in which powerful actors strive to preserve their domination by limiting access to decision making, while peripheral and subordinate players want to open up the political game. Typically, the former frame their interests in terms of efficiency, and the latter, in terms of democratization.[22] This patterned form of confrontation helps explain why international practices produce complex political effects: just as ways of governing globally serve to structure world politics, they are also objects of struggle in and of themselves.

How, exactly, do international practices produce inclusion and exclusion? In broad terms, practices shape the social configuration of global governance: they generate new social ties and diversify the array of actors while also reinforcing existing structures and enabling power relations. If we are to capture this twofold movement, we must think of "the structure of global politics as a complex web of relationships among different authorities, accomplishing different tasks and dependent on one another for outcomes."[23] Ways of governing globally set

---

[18] Adler and Pouliot 2011.   [19] Avant, Finnemore, and Sell 2010b.
[20] See also Viola 2020.   [21] Fligstein and McAdam 2012.   [22] Koppell 2010.
[23] Avant, Finnemore, and Sell 2010a, 4.

Table 2.1 *The dual political effects of global governance practices*

Inclusion	Exclusion
Give voice to new and more diverse actors	Rest on arbitrary selection criteria and processes
Level up the playing field via flatter forms of cooperation	Reproduce or reinforce existing inequalities and cleavages
Enhance accountability by fostering public debate and transparency	Marginalize certain viewpoints and disempower certain positions

and reset the parameters of interaction, fostering forms of cooperation that are open to some actors but not to others. For instance, the broadening of participation in global fora is generally accompanied by club dynamics. The representation of more heterogeneous interests and values thus tends to be counterbalanced by other selective practices based on a quest for cohesiveness. Similarly, more transparent procedures may lead to the development of new ways of preserving secrecy. Often enough, practices that heighten accountability elicit defensive reactions from those in power, just like the formalization of procedure creates opportunities for arbitrariness in the implementation of policy.

Our argument is that most, if not all, practices generate such a combination of inclusion and exclusion. While the specific processes by which this dialectic obtains vary from one case to the next, there are a number of common features that are worth identifying. This is not only a useful way of better understanding the power politics at the heart of global governance. It also counters the widely held notion that novel ways of governing globally are necessarily inclusive because they open the political stage to new voices. Indeed, several practices that characterize contemporary global governance are legitimized on the very basis of their democratizing potential, as they are said to contribute to an extension of global political deliberations and amplify the voices of nonstate actors. Yet, despite these purported gains in inclusiveness, the balance sheet is altogether more mixed than such a view would suggest (see Table 2.1). Even as they expand participation to additional categories of actors, many of the emerging global governance practices may also encourage co-optation, elitism, and nontransparency.

This common dialectic of inclusion and exclusion provides an analytical key to better understand the politics of global public policymaking, including its power dynamics.

Take, for example, the practice of forming a multistakeholder partnership, which consists in establishing a loose, enduring, voluntary, and nonhierarchical association of heterogeneous agents with a common interest in resolving a problem of shared concern. In the twenty-first century, such "global policy networks"[24] have become all the rage in global governance. Yet, by fixing social ties across various categories of actors, multistakeholder partnerships lead to contrasting outcomes. For some, the idea that partnerships are flat and nonhierarchical suggests that their prevalence could signal more equality between participants. And yet, "often [these] networks are just another way for already powerful players, such as major powers and multinational companies, to achieve their goals."[25] In addition, multistakeholder partnerships tend to be characterized by "normative homogeneity,"[26] meaning that those who join already share a particular worldview, often at the exclusion of dissident voices.

Similarly, due to the prevalence of so-called revolving doors between one initiative and another, there tends to be a high level of "homophily" among participants.[27] As a result, one finds few partnerships that bridge the North–South divide, and even fewer South–South initiatives. The informality of participation rules, while ensuring more flexibility, also opens the door to arbitrariness, self-mandating, and exclusion.[28] Last, as a form of semiprivate governance, the practice of forming multistakeholder partnership presents significant accountability challenges. The lack of public oversight and transparency often makes it difficult for outsiders to evaluate the procedural legitimacy of these initiatives. Overall, there is little doubt that, as Avant puts it, "[g]lobal governance is more likely when participants represent multiple competencies."[29] That said, the ways in which these relations are organized are never neutral. As such, the practice of forming multistakeholder partnerships, beyond the "appearance of inclusivity" upon which it rests, comes with contradictory political effects.[30] We think that similar patterns obtain in most, if not all, contemporary global governance practices.

---

[24] Reinicke 1998.   [25] Avant and Westerwinter 2016, 17.   [26] Bob 2012.
[27] Murdie and Davis 2012.   [28] Bexell and Mörth 2010, 13.
[29] Avant 2016, 340.   [30] Bexell and Mörth 2010, 14.

Clearly, the practice perspective cannot fully replace other approaches centered on actors, institutions, rules, or ideas. In and of itself, it offers no more – and no less – than any other unit of analysis we might use to examine how global politics is structured and constructed. Yet, the value added of the practice approach can hardly be overstated. As they draw our attention to informal social relations, practices help uncover a largely hidden layer in the texture of global governance.

1.2 Studying Global Governance Practices: A Methodology

Identifying and making sense of global governance practices is a major intellectual challenge. For one thing, the task requires deep induction and sophisticated interpretation. In addition, the act of formulating a list of global governance practices will always be subject to debate. In any event, practices should be analyzed with methodological rigor. In what follows, we present a three-step process for identifying portable guidelines that seek to restore the contingency and idiosyncrasies of different practices while also attending to their common patterns.

As a sort of initial ground-clearing exercise, step 1 in this process consists of mapping the global policymaking space. This essentially involves identifying the key actors and sites of policymaking. For both, we recommend casting a wide net so as to go beyond formal processes and highly visible actors. Three tips seem useful here. First, include prenegotiations and implementation phases as integral parts of the policymaking process. Second, target not only dominant and powerful actors but also marginal ones, be they small states, NGOs, or marginalized civil society actors. As Weiss and Wilkinson rightfully point out, the "globally governed" remain a blind spot in global governance studies.[31] Third, expand the notion of the policymaking site beyond the formal chambers of IOs to cover less obvious venues and forms of policymaking. Civil society activism, op-eds by the heads of IOs, informal gatherings of states, and NGO petitions are all potentially relevant examples of the dispersed and fluid process of global policymaking.

Overall, the point is to espouse as broad a view of policymaking as possible. In order to capture the political dynamics at play, this first step should also include policy "unmaking," which describes "policy

---

[31] Weiss and Wilkinson 2018.

opponents' efforts to attack, eviscerate or kill policy processes."[32] In general, policymaking is a messy and contentious affair involving various practices of spoiling, contesting, or gatekeeping.[33] The main outcome of this first step should be a detailed timeline plotting key initiatives and turning points in the process. Crucially, reconstructing what the process looked like from the practitioners' perspectives – in the thick of it, as it were – allows us to include the "roads not taken,"[34] the dead ends, and parallel processes that took place without necessarily influencing the final outcome. Instead of starting from the adopted policy and reverse engineering its particular shape, then, the approach should be forward-looking so as to capture the contingent nature of the global policymaking process.

Step 2 consists of systematically inventorying the key practices that structure the global policymaking case at hand. Recall that practices are structured ways of doing things: recognizable and meaningful patterns of action that tend to recur in specific settings, while also allowing for some improvisation.[35] Once policymaking sites and actors are identified, the challenge is to organize the (usually chaotic) chain of events into a set of interlocking governance practices. Once again, where patterns of action are already labeled by practitioners, the job is easier: for example, one can easily locate the much-celebrated Millennium Summit of 2000 as an instance of global summitry. In some circumstances, however, identifying the pattern of global governance to which a particular event belongs can be tricky, especially for unexperienced researchers who lack insider understanding. Here, we recommend asking the fundamental social scientific question: What is this a case of? For example, when an NGO like Human Rights Watch seeks to address the Security Council, what pattern of action is it following? Insiders would respond that it is participating in an Arria-formula meeting (a recurring practice in UN diplomacy), but at a higher level of aggregation, seeking to address the Security Council could also be understood as a case of civil society briefing an IO. By locating specific exercises in broader patterns of action, practice analysis helps us climb the so-called ladder of abstraction and group together ways of governing globally.

---

[32] Bob 2010, 185.   [33] E.g. Carpenter 2010; Mundy 2010.
[34] Steffek 2006, 35.   [35] Adler and Pouliot 2011.

We break down step 2 – the inventory of global governance practices – into two subcomponents. First, global governance rests on a
limited set of policymaking practices: global conferences, the issuance
of reports, the setting up of commissions, etc. These recurring patterns
of actions on the global stage are mobilized as part of the consultation,
decision-making, and possibly implementation processes. New or idiosyncratic practices also emerge from time to time – take global surveys,
for instance, which were utilized for the very first time in the making of
the SDGs (see Chapter 3). Identifying global policymaking practices
thus requires an inductive approach that pays attention to established
as well as emerging patterns. Recall that practice analysis necessitates
going beyond formal procedures, even though most of what global
actors do, in fine, relies on forms of textualization and codification. In
general, global rules are incomplete, sometimes even contradictory; in
any event, there is ample room for maneuver in their interpretation and
implementation.[36] It is this space for improvisation and political work
in the policymaking process that practice analysis should magnify.
Once key policymaking practices have been identified – usually ranging
in number from three to ten, depending on the intricacies of each
policymaking process – they should then be put in relation with
one another. After all, it is not rare to find overlapping initiatives
happening simultaneously and forming a "web of practices."[37]

The second subcomponent of practice identification has to do with
what Swidler calls "anchoring practice"[38] – that is, the central pattern
of action structuring how a policy actually works. Identifying the
anchoring practice(s) of a global policy can be challenging and requires
scholarly judgment. The goal here is to identify the key way of doing
things that structures the proposed (or adopted) policy as such. As a
rule, anchoring practices exert gravitational effects akin to a star's
influence on its planets: other processes involved in the policy tend to
revolve around, or at least occur in reference to, them. Put differently,
anchoring practices make possible some related patterns of action but
not others. In general, an anchoring practice belongs to a particular
governance model or ideology, and as such, it ends up displacing
alternative organizing schemes for a particular policy. For instance,
Sending and Neumann contend that the World Bank's Country Policy
and Institutional Assessment is the "reference-point for interaction" in

[36] Pouliot 2021.   [37] Pouliot 2020.   [38] Swidler 2001.

the field of international assistance: "This infrastructure renders some 'strategies for action' available, and closes off others."[39] The bank's patterns of fund allocation, evaluation, and management all tend to revolve around this anchoring practice, as opposed to other development approaches. Any global public policy is similarly structured as a constellation of practices that are centripetally clustered.

Step 3 of our method requires documenting the political effects stemming from the fact that certain ways of doing things are more prevalent than others. The general focus should be on the dialectics of inclusion and exclusion: Who gets to participate? Issues of access, influence, and accountability should be central to such an analysis, because policymaking practices generate an unlevel playing field. How are conflicts settled? Here, practices of arbitration, consensus building, and decision making seem particularly salient: Which voices get amplified (or muted) and through what mechanisms? Are there forms of co-optation or normative homogeneity, and if so, what do they rest on? What kind of criteria must actors fulfill to be part of the policymaking process? Who gets to draft reports and select participants? Importantly, global policymaking practices often generate contradictory social effects: the analysis should tease them out carefully so as to capture the political complexity of global governance.

Take, for example, the practice of mandating a group of experts or a commission, which refers to the establishment by a global actor of a panel of specialists charged with investigating a global issue and providing political recommendations. Typically, such a body is legitimated by way of an opening up of the policy process and the valuing of technical knowledge. The goal is to enlarge the political debate beyond the bureaucratic or intergovernmental spheres to include individuals whose expertise renders them seemingly impartial. The stated objective of inclusion, however, cannot be properly understood without questioning what the experts' impartiality really means. Most commission members come from governments, and few from civil society. Critics describe international commissions as "exercises driven by a global managerial class."[40] While several commissions have been structured around a dual, North–South presidency, their membership has frequently been "Northern or Western-centric."[41] In terms of gender,

---

[39] Sending and Neumann 2011, 232.   [40] Cooper and English 2005, 11.
[41] Evans 2013, 292.

women have never been but a tiny minority of commission members, raising the specter of "'old boys club' diplomacy."[42] In terms of ideology, international commissions have systematically sought middle-of-the-road approaches that exclude "both the far left and more conservative elements,"[43] and favor recommendations consistent with the liberal internationalism of major IOs. Admittedly, international commissions have striven to become more open and participatory in recent years; yet, public staging only partially offsets their selective and arbitrary functioning.

Overall, the methodology we develop in the practice analysis of global governance has several advantages. First, it helps uncover the social texture of global policymaking by locating specific events and happenstances as part of the recurring forms of governance. Second, practice analysis sheds light on what makes a given policy hang together, as well as the anchoring mode of action that pushes alternatives to the sidelines. And third, practice analysis captures the politics of global governance by emphasizing the dialectics of inclusion and exclusion and the many ways in which power structures the making of global policies at every step of the way.

2 Global Policymaking as a Struggle over Universal Values

The second part of our analytical framework proposes to make sense of global governance as a patchwork of competing and polysemous value claims. To begin, it is crucial to recall that politics always entails a contest over values. The global stage is no exception to this social fact. To go back to our teleportation thought experiment, it is easy to imagine the kind of normative debates that our imagined scenario would trigger. Some would argue that the new technology is a private good that must be protected by current intellectual property laws; others would see it as a public good that should be made available to both poor and rich. Some would maintain that access to the teleportation equipment should be regulated by markets; others would argue that such a revolutionary machinery should be managed by a multilateral authority.

What this example suggests is simply that global actors do not all aspire to the same thing. Whether public discourse reveals sincere

---

[42] Ibid., 293.   [43] Cooper and English 2005, 14.

aspirations or cover for private interests, the fact remains that on the action floor, global policymaking is consistently structured around contending normative positions. It is important to note that at the global level, values are not simply plural or diverse – they are also inherently conflictual, which means that their pursuit often leads to intense debates and political clashes. Building on these insights, we argue that the definition of global problems, the establishment of collective goals, and the evaluation of joint solutions generate conflict because all of these processes involve choices, not only among possible actions but also between distinct values. As such, global governance is always the product of competing ideologies.

Here, our framework draws on a rich tradition in both political theory[44] and IR theory[45] that demonstrates how the foregrounding of normative conflicts highlights the political dynamics of global governance. This kind of approach seems all the more relevant when we consider that the globalization of ideologies in recent decades has intensified the global competition of values.[46] From this perspective, the key reason why global governance is so "poorly done,"[47] to borrow Murphy's description, concerns the value divides that pervade the global policymaking process.

Compared to openly normative perspectives, more conventional approaches appear incomplete at best. One popular view, for instance, explains global governance failings by the lack of political will and leadership at the international level. This is what the Commission on Global Governance had in mind when, in 1995, it deplored "the lack of leadership over a wide spectrum of human affairs."[48] A second line of explanation has to do with international organizations' malpractices. Noting that "every bureaucracy has the potential for pathology," Barnett and Finnemore show how "international organizations, too, are prone to dysfunctional behaviors."[49] Finally, a third way to account for the failures of global governance is to refer to the sheer complexity of the "wicked problems" it faces.[50] Following this view,

---

[44] E.g. Beitz 1979; Held 1995; Lu 2017.
[45] E.g. Reus-Smit 1999; Bernstein 2001; Steffek 2006; Hurrell 2007; Zürn 2018.
[46] Noël and Thérien 2008; Steger 2009; Stuenkel 2016; Voeten 2021.
[47] Murphy 2000.   [48] Commission on Global Governance 1995, 353.
[49] Barnett and Finnemore 2004, 35 and 41.   [50] Stone 2020.

the growing number of players, the highly technical nature of trans-sovereign issues, and the fragmentation of the institutional infrastructure of global governance have led to "gridlock."[51]

Problematically, none of these conventional explanations takes seriously the possibility of substantive value conflicts on the global stage. To redress this oversight, we argue that political actors constantly clash over the worth of different universal principles – over their meanings and implications – as well as their alternatives. By unpacking the dynamics of these ideological battles, we seek to offer a more comprehensive explanation for why it is so complicated to reach deals across a variety of constituencies on the global stage. While several analysts have taken note of the normative nature of global governance,[52] few have thus far specified the nature, the scope, and the mechanics of the value struggles upon which it rests. With Bernstein, we strive to avoid any "a priori basis for legitimacy" in order to ask, "not what should count as justification for recognizing the authority of an institution of global governance, but how particular requirements came to be viewed as justifications."[53]

We contend that references to the general interest or the common good, generally put forward in the form of so-called universal values, form the basic discursive structure of contemporary global governance. Appeals to the general interest are of course widespread in politics, across both time and space, but we start from the observation that they have become simply unavoidable on the world stage. The issue is not whether proclaimed values are truly universal or not, but what politics they generate. As Bartelson correctly notes, "a real and genuinely inclusive world community is a dream incapable of realization, since every attempt to transcend the existing plurality in the name of some set of universal values is likely to create conflict rather than harmony."[54] Our claim is not that genuine universality is possible or real, but rather that, at the empirical level, references to alleged universal values constitute an intrinsic component of the politics of global policymaking.

---

[51] Hale, Held, and Young 2013.
[52] E.g. Bernstein 2001; Ba and Hoffmann 2005; Steffek 2006; Bartelson 2009; Weiss and Thakur 2010; Weiss and Wilkinson 2014; Hofferberth 2015.
[53] Bernstein 2011, 19.   [54] Bartelson 2009, 8.

2.1 The Idiom of Universal Values

The notion of legitimacy offers a good starting point for highlighting the importance of universal values in global governance. As noted by Dingwerth and his coauthors, the legitimacy of international institutions has long been an object of debate. These contests can be interpreted as "negotiations about the acceptable reach and specific form of governance, about its protagonists, and about the inequalities that are accepted, (re)produced or deepened by it."[55] What needs to be added to this insight is that competing discourses concerning international institutions' legitimacy generally share one common trait: an appeal to ostensibly planetary ideals. On the face of it, there is nothing particularly surprising about the fact that political actors would appeal to the common good to publicly justify their positions and policies. However, what is missing from existing accounts is an understanding of the implications of the prevalence of such an idiom. We argue that attempts to depoliticize global debates by appealing to the general interest actually serve to reintroduce politics in a new guise.[56] To paraphrase Cox, universal values are always for someone and for some purpose.[57]

Consider the scholarly literature on the subject. Cosmopolitan theorists, for example, argue that democratic norms – such as participation, fairness, and transparency – are the key sources of global legitimacy.[58] In the words of Scholte, "to be effective and legitimate, governance needs to be accountable."[59] In a similar vein, Beitz defends individual autonomy and human rights as the bases for normative judgment in world politics.[60] Alternatively, the legitimacy of global governance is sometimes grounded in universal moral principles of justice and social ethics. Hurrell, for instance, claims that humanity forms a "global moral community"[61] whose main challenge is "to create a morally more satisfactory form of international society."[62] Whichever overarching value they promote, these scholars rest on various universalizing aspirations.

Contrary to common assumptions, references to universal values as sources of global legitimacy are not exclusive to overtly normative

[55] Dingwerth et al. 2019a, 11.
[56] See also Petiteville 2018; Louis and Maertens 2021.   [57] Cox 1981.
[58] Held 1995; Woods 1999.   [59] Scholte 2011a, 2.
[60] Beitz 1979; Beitz 2009.   [61] Hurrell 2007, 287.   [62] Ibid., 315.

literatures. They are also notably observable in other accounts that locate the legitimacy of IOs in rational-legal authority. As Steffek defines it, "[r]ational-legal rule is the rule of abstract laws that generally do not make any difference between their subjects."[63] Rational-legal authority is often presented as impartial because it is founded on expertise. According to Barnett and Finnemore, "The authority of IOs ... lies in their ability to present themselves as impersonal and neutral – as not exercising power but instead serving others."[64] Impartiality is thus often conceived as a legitimating principle whose worth is greater than others. In Zürn's words, "the fundamental condition for any belief in legitimacy in modernity [is] non-arbitrariness."[65]

As substantively distinct as they may be, there is a common feature among these competing views that needs to be underlined. Whether or not it is conveyed explicitly, the arguments advanced about the sources of global legitimacy often take a universalizing tone that seeks to detach them from any particular point of view, moment in time, or place of origin. In other words, in global governance, legitimacy is generally sought by recourse to a rhetoric of planetary aspirations. This presumes that the social acceptability of a given position flows not simply from its substance (promoting sustainable peace, alleviating poverty, etc.) but primarily from its form – that is to say, from the language in which a given claim is couched, as well as its purportedly generic scope. Our analytical framework seeks to understand how the language of universal values, which purports to be all-inclusive and to stand above politics, actually comes with a diversity of political priorities that often clash with one another. In our view, there is no better way to flesh out the normative and political nature of global governance than by examining the struggles over universal values that bring global actors together – and simultaneously pit them against each other.

Nearly all global actors speak the idiom of universal values. This observation is crucial because universal values are often thought to be the preserve of moral actors (e.g., humanitarians), experts (e.g., scientists), or international organizations (often described in abstract terms

---

[63] Steffek 2003, 260–1.

[64] Barnett and Finnemore 2004, 21. See also Seabrooke 2006; Avant, Finnemore, and Sell 2010b; Best 2014; Sending 2015.

[65] Zürn 2018, 11.

as the "international community"). However, even states – those self-regarding, egoistic units, according to IR textbooks – tend to formulate their positions in terms of the greater good. When national governments struggle to legitimize their positions on the global stage, they generally adopt the idiom of universal values (freedom, equality, the rule of law, sovereignty, etc.), thereby echoing the language of NGOs, experts, and IOs. Further, we contend that the idiom of universal values is not simply a cloak with which the dominant global actors can conceal their ulterior aims and thereby legitimize their superior positions, as realists and some critical scholars would suggest. Weaker parties also base their positions on particular visions of the common good as they seek to contest and disrupt the established order. Put differently, the idiom of universal values is used to oppose, just as much as to support, existing power structures. Even though it is sometimes rejected by some players, this language has come to form the core currency of global governance debates. Today, regardless of their specific nature, origins, or ambitions, global actors of all stripes tend to defend their positions with reference to universal values.

It should also be stressed that such references to universal values come in a variety of flavors as part of competing legitimacy discourses. At times, appeals to universal values remain rather inconspicuous, as in the technical language of expertise, which is usually draped in the veneer of scientific evidence.[66] And at other times – when they invoke democratic principles, for instance – global actors' claims to universality are openly normative and axiological. Our approach seeks to draw a connection between these distinct yet germane ways of framing legitimacy arguments in the global arena. As such, it helps us to better convey what Avant, Finnemore, and Sell call "principled authority," which is "legitimated by service to some widely accepted set of principles, morals, or values."[67] Extending this insight, we argue that the idiom of universal values upon which principled authority rests is articulated in a variety of ways – moral, technical, legal, etc. – whose common trait is an appeal to "noncontingent principles."[68]

To be sure, the rhetoric of universal values is not exclusive to the international realm. And yet, this type of argumentative strategy seems to be more prevalent in global affairs than in other spheres of political

---

[66] Best 2014; Sending 2015.   [67] Avant, Finnemore, and Sell 2010a, 13.
[68] Sending 2015, 131.

life.[69] Three decades ago, Soroos had already noted that in global policymaking, "[v]alues are often expressed in such terms as peace, economic development, social justice and sovereignty that are so widely embraced as to have become mere platitudes that are politically awkward to argue against."[70] Trite as they may be, though, these terms keep getting bandied about, with major implications for the politics of global governance. As they clash over global policies, the various actors involved – state and nonstate, weak and strong – draw on a shared vocabulary that seeks to stand above politics by appealing to collective ideals that are normally thought to transcend national preferences and sociocultural differences. In so doing, particular interests get clothed in the mantle of the public good.

How does the value struggle work in global governance? To answer this question, it seems useful to first define what values are. We conceive of values as the publicly debated political ideals of a given collective. As such, values are inherently axiological and normative. We prefer the concept of values over that of norms, however, for three basic reasons. First, we are less interested in the dynamics of rule-following (i.e., norms as standards of appropriate behavior) than in the political aspirations that structure global debates. Second, compared to norms, value claims have a distinctly "bottom-up" relationship with structures of authority, which facilitates the study of exclusion and discarded alternatives. Third, while the logic of appropriateness operates at the individual level and often gets difficult to track empirically, value debates are generally conducted out in the open, which makes their reconstruction easier.[71] Indeed, the public nature of values is of central importance to us, because as Elster notes, "the effect of an audience is to replace the language of interest by the language of reason.... Publicity does not eliminate base motives, but forces or induces speakers to hide them."[72] In global governance, which takes place in (semi)public settings such as multilateral organizations, global conferences, and other deliberative fora, actors are required to justify their stance in front of others – a process of reason-giving that has constitutive effects.[73]

[69] Bartelson 2009.   [70] Soroos 1986, 115.

[71] Krebs and Jackson 2007. For an application to UN debates, see Gray and Baturo 2021.

[72] Elster 1998, 111.   [73] Mitzen 2013.

Our focus on normative claims and clashes in no way implies that other factors, starting with material interests, do not play a role in global policymaking. We do not presume that values trump interests, as suggested for example in the debate between the logic of consequences and that of appropriateness.[74] Instead, we argue that interests simply cannot be expressed outside of some normative framework. Actors may long for wealth, power, and influence as much as they want, as soon as they step onto the global stage they are compelled to use universal value frames. As Elster puts it, "Rhetorics and strategic manipulation are parasitic upon the validity of social norms."[75] He further explains that such a mode of justification has to conform to the "consistency constraint" that derives from "the civilizing force of hypocrisy." In sum, when they partake in deliberations, global actors come to frame their interests – self-regarding as they may be – in terms that resonate with the audience.[76]

In IR, constructivists similarly argue that public speech leads to "rhetorical entrapment"[77] and "tongue-twisting."[78] For rationalists, alternatively, "arguing publicly [may] reshape one's private desires."[79] According to both approaches, deliberation transforms the pursuit of individual interest into something qualitatively different. A good example of how this publicity works at the global level may be found in Johnstone's analysis of Security Council deliberations. As he observes, within this body, an argument "is more likely to succeed if pure self-interest is diluted."[80] At the Security Council, Johnstone continues, "[h]aving to pay lip service to the collective interest and shared principles does not turn states into paragons of virtue, but it does force them to moderate the rhetorical positions they take."[81] In other words, a key distinctive trait of global governance is that its competing discourses generally refer to the world's welfare in order to legitimize global policies.[82] As they pursue their interests, states, IOs, and civil society organizations are faced not only with contending preferences but also with the need to communicate their own position in a way that will make sense to their counterparts. In so doing, they

---

[74] March and Olsen 1998.   [75] Steffek 2006, 14.   [76] Elster 1998, 104.
[77] Schimmelfennig 2001.   [78] Krebs and Jackson 2007.
[79] Fearon 1998, 54. See also Voeten 2011.
[80] Johnstone 2003, 454. See also Nuñez-Mietz 2018.   [81] Johnstone 2003, 454.
[82] See Steffek 2003; Bernstein 2011; and Zürn 2018.

resort to a peculiar kind of discourse in which universalizing aspirations serve as a shared format.

As soon as they enter public debate, values produce effects that are irreducible to the question of whether people "really" adhere to them or simply use them as part of a window-dressing strategy. Our argument, then, seeks not to invalidate but rather to complement interest-based approaches, which explain global governance bargains in terms of the distribution of preferences. Without a doubt, actors are subject to a variety of material and symbolic incentives, often making multilateral negotiations difficult. Far from mere cheap talk, the idiom of universal values has constitutive effects vis-à-vis the politics of global governance: its normative structure frames exchanges by legitimizing certain viewpoints and invalidating others. In short, distinct repertoires of universal values feed into alternative ideologies of global governance. Through this conflict of worldviews, global legitimacy is produced, reproduced, and contested.

Conceiving of universal values as public objects of struggle leads us to highlight, first, their relationships with alternatives, and second, their polysemy or inherent ambiguity. As it unfolds, global policymaking exposes distinct combinations of collective ideals stemming from competing ideologies. This contest of worldviews is what makes multilateral negotiations so difficult. To move forward, global policymaking needs to find a compromise that will typically favor one set of universal values over others while leaving space for interpretation from all sides. Normative cleavages are thus diluted in what some scholars have called "constructive ambiguity." We prefer the term "polysemous compromise" since it allows us to emphasize how value cleavages can be subsumed into a wide range of meanings, none of which is deemed ambiguous by its defenders.

Take, for example, Steffek's study of the making and unmaking of the compromise of embedded liberalism.[83] This normative assemblage, primarily promoted by the US after the Second World War, rested on "a certain division of labor between the national and international level of policymaking," with the latter strictly focused on liberalization.[84] Interestingly, Steffek adds, "embedded liberalism was defended against an alternative program ... of 'redistributive multilateralism' ... a vision of international cooperation in which goals such as employment,

---

[83] Steffek 2006; also Ruggie 1982.   [84] Steffek 2006, 4.

welfare and socio-economic development are pursued by the institutions of global governance through (re-) distributive political measures."[85] In a related vein, Bernstein analyzes the rise of the "compromise of liberal environmentalism" in the wake of the 1992 Rio Conference, and shows how the vagueness of the sustainable development ideology has made it a favorite reference point in global environmental governance, including in squaring off with its alternative value systems such as the so-called Washington Consensus.[86] Along the way, alternative ideologies such as the green economy, command-and-control, or common property ownership got pushed to the wayside of history.[87]

To be sure, our approach does not deny the possibility of consensus in global affairs. But it does suggest that consensus is seldom based on truly shared understandings. In that sense, the very existence of universal values remains a matter of debate. For some, universal values that transcend culture are indeed possible; for others, such a position is nothing but a reflection of "ideologies of empire."[88] For our purpose, it will suffice to observe that, by serving as a focal point in global debates, notions of the common good tend to create an intriguing paradox: as it attempts to depoliticize global governance, the idiom of universal values actually ends up returning politics to the fore.

2.2 *Studying Global Value Debates: A Methodology*

On top of practice analysis, our methodology for the study of global governance involves mapping the key value debates that structure the public policymaking process. Empirically, value claims may be located by looking for the normative assumptions that inform actors' positions. Sometimes, the value claims are explicit ("we support free trade"); sometimes, they have to be inferred from what a given statement takes for granted ("trade is good for the poor"). In any event, universal values form the bedrock of political argumentation since they are asserted as good though rarely demonstrated as such.

In order to document value cleavages, we recommend discourse analysis based on deep immersion in policy debates. Building on the timeline constructed for the study of practices, key moments of policymaking may be identified in order to access declarations, reports, and

---

[85] Ibid., 5.   [86] Bernstein 2001.   [87] Ibid., 178.   [88] Bartelson 2009, 2.

communiqués from global governors and globally governed alike. It is critical to cover a wide variety of constituencies, in terms of the size, origin, and nature of the actors, ranging from powerful states to small island countries, from formal IOs like the World Bank to informal groups like the G77, from large NGOs headquartered in the North to community associations based in the South, from multistakeholder partnerships to think tanks, and from major cities to private corporations. A key objective here is to counter the post hoc rationalizations by which policy outcomes come to look like inevitable solutions to technical problems (see Chapter 1). While powerful actors tend to have much more visibility and leave a greater number of discursive traces, more marginal actors are often the ones advocating substantive change. The latter should never be dismissed simply because they are less visible or influential.

By emphasizing alternative views, including radical ones, value analysis throws light on widespread power dynamics and persistent ideological conflicts that are too easily brushed under the carpet when one looks at policymaking retroductively. In mapping value debates, then, equal emphasis should be given to dominant and weaker actors, and particular attention should be paid to discarded ideas. Worldviews are often positionally derived, as Kennedy illustrates: "We should not be surprised to learn that people in the global North and the global South understand the nature of global power and order quite differently."[89] Another important step is to look for the evolution of viewpoints and documents over time. Drafts of agreements or communiqués often contain excerpts eliminated at a later point, suggesting once again that the final outcome embodies the triumph of one position over a number of discarded variations.

A similar balancing act should guide text selection. By going back and forth between primary documents and scholarly literatures, one may start to glimpse patterns in value positions, as well as further references that ratify such findings. Even within a given social group, it is important to remain attentive to diverging voices. It is well known, for instance, that ministers of finance and ministers of international development have different agendas and priorities. The goal is to read enough to reach what ethnographers call the "saturation point" – the moment at which the marginal benefits of each additional text

---

[89] Kennedy 2008, 832.

approaches zero in terms of supplementary insight. This benchmark is obviously relative, especially since we emphasize the need to cover marginal and liminal positions, which may be hard to come by. Here, Hansen's methods of reading and textual selection provide apt guides in terms of which materials to consult and how to infer value debates from them.[90] As always, multiple interpretations of the discursive space of policymaking are possible, yet the quality of evidence as well as the diversity of views taken into account should help adjudicate between them.

Global policymaking typically results from value debates that, for heuristic purposes, we reduce to three dimensions. First, actors disagree on the very nature and magnitude of the global problems they are confronting. Second, they debate the end goal or social purpose with which the chosen policy should align. And third, actors face off on the ways and means by which their end goals should be implemented in order to obtain. These three dimensions of policymaking – problem, ends, and means – generate conflict because they all involve choice, not only among possible actions to be taken but also between distinct values. As such, global governance is always the product of competing ideologies.

On top of these three dimensions, we distinguish between two types of value claims in global policymaking. First, as mentioned earlier, initial discussions generally exhibit value cleavages: two positions clash and are presented as "policy alternatives."[91] Sometimes, debates are more about shades of gray – a matter of emphasis and prioritization – but this should not obscure the ideological differences running through them. The second aspect consists of what we have termed polysemous compromises – that is, formulations that global actors come up with in an effort to paper over their disagreements. In diplomatic settings, insofar as diverse audiences espouse different worldviews, actors often move forward through the use of constructive ambiguity. Polysemous compromises thus abound in global governance because as Steffek[92] underscores, "Diplomacy is a practice of containing rather than resolving fundamental disagreement." As multivocal statements, value claims inherently contain (in both senses) multiple meanings that reflect a certain flexibility, if not plasticity in admitting competing interpretations of the same words.

[90] Hansen 2006.   [91] Soroos 1990, 312.   [92] Steffek 2005, 229.

Table 2.2 *Values analysis grid (with exemplars)*

	Value cleavages	Polysemous compromises
What is the problem?	Bad governance vs. systemic inequality	Global responses to global challenges are inadequate
What are the ends?	Global governance needs to be more efficient vs. global governance needs to be more democratic	International cooperation and rule of law must be strengthened
By what means?	Fine-tuning vs. structural reform of multilateral institutions	UN Charter principles must be upheld

These sorts of surface consensuses, which tend to take the form of buzzwords or rhetorical commonplaces that mean different things to different people, typically emerge as the policymaking process unfolds. Likewise, value cleavages tend to gradually fade away as negotiations progress. That is generally the result of one side winning over the other, which should not be mistaken for the absence of alternative viewpoints. Overall, then, the value claims made during the policymaking process assume something of a temporal sequence, from stark divisions to polysemous compromises. As our case studies will later demonstrate, synthesizing value debates in a table that identifies cleavages and compromises regarding the three dimensions of policymaking is helpful. While it is impossible to account for all potential positions in such a graphic synthesis, the goal of this exercise is to capture as broad an array of views as possible (see Table 2.2 for generic examples).

The goal of a values analysis grid is synthesis: the researcher should seek to boil down political debates to a handful of value cleavages per question, with the attendant polysemous compromises presenting themselves as they emerge in the policymaking process. The table should contain recurring formulations and expressions of normative stances as found in the primary and secondary literatures. It is important to substantiate the table with a representative sample of direct quotations from global actors and subjects; this is why using a variety of documents, including speeches, reports, and position papers, is so useful. These should not only come from a variety of actors but also represent different phases of the policymaking process. After all, if we analyze global policies based on the final outcome, it almost always seems like everyone wanted the same thing from the get-go, as though the process was governed by a simple functionalist logic. But such post hoc rationalization is an illusion created by the fact that political entrepreneurs work very hard to create the "gloss of harmony"[93] that often characterize global governance. By focusing on the process, the researcher is better able to see how competing worldviews clash until some get sidelined and a more or less uneven compromise emerges.

The biggest challenge of values analysis rests in organizing disparate political statements into limited sets of values. There is no magic wand on offer here: the best solution is to proceed inductively, by reading a lot and from a wide array of sources, until family resemblances (in Wittgenstein's sense) start to emerge. The logic of family resemblance is that people who look alike should be grouped together. In terms of values, this means that actors who take stands with a similar political orientation or aspiration, despite apparent differences in wording and style, are probably espousing the same value claim. When actors explicitly name this value, the analysis is made much easier (although one should never take value statements entirely at face value). In many cases, though, it is up to the analyst to label the value that bridges various positions. Likewise, family "dissemblances" also become clearer, paving the way for the identification of normative cleavages.

Heuristically, one may conceive of values in opposing pairs. Among the most classic divides are order vs. justice, freedom vs. equality, responsibility vs. solidarity, economic vs. social priorities, and individual vs. collective rights. Above all, however, it is important to remember that values do not exist in a void. They are hierarchically organized as elements of a system of values or an ideology. Particularly visible in the history of East–West and North–South policymaking, the Left–Right opposition has long been a key driver of global governance.[94] Although ideological coherence is no more than an analytical construct, all global actors seek to display some form of normative consistency.

In order to illustrate the difference between value cleavages and polysemous compromises, we resort to a short empirical vignette. As

---

[93] Müller 2013.   [94] Noël and Thérien 2008; and Noël and Thérien 2023.

a global policy, the reform of the UN Security Council has long been in the making. Started in 1992, the debate has since taken many twists and turns without resulting in any tangible result. The main issue at stake is how to legitimize (and delegitimize) the different proposals put forth, with options ranging from new permanent members to renewable elected terms through veto abolition. Universal values have proven a very useful rhetorical device in advancing and undermining the various positions. While the main normative cleavage opposes output-oriented with input-oriented forms of legitimacy, most of the contemporary debate actually focuses on subtle variations in the meaning of the central value of representativeness.

Let us start with the fundamental value cleavage at stake: output-oriented vs. input-oriented legitimacy. For advocates of the former, the rallying cry is the value of efficiency: the need for the Council to deliver the goods in terms of maintaining international peace and security. In 2004, a high-level panel report observed that the Council "was created to be not just a representative but a responsible body, one that had the capacity for decisive action."[95] In order to "combine power with principle,"[96] the report suggested an "increase [in] the involvement in decision-making of those who contribute most to the United Nations financially, militarily and diplomatically."[97] Among states, the main advocates of efficiency include Western countries as well as current permanent members of the Council. To use Australia's words, "The principal concern in any review should be to maintain and, where possible, enhance the effectiveness of the Security Council."[98]

More recently, the value of efficiency has receded from Security Council debates, with the normative framework shifting perceptibly toward input-oriented notions of legitimacy. Ever since the failure of the UN's World Summit, organized to celebrate the sixtieth anniversary of the UN in 2005, the value of representativeness has come to dominate the negotiations, forming a new polysemous compromise on the issue of Security Council reform. However – and this is the second component of our values analysis – this allegedly universal value is interpreted in a wide variety of ways. Empirically, the very same value of representativeness gives way to a range of competing views from credibility to diversity, inclusiveness, equality, and accountability.

---

[95] UN General Assembly 2004, para. 244.   [96] Ibid., 77.
[97] Ibid., para. 249.   [98] UN General Assembly 1993, 8.

One of the most dominant concepts in the debate is credibility: a more representative Council would enjoy more credibility, which in turn would mean that it is better positioned to remain a central actor in the global governance of international security. So-called rising powers are among the loudest voices here, with Brazil calling on the Council "to reflect today's geopolitical realities."[99] During his tenure as Secretary-General, Ban Ki-moon similarly argued that the Council would boost its credibility by "reflect[ing] today's political and economic realities, not those of more than half a century ago."[100]

Other interpretations of representativeness depart more significantly from output-oriented legitimacy. A group of states under the banner of Uniting for Consensus (UfC) calls for a Council that better reflects the world's diversity and pluralism. In parallel, the Non-Aligned Movement has made clear that Council reform should be targeted "at augmenting the power of the countries of the South."[101] Meanwhile, building on article 23 of the UN Charter, which provides for "equitable geographic distribution" of (elected) Council members, other actors interpret representativeness in terms of geographical diversity.

Harping on the polysemy of representativeness, some countries argue in favor of inclusiveness as a key value in reform debates, especially when it comes to more marginalized states. Denmark advocates a greater voice for small states because they "form the majority of the membership of the United Nations."[102] For its part, Nigeria laments the underrepresentation of African nations on the Council, which it calls a "historical injustice ... to the African continent."[103] Alternatively, some member states emphasize cultural diversity as the basis for representativeness. For instance, the Organization of the Islamic Conference calls for "the representation of the main forms of civilization in the Security Council."[104]

Adding to the debate's complexity, the value of equality is championed by many poor and small countries, as well as by larger ones. India invokes demography to argue that "population ... represents

---

[99] Unpublished statement by Brazilian representative, New York, December 8, 2009.
[100] UN Secretary-General 2009.   [101] Quoted in Bourantonis 2005, 55.
[102] Unpublished statement by Danish representative, New York, June 11, 2009.
[103] Unpublished statement by Nigerian representative, New York, January 19, 2010.
[104] Unpublished statement by Syrian representative, New York, undated (presumably January 2010).

both an expression of the principle of democracy and an element of power."[105] Among aspiring permanent members, equality rather involves obtaining the same privileges as current veto-wielders: the G4's 2005 draft resolution, for instance, states that "[n]ew permanent members should have the same responsibilities and obligations as the current [ones]."[106] In a similar spirit, the African Group invokes justice and fairness to argue that its members should "enjoy all the prerogatives and privileges of permanent membership."[107] By contrast, for Pakistan, Council reform "should avoid perpetuating the current inequities by creating new centres of privilege."[108]

Indeed, countries that oppose new permanent seats emphasize the importance of the electoral mechanism and of accountability as a source of representativeness: "For UfC the principle of standing for election, periodically, in front of the General Assembly must be included in any proposal to enlarge the Security Council."[109] By a similar logic, the World Federalist Movement opposes new permanent seats, which it portrays as "a retrograde step that would condemn the Council to greater inefficiency and less accountability. Per definition, permanent members risk no democratic elective repercussions for failure or misconduct."[110] The Global Policy Forum adds that a truly representative decision-making body should include the constituents who are directly affected by global governance schemes: "[t]oo often [the Council] seems the captive of great power politics with little connection to the needs of the world's peoples."[111]

Overall, it seems fair to say that reform debates have for the most part pitted the proponents of two distinct sets of universal values against each other: those who want a more efficient Council and those who favor its democratization. As a value discourse, however, the output-oriented notion of legitimacy has almost completely given way to an input-oriented discussion about what representativeness actually means. Needless to say, these distinct positions – which refer

---

[105] UN General Assembly 1993, 47.   [106] UN General Assembly 2005f, 3.
[107] Unpublished statement by Sierra Leone representative, New York, December 23, 2009.
[108] UN General Assembly 1993, 74.
[109] Unpublished statement by Italian representative, New York, March 31, 2009.
[110] Conference room article submitted on behalf of Colombia and Italy, New York, January 21, 2010, 2.
[111] James and Nahory 2005.

Table 2.3 *Global policy analysis: A methodology*

Tasks	Steps	Advice
Practice analysis	Mapping the policymaking space	Cast a wide net: include prenegotiations and implementation phases, target powerful and marginal actors, expand beyond formal chambers, and include policy "unmaking" Generate a detailed timeline of events, including roads not taken
	Inventorying governance practices	Identify policymaking practices (both established and innovative) Point out the anchoring practice(s) around which the policy revolves
	Unpacking governance practices	Delineate the inclusionary and exclusionary effects of practices Pay attention to issues of access, influence, and decision making
Values analysis	Identify textual sources covering a broad range of actors (weak and strong)	Use the timeline constructed during practice analysis to identify key moments of debate Pay special attention to alternative views and marginal positions Reconstruct the debate as it happened – e.g., by looking for evolutions in documents
	Construct the values table (problem, ends, means) and gather evidentiary quotes	Identify the most important value cleavages that structure the debates by looking for family resemblances between positions Locate the polysemous compromises that are eventually adopted by most actors

to fairly different views of the general interest – would obviously lead to contrasting reform policies.

Summing up this chapter, Table 2.3 captures the different steps, components, and advice of our methodology. In Chapters 3, 4, and 5, we will apply and illustrate our approach with three in-depth case studies.

Conclusion: The Normativity of Practices, the Practicality of Values

The theoretical and methodological framework developed in this chapter helps recover the political nature of global governance. In the bricolage of global policymaking, a variety of practices, generally established but sometimes new, are combined in order to create a variety of contingent patchworks. Privileged patterns of action not only create unequal political effects, specifically by favoring the participation of some while marginalizing others; they also push alternative modes of action to the sidelines. By identifying prevalent practices, then, our framework captures the dialectics of inclusion and exclusion, while also making sense of historical shifts in dominant modes of global governance.

When it comes to value debates, our framework illuminates the persistence of social conflict as the normal and expected condition of global policymaking. Normative patchworks are generated by global governors out of multidimensional ideological cleavages. Accounting for such polysemous compromises, global governance may be read as a shifting normative terrain on which some worldviews triumph over others, often repeatedly, in a process that sees alternatives discarded along the way. By reconstructing value debates, we better understand the structure of global ideologies, and we can even point at historical trends in terms of who (and what options) tend to win or lose more often than others in never-ending normative struggles.

At the risk of simplifying, then, one could say that while values orient global policymaking, practices organize the overall process. In this ontology, ideas and material forces combine at every step of the way to shape the normative and practical patchwork of global governance. Ideationally and materially, global policymaking follows the logic of bricolage as outlined in Chapter 1. On one hand, actors paper over their value differences via constructive ambiguity and polysemous compromise; such normative muddling through helps participants claim a common ideal, even when it is clear that the consensuses reached are biased in favor of some players over others. On the other hand, actors piece together global policies by improvising shifting patchworks of practices; these established ways of governing the global stage allow claims of inclusiveness and equality, even though the playing field remains highly exclusive and unequal. Throughout the process of global policymaking, social conflict is everywhere, although it is often hidden below the surface.

As possible extensions of our framework, there are several other ways in which global policymaking practices and value debates interact. First, any given practice tends to instantiate some values at the expense of others. Intergovernmental negotiations, for example, privilege sovereignty over democracy. Second, anchoring practices are normatively situated. Benchmarking, to take a contemporary example, falls on the side of soft law, as opposed to fully fledged regulation. Third, policymaking practices, by amplifying certain voices and excluding others, play a large role in defining the breadth of values being represented in the process. It is often decried, for instance, that indigenous worldviews are left out of the global conversation, in part because of exclusive policymaking practices. Fourth, values enable and constrain the selection of certain policymaking and anchoring practices. For instance, Bernstein shows how the compromise of "liberal environmentalism" promotes practices such as tradeable pollution permits over "command-and-control" methods.[112] Fifth and finally, political values are by definition oriented toward action and thus practice. When one advocates justice over order, to pick a classic example, this normative program points toward more practice upheaval than its opposite. By contrast, the narrative of "best practices" favors new forms of public management.[113]

In the three case studies that follow, we intend to put our framework to work. While the making of the SDGs, the HRC, and the PoC doctrine each present their own idiosyncrasies, they also share striking similarities, especially when it comes to the bricolages of practices and values on which they are based. Following our three case studies, we will return in Chapter 6 to these broader trends in the contemporary evolution of global governance.

---

[112] Bernstein 2001, 7.   [113] Bernstein and van der Ven 2017.

3 | The Sustainable Development Goals

Planning without a Blueprint

As the centerpiece of the 2030 Agenda adopted by the UN in September 2015, the SDGs provide an excellent case study with which to demonstrate the usefulness of our analytical framework. Designed as a follow-up to the Millennium Development Goals (MDGs), which guided international development policies from 2000 to 2015, the 2030 Agenda proposed a new development road map for the subsequent fifteen-year period. According to the official rhetoric, this road map lays out "a supremely ambitious and transformational vision" revolving around seventeen SDGs as well as 169 specific targets spanning the social, economic, and environmental aspects of development.[1] The most iconic SDGs deal with the eradication of poverty and hunger, the fight against climate change, and the creation of a global partnership for sustainable development. Many people saw the adoption of the SDGs as a "game changer" capable of "transition[ing] development [away] from a post-colonial to a global project."[2]

As could be expected, recent scholarship has focused on the implementation of the SDGs.[3] Yet, one should not forget that the SDGs were first and foremost "the result of political negotiations."[4] And as we shall see, by unpacking the making of the SDGs as an assemblage of practices and values, we can gain a unique perspective on the *political* content of that global policy. Importantly, the bricolage of practices and the values struggles through which the SDGs emerged were not programmed through a formal set of procedures. Rather, as our analysis shows, the SDGs' script was not written in advance for the UN supertanker does not follow a predetermined route. The 2030 Agenda

---

[1] UN General Assembly 2015, para. 7. See also Dodds, Donoghue, and Leiva Roesch 2016.

[2] Fukuda-Parr and Muchhala 2020, 9.

[3] Hanson, Puplampu, and Shaw 2017; Meuleman 2019; Hazra and Bhukta 2020; Bexell and Jönsson 2021.

[4] Bexell and Jönsson 2021, 1.

is also a useful reminder that for every global public policy adopted, alternative courses of action that were once part of the conversation are discarded along the way. The air of improvisation that prevailed in the negotiations over the SDGs was well summarized by Kenyan Ambassador Macharia Kamau, who, along with his Irish counterpart David Donoghue, was in charge of the final negotiation of the 2030 Agenda. When diplomatic discussions on the SDGs began, Kamau explains, "no one had any clear idea what shape or character they would take nor how many there would be."[5]

This chapter examines the making of the SDGs as a global policy. It analyzes the bricolage of practices and values that structured the "global conversation" leading up to the adoption of the 2030 Agenda.[6] Our analysis illuminates not only the experimental nature of the SDGs' creation but also the power relations and the political choices that the SDGs reflected.

1 The Making of the SDGs: Open-Ended Improvisation

From the get-go, the SDGs' raison d'être was understood as addressing the "unfinished business" of the MDGs,[7] which had previously been described as the "world's biggest promise" and the most ambitious effort to fight poverty in history.[8] Considering the immense political significance of the 2030 Agenda, examining its practical underpinnings can help us make sense of the evolution of global public policymaking as well as its political nature. As Table 3.1 shows, the SDGs were structured around a set of seven key practices, some of which are well established in global governance while others are more innovative. We group these patterns of action in two categories: first, the practices that organized the negotiation process, and second, the "anchoring practice" of the SDGs as a public policy – that is, goal-setting. Haphazardly enacted over a period of five years, this bricolage of practices defined the patterns of inclusion and exclusion that would ultimately characterize the SDG process.

---

[5] Dodds, Donoghue, and Leiva Roesch 2016, xviii.
[6] United Nations Development Group (UNDG) 2013a.
[7] UN General Assembly 2015.　　　[8] Hulme 2009.

Table 3.1 *Key practices in the making of the SDGs*

Practices	Instances	Political effects
Holding a high-level plenary meeting	General Assembly (2010, 2015)	States control the initiation and completion of policymaking
Creating an interagency coordination mechanism	UN Task Team (sixty United Nations agencies)	International public servants provide background analysis
Holding public hearings	United Nations Development Group (eighty-eight countries)	Consultation with national stakeholders mediated by international public servants
Launching a worldwide survey	"My World" (2013)	Outreach to parts of global civil society
Establishing a panel of eminent persons	High-Level Panel of Eminent Persons on the Post-2015 Development Agenda (2012)	Elder statesmen give strategic advice for the production of draft texts
Establishing an experts group	Sustainable Development Solutions Network (2012)	Expertise from scientific community facilitates operationalization and implementation of agreement
Goal-setting (anchoring)	Open Working Group (2013–14); Intergovernmental Negotiations (2015); Inter-Agency Expert Group (2015)	Diplomats provide leadership on goals, while experts define indicators; alternative courses such as rulemaking get discarded

1.1 An Unscripted Negotiation Process

The making of the SDGs started and ended with a High-Level Plenary Meeting of the General Assembly. The SDGs thus constituted a typical example of how states exercise control over the production of global policies, in this case by initiating the process and preserving ultimate decision-making authority. Although concerns about what would happen after 2015 surfaced right after the adoption of the MDGs in 2000, it was only during the 2010 High-Level Meeting – which had sought to give momentum to the MDGs – that UN member states formally asked the Secretary-General to formulate a new development framework for the post-2015 period. The resulting resolution, though vague, requested that the Secretary-General "make recommendations in his annual reports, as appropriate, for further steps to advance the United Nations development agenda beyond 2015."[9]

It was during another High-Level Plenary Meeting of the General Assembly, attended by 136 heads of state, that the SDGs were adopted in 2015.[10] Of course, the presence of such a large number of world leaders was in no way mandatory. Indeed, their involvement was mostly symbolic, as the approval of heads of state added to the legitimacy of the UN decision. This way of crafting policy was all the more relevant given that it was based on the precedent established in 2000, when political leaders from around the world adopted the Millennium Declaration, from which the MDGs emerged. Clearly, summitry has gradually become one of the most prevailing practices of global policymaking.

Alongside this state-centric dynamic, attempts to design inclusive practices appeared early on in the SDG negotiating process. This took shape through a variety of consultation mechanisms spearheaded by the UN Secretariat. Internally, the Secretary-General deviated from established practices by creating a Task Team composed of sixty UN agencies, which he invited to clarify the organization's development priorities.[11] This innovation was deemed essential in order to define a coherent institutional perspective on the post-2015 agenda. The three reports released by the Task Team fed into many of the subsequent discussions on the post-2015 period.[12]

---

[9] UN General Assembly 2010b, para. 81.
[10] Kamau, Chasek, and O'Connor 2018, 242.
[11] UN Department of Economic and Social Affairs 2010.
[12] UN System Task Team on the Post-2015 UN Development Agenda 2012; UN System Task Team on the Post-2015 UN Development Agenda 2013a; UN System Task Team on the Post-2015 UN Development Agenda 2013b.

Externally, the United Nations Development Group (or UNDG, the organ that coordinates UN development activities) and the Secretary-General initiated several forms of consultation. While this was in line with standard practice, the UNDG also went beyond that. First, it consulted stakeholders in close to 100 countries.[13] Interestingly, this outreach increased the process's transparency and legitimacy, but it had few concrete inclusionary effects. Indeed, the results from the national meetings were barely taken into consideration by the diplomats who negotiated the SDGs' final wording in New York.[14]

Second, in a move unprecedented in global governance, the UNDG launched in 2013 the "My World" survey to assess international public opinion on the post-2015 agenda. Described as "the largest global survey ever held," the initiative collected seven million responses.[15] This number, however, should be pondered against the fact that 80 percent of respondents came from only five countries (India, Mexico, Nigeria, Pakistan, and Sri Lanka). While it is impossible to measure the survey's impact on the making of the SDGs, it did serve as a political resource for a number of state interventions during the intergovernmental discussions.

Third, in line with much recent global policymaking, the Secretary-General established a High-Level Panel of Eminent Persons on the Post-2015 Development Agenda (HLP) in July 2012. The HLP, which was cochaired by Indonesian President Susilo Bambang Yudhoyono, Liberian President Ellen Johnson Sirleaf, and British Prime Minister David Cameron, gathered twenty-seven experts from both the Global North and the Global South. After leading a series of consultations throughout the world, the group delivered its report in May 2013. One of the document's main achievements was to popularize the objective of "leaving no one behind." Largely inspired by NGOs, this objective later became a key reference in the post-2015 agenda.[16]

A fourth initiative was the creation of the Sustainable Development Solutions Network (SDSN), which exemplified the well-established practice of spurring the growth of policy networks in governance circles. Established under the auspices of the Secretary-General and

---

[13] United Nations Development Group (UNDG) 2013b, 43.
[14] Dodds, Donoghue, and Leiva Roesch 2016, 49.
[15] United Nations Development Program (UNDP) 2014, v.
[16] High-Level Panel of Eminent Persons on the Post-2015 Development Agenda 2013; Save the Children 2012.

headed by US economist Jeffrey Sachs, the SDSN presents itself as a network of scientific experts that seeks to promote "practical solutions" in the realm of sustainable development.[17] Its 2013 report was unanimously viewed as a "high-profile contribution to the public debate regarding the Sustainable Development Goals."[18]

While these consultation practices defined the broad contours of the policy debate, the basic structure of the post-2015 agenda was shaped by two global conferences that were planned separately: the 2012 Rio Conference on Sustainable Development and the 2015 Addis Ababa Conference on Financing for Development. By their very nature, the two events were dominated by states, but they nevertheless allowed for ample interactions between government officials and nonstate actors. Of the two, the Rio meeting, which was organized to mark the twentieth anniversary of the Earth Summit, was by far the most decisive. Following a Colombian initiative, one of the main decisions taken in Rio was to propose the establishment of a General Assembly Open Working Group (OWG) to formulate a set of sustainable development goals.[19] Remarkably, when the OWG started its activities, the link between its role and the post-2015 process was tenuous at best. Many feared that the Rio follow-up and the post-2015 agenda would remain disconnected, thereby generating confusion.[20] It was only halfway through the Rio group's work that a formal connection with the post-2015 agenda was established.

Though it was the subject of less media attention than the Rio Conference, the Addis Conference also had a major impact as it defined the means by which the 2030 Agenda would be implemented. Strangely enough, however, the Addis meeting was held in July 2015, by which point the post-2015 negotiations had entered their final push. Following conferences in Monterrey (2002) and Doha (2008), the Addis Conference was meant to establish an action plan to promote the mobilization of financial resources for development. Although many developing countries were disappointed by the firm refusal of developed countries to create an intergovernmental committee on tax

---

[17] UN Secretary-General 2012.
[18] Young 2017, 46. See also Sustainable Development Solutions Network 2013, 28.
[19] UN General Assembly 2012, para. 248.
[20] Kamau, Chasek, and O'Connor 2018, 99.

cooperation,[21] the agreement struck in Addis nevertheless managed to establish an ambitious strategy for financing development in the future. Based on financial needs estimated to be at least a trillion dollars per year, this strategy was integrated into the post-2015 agenda at the last minute.[22]

While the Rio and Addis Conferences provided substantial input, the actual negotiation of the 2030 development program unfolded in two distinct processes that some observers considered almost "antagonistic."[23] The first, which took place from March 2013 to July 2014, centered around the activities of the OWG established in Rio. The second, formally known as Intergovernmental Negotiations on the Post-2015 Development Agenda (IGN), lasted from January to July 2015 and dealt specifically with the negotiation of the post-2015 agenda. One of the main challenges of this second process was to define the nature of its connection with the strategy outlined in Rio. The need for this connection had officially been recognized in September 2013, during the Special Event to Follow up Efforts Made Towards Achieving the Millennium Development Goals, held by the General Assembly.[24] Indeed, the final document produced at the Special Event was a turning point as it supported "a single framework and set of goals that are universal in nature and applicable to all countries."[25] Only then did it become clear that the post-2015 agenda was going to be built on the goals proposed by the OWG created in Rio. Yet, the exact nature of the link between the two processes remained ambiguous until early 2015 – a strikingly late development given the high stakes involved.

The document adopted during the 2013 Special Event also set the upcoming schedule in conformity with established global governance practices. First, the Secretary-General was invited to deliver a synthesis report on the state of discussions regarding the post-2015 development agenda at the end of 2014.[26] Second, intergovernmental negotiations on the agenda were to be initiated in early 2015.[27] Finally, a head-of-state

[21] Anyangwe 2015.

[22] See United Nations 2015a, 8; and UN General Assembly 2015, para. 40 and para. 62.

[23] Fukuda-Parr and McNeill 2019, 10.

[24] Dodds, Donoghue, and Leiva Roesch 2016, 47.

[25] UN General Assembly 2013b, para. 19.   [26] Ibid., para. 25.

[27] Ibid., para. 20.

summit was to be organized in September 2015, at which the negotiated development program would be approved.[28]

The way in which this two-phase process unfolded in practice provides further evidence of the haphazard construction of the SDGs. After the decision in Rio to create an OWG to establish the SDGs, it took six months "of hard negotiations on how [the group] should be structured and function."[29] In Rio, it had been agreed that the OWG would include thirty seats representing the five regional groups recognized at the UN. But given the high number of countries that wanted to participate, it was decided in an unprecedented move that each seat could be occupied either by a duo of states or by "troikas."[30] Although this decision enlarged the OWG membership to seventy states,[31] it was nonetheless contested for its lack of transparency. In the end, "member states who were not included in the OWG asked that all OWG meetings be open to all."[32] Reflecting on this gradual process of enlargement, Ambassador Kamau aptly pointed out that it "tested the limits of tolerance in terms of what innovations could be used and where new arrangements could be accepted."[33]

In the course of the OWG negotiations, which were fueled by the technical input of the UN Task Team, the themes covered expanded beyond environmental issues in some unexpected ways. In February 2014, after eight meetings, the chairs, building on established multilateral practice, released a stocktaking document as well as a document outlining nineteen "focus areas" for further discussion.[34] Then, in July 2014, the OWG adopted a document that included seventeen SDGs and 169 targets.[35] A few weeks later, in September 2014, the OWG report was approved by the General Assembly, which also decided that the OWG proposal would constitute "the main basis" of the 2030 Agenda.[36] However, it took several months to elucidate what the expression "main basis" meant.

---

[28] Ibid., para. 26.   [29] Dodds, Donoghue, and Leiva Roesch 2016, xvii.
[30] Chasek et al. 2016, 10.   [31] Dodds, Donoghue, and Leiva Roesch 2016, 31.
[32] Ibid., 32.
[33] Macharia Kamau, Permanent Representative of Kenya to the UN, cited in Chasek et al. 2016, 11.
[34] UN Open Working Group for Sustainable Development Goals 2014a.
[35] UN Open Working Group for Sustainable Development Goals 2014b.
[36] The report as it was adopted by the UNGA in September 2014: UN General Assembly 2014b.

After the publication of the Secretary-General's synthesis report, which had been requested at the 2013 Special Event, the IGN committee was left with four main tasks: the final formulation of the SDGs, the writing of a political declaration, the definition of the means by which the agreement would be implemented, and the elaboration of a follow-up review process. In spite of a variety of hurdles on its way, the IGN managed to reach a consensus on each of these items by July 2015, setting the stage for the historic SDGs summit held from 25 to 27 September, 2015.

The negotiations around the Agenda 2030 have often been deemed the "most participatory process ever in the history of the UN."[37] This inclusive dynamic materialized in a variety of policy practices, some of which we have already discussed. Broad inclusion was also apparent in the work of the OWG and the IGN committee. For instance, the OWG chairs had introduced an inclusive procedure, according to which each day of OWG meetings would start with an hour of informal exchanges with civil society representatives. This dialogue mechanism was later preserved in the IGN. Indeed, the fact that many governmental and nongovernmental participants knew each other from the Rio Conference contributed to the creation of a rare climate of trust between the two groups. The 2015 summit, which was symbolically headed by two diplomats representing the North (Denmark) and the South (Uganda), was also an opportunity to send a message of openness that relied on innovative practices. Before the opening plenary session, Pope Francis addressed the General Assembly with a highly publicized speech. "Interactive dialogue" sessions gave civil society representatives an opportunity to speak.[38] Finally, performances by UNICEF goodwill ambassadors Shakira and Angélique Kidjo, as well as a message from Malala Yousafzai, aimed to strengthen the SDGs' popular legitimacy.[39]

In light of these efforts to enhance inclusion, it is easy to forget that decision making ultimately reflected entrenched power dynamics. In the IGN, in particular, following the abandonment of the troika system and a return to classical coalitions, "negotiations were more polarized and the North-South divide almost threatened the agenda."[40] Also, the

---

[37] König-Reis 2017.   [38] Kamau, Chasek, and O'Connor 2018, 242–3.
[39] International Institute for Sustainable Development 2015, 1.
[40] Chasek et al. 2016, 11.

use of contact groups marginalized small delegations, in particular those that lacked fluency in English.[41] Furthermore, the actual influence of civil society on issue framing, its ability to shift states' views and to exert a meaningful impact on the wording of the final text, has been described by one analyst as "marginal."[42] Significantly, the final negotiations, which raised many delicate political issues, unfolded behind closed doors, out of sight from civil society representatives. As the moment of truth approached, inclusion thus tended to decline.

In sum, the practices that shaped the SDG negotiation process were politically meaningful in at least two ways. First, they demonstrated that global governance is a work in progress in which diplomatic creativity plays an important role. In other words, they have shown that "UN negotiations can experiment with new procedures and do not have to be wedded to the past."[43] Second, negotiation practices were meaningful in the sense that they helped to considerably widen the spectrum of participants in the SDG debate. Although the making of the 2030 Agenda was strongly influenced by the most powerful states, it is likely to be remembered as "the most inclusive process in UN history."[44]

1.2 Anchoring Sustainable Development in Goal-Setting

The 2030 Agenda was also profoundly marked by a set of practices related to goal-setting. With the SDGs, notes Fukuda-Parr, global goal-setting has become "the dominant method for formulating the international development agenda."[45] In a similar manner, one group of scholars argues that the SDGs represent "the most ambitious effort yet to place goal setting at the center of global governance and policy."[46] To a large extent, goal-setting can thus be seen as the primary "anchoring practice" of the SDGs.[47] This is unsurprising given that goal-setting, which as a governance technique grants a central role to experts, has come to affect all forms of political activity. According to its proponents, it has the advantage of setting a clear direction for political action and creating momentum in the pursuit of collective objectives.[48]

---

[41] Ibid., 12.   [42] Sénit 2020, 708.
[43] Kamau, Chasek, and O'Connor 2018, 265.   [44] Caballero 2019, 140.
[45] Fukuda-Parr 2017, 2.   [46] Kanie, Bernstein, Biermann, and Haas 2017, 1.
[47] Swidler 2001.   [48] Jolly 2004; Sachs 2015; Browne 2017.

It is worth recalling here that, although it acquired an unprecedented importance with the SDGs, the practice of establishing voluntary goals and standards has long been a policy instrument in international development. For instance, the four Development Decades declared by the UN between 1960 and 1990 were linked to a series of time-bound, quantitative social and economic objectives.[49] In 2000, the UN further emphasized development goal-setting by establishing twenty-one targets and sixty indicators to define the eight MDGs.[50] Although the MDGs have been criticized for the lack of transparency behind their creation and their narrow vision of development, their general approach to social engineering has seldom been an object of contestation.[51] For a majority of global decision makers, it thus seemed natural that the post-2015 agenda would follow a similar method. From the beginning, then, the SDG process was conceived as an exercise in identifying development priorities and a number of bench-marks by which to track the progress made.

Already at the 2012 Rio Conference, it was agreed that goal-setting could be "useful for pursuing focused and coherent action on sustainable development."[52] The conference's outcome document also mentioned that "sustainable development goals should be action-oriented, concise and easy to communicate, limited in number, aspirational, global in nature and universally applicable to all countries."[53] The HLP and the SDSN reports reinforced this idea by calling for the post-2015 agenda to be structured around a short list of precise objectives. In particular, the HLP report argued that "goals can be a powerful force for change," and that "they are most effective where a clear and compelling ambition can be described in clearly measurable terms."[54] In addition to recommending that the post-2015 development program be extended to 2030,[55] the HLP expressed great enthusiasm for the data revolution, noting that it would allow governments and civil society to better monitor development goals.[56]

Putting goal-setting to work required the pooling of experts from the "three UNs."[57] In this process, the UN Task Team played a decisive

---

[49] Browne 2017, 69–76.   [50] United Nations 2008.
[51] A stimulating exception is Fukuda-Parr 2017.
[52] UN General Assembly 2012, para. 246–7.   [53] Ibid., para. 247.
[54] High-Level Panel of Eminent Persons on the Post-2015 Development Agenda 2013, 13.
[55] Ibid.   [56] Ibid., 23.   [57] Jolly, Emmerij, and Weiss 2009.

role. In 2012, it created a Technical Support Team (TST) gathering forty UN entities to help the OWG's negotiators get a better sense of the stakes. The TST produced twenty-nine issue briefs dealing with each of the themes debated in the OWG.[58] The UN Statistical Commission subsequently provided statistical notes for each of the briefs. Seeking to avoid any form of conflictual terminology, these notes aimed to provide a "neutral picture of the statistical possibilities of measuring and monitoring the main issues identified in the issue briefs."[59]

The role of experts increased with the definition of SDG indicators. Indeed, it was decided early on that diplomats would define the agenda's goals and targets while the elaboration of indicators would be left to specialists.[60] This division of labor was of course based on the relatively abstract distinction between political and technical matters. In any event, in March 2015, the UN Statistical Commission created the Inter-Agency Expert Group on SDG Indicators. Made up of twenty-seven representatives of national statistical offices, this body oversaw the development of a global indicator framework to help monitor the SDGs.[61] It was expected that this framework would not "reinterpret the targets" and "should not introduce any new or contentious issues."[62] In a particularly stark illustration of policy bricolage, an incomplete version of the global indicator framework – including 230 indicators – was adopted by the UN General Assembly in July 2017.[63] Since then, the framework has been regularly amended to include a number of "replacements, revisions, additions and deletions."[64]

While this sort of definitional work was still in its early stages, in August 2014, the Secretary-General established the Independent Expert Advisory Group on a Data Revolution for Sustainable Development (IEAG), composed of twenty-four experts, including chief national statisticians, specialists from the private sector, and international public servants. The IEAG's mandate was to make recommendations on how to strengthen statistical capacity-building to monitor the post-2015 agenda. Revealingly, the IEAG's first report

---

[58] Inter-Agency Technical Support Team for the UNGA OWG 2014.
[59] UN Statistics Division 2014, 1–2.
[60] Dodds, Donoghue, and Leiva Roesch 2016, 83.   [61] United Nations 2015c.
[62] UN Department of Economic and Social Affairs 2015.
[63] UN Economic and Social Council 2017.
[64] UN Department of Economic and Social Affairs 2021.

was entitled *A World that Counts.*[65] The report reinforced the idea that the data revolution should be harnessed for sustainable development. Shifting from technical language to a decidedly more political tone, the IEAG argued that "[n]ever again should it be possible to say 'we didn't know.' No one should be invisible. This is the world we want – a world that counts."[66]

The Secretary-General also picked up the HLP's proposal to create a Global Partnership for Sustainable Development Data. Launched on 1 October, 2015, this partnership defines itself as "a multi-stakeholder network of Data Champions ... working to harness the data revolution for sustainable development."[67] The partnership aims to address the problem of unreliable or nonexistent data by connecting official statistics, big data, geospatial data, and citizen-generated data. It also created the World Forum on Sustainable Development Data, an institution that brings together the various constituent parts of the data ecosystem to share ideas and experiences. The first UN World Data Forum was held in Cape Town from 15 to 18 January, 2017, thus cementing the role of experts and benchmarking in the SDG process.[68]

A central component in the bricolage of practices that brought the 2030 Agenda to life, goal-setting came with important political effects. These effects can be described according to their methodological, sociological, and institutional dimensions. Methodologically, it is crucial to note that "the ideal concept of goal setting relies on measurable targets and indicators."[69] By overvaluing quantification, goal-setting creates the impression that the production of knowledge is a neutral process.[70] The negotiation of the SDGs also contributed to such an impression insofar as participants pretended that the diplomats' political discussions and the statisticians' technical work could be neatly distinguished. Cloaked in an aura of expertise and objectivity, though, goal-setting conceals the values and the worldviews that undergird it.[71] In spite of its declared objective of depoliticizing sustainable development, then, the technocratic language of goal-setting in fact obscured the power relations that animated the SDG process. Because it reifies the common good through numbers and data, goal-setting also departs from more

---

[65] Independent Expert Advisory Group on a Data Revolution for Sustainable Development 2014.
[66] Ibid., 3.   [67] United Nations 2015c.   [68] United Nations 2017.
[69] Fukuda-Parr and McNeill 2019, 6.   [70] Ibid., 7.   [71] Ibid.

qualitative practices, such as human rights-based approaches to development.[72] Sometimes denounced as radical, these approaches insist on empowerment and social justice, while goal-setting emphasizes a notional view of efficiency. Navi Pillay, the former head of the Office of the United Nations High Commissioner for Human Rights (OHCHR), succinctly exposed the methodological assumptions behind goal-setting as well as an alternative perspective on the SDGs when she argued that global policymakers should not "treasure what we measure" so much as "measure what we treasure."[73]

Sociologically, goal-setting also tends to favor the viewpoints of certain social groups while excluding others'. The selection of SDG indicators was largely dominated by state actors, thus leaving a very limited role to UN specialized agencies and civil society representatives.[74] And among these state actors, the representatives of developed countries, who enjoy more resources and greater technical prestige than their counterparts from the developing world, clearly had the biggest influence. Moreover, the indicators that were selected often gave the goals a conservative orientation. "With some exceptions," explained one group of experts, "the set of goals are more ambitious than the targets, and the targets are more ambitious than the indicators."[75] Fukuda-Parr aptly shows how this kind of distortion affected SDG 10, which calls for the reduction of inequality. Although the introduction of a stand-alone goal on inequality was in itself a significant innovation of Agenda 2030, its formalization gave way to a statistical debate in which the conservative camp prevailed. Rather than considering inequality as an issue of distribution that concerns a country's entire population, the main indicator chosen to assess progress toward SDG 10 emphasized the need to increase the income of the bottom 40 percent of the population. In other words, the fight against inequality was subsumed into the fight against poverty.[76] Similar "technocratic" battles, whereby the transformative potential of Agenda 2030 was diluted through the choice of certain indicators

[72] Fukuda-Parr 2014; Fukuda-Parr, Yamin, and Greenstein 2014; Fukuda-Parr and McNeill 2019.
[73] UN Office of the High Commissioner for Human Rights 2013b, 13.
[74] Kapto 2019.   [75] Adams, Bissio, and Judd 2016, 147.
[76] Fukuda-Parr 2019, 65–6.

over others, have been documented for a variety of SDGs dealing with the environment, sexual and reproductive health, education, justice, and agriculture.[77]

Finally, from an institutional perspective, the SDG policymaking process reinforced the supremacy of goal-setting over other techniques in the global governance toolbox. This came at the expense of alternative approaches, including rulemaking and norm creation.[78] For its proponents, goal-setting offers a middle-of-the-road strategy in which "governments signal their interest in achieving such goals and possibly being accountable for doing so."[79] According to this perspective, goal-setting appears as a useful compromise between the purely aspirational character of norm creation and the almost insurmountable task of formulating binding international agreements among sovereign equals. Yet, because of its strong reliance on expertise and technical knowledge, goal-setting often drove the negotiation of the SDGs in a top-down rather than a bottom-up direction. As a consequence, it tended to draw the SDG process toward managing the established order rather than transforming it. Overall, goal-setting thus appears as a global governance practice that, far from transcending ideologies and power relations, remains deeply determined by political struggles.

2 Debating Sustainable Development in "a World That Counts"

The 2030 Agenda was built around a set of values that were expressed by a wide range of state and nonstate actors. To some extent, these values reflected the quest for consensus that is often found in global policymaking. The most basic area of agreement in the context of the 2030 Agenda concerned a shared belief that the MDG experience had for the most part been a positive one. This assessment was in fact the precondition for the SDGs to emerge on the international agenda. As the MDG experience was widely deemed a success, the idea of replicating – indeed improving upon – this type of public policy after 2015 was rarely contested. At the same time, the 2030 Agenda obscured many ideological cleavages. These sometimes grew out of

---

[77] Elder and Olsen 2019; Fukuda-Parr and McNeill 2019; McNeill 2019; Satterthwaite and Dhital 2019; Unterhalter 2019; Yamin 2019.
[78] Kanie and Biermann 2017, 1–27.   [79] Ibid., 5.

Table 3.2 *Main value debates in the making of the SDGs*

	Value cleavages	Polysemous compromises
What is the problem?	Poverty as structural challenge vs. as individual exclusion	Global poverty as multidimensional
	Domestic vs. international sources of inequality	Unequal development
What are the ends?	Ensuring economic growth vs. protecting the environment, fostering good governance and/or promoting human rights	Sustainable development and poverty reduction
	Democracy vs. efficiency in reforming global institutions	Global partnerships
By what means?	International solidarity vs. national responsibility	Policy must be universal
	Technical vs. deliberative decision-making process	Design of policy must be inclusive and transparent

unexpected political alignments, but in the end, they mainly illustrated the depth of the North–South divide.[80]

The normative stakes that punctuated the creation of the 2030 Agenda revolved around three main questions: (1) What is the problem? (2) What are the ends to be achieved? (3) By what means are those ends to be reached? As Table 3.2 shows, our analysis reveals a complex mix of convergence and disagreement in which positions were typically formulated in an idiom of universal values. Like other global policies, Agenda 2030 and the SDGs may be seen as a political bricolage combining competing conceptions of the common good.

2.1 What Is the Problem?

The key problem underlying the SDGs was generally portrayed as the persistence of global poverty. In the final agreement, for instance, UN

---

[80] Muchhala and Sengupta 2014; Kamau, Chasek, and O'Connor 2018; Fukuda-Parr and Muchhala 2020.

member states recognized that "eradicating poverty in all its forms and dimensions, including extreme poverty, is the greatest global challenge and an indispensable requirement for sustainable development."[81] And by acknowledging the multidimensional nature of poverty, the international community implicitly agreed that "poverty is not, of course, just about income."[82] This emphasis on poverty was widely shared not only by governments from the Global North and South but also among civil society. The general feeling was that the MDGs were only the first step in a more ambitious undertaking. This feeling was described by a representative from Greenpeace as "a broad consensus around a core set of issues. Poverty eradication is an overarching goal to which all SDGs must contribute."[83]

The 2030 Agenda was also built through convergence around the idea that global poverty is linked to unequal development. Unsurprisingly, it was the rich countries that formulated the lowest common denominator on this issue. Speaking as a duo, the US and Israel recognized that "the world is wealthier than ever before, but not all people have benefited and many have been left behind."[84] Another group of northern countries acknowledged that "the MDGs clouded the challenges of growing inequalities within countries and between countries."[85] The 2030 Agenda integrated these viewpoints on development by condemning "enormous disparities ... of wealth and power," and noting that in the past years, "progress has been uneven, particularly in Africa, least developed countries, landlocked developing countries and small island developing states."[86] In the end, all participants could get on board with Amnesty International's condemnation of the "huge gap between the world we live in and the world we want."[87]

However, behind this apparent consensus on poverty and developmental inequality, the 2030 Agenda was the site of deep value clashes. Because of its polysemous nature, the adjective "multidimensional" was used as a catchall term to define poverty in different ways. For instance, governments from the Global North and international

---

[81] UN General Assembly 2015, para. 2.
[82] High-Level Panel of Eminent Persons on the Post-2015 Development Agenda 2013, 23.
[83] Lerner 2012, 2.   [84] United States of America and Israel 2014, 1.
[85] Denmark, Ireland, and Norway 2013, 2.
[86] UN General Assembly 2015, para. 14 and 16.
[87] Amnesty International 2015, 3.

institutions generally presented poverty as the result of individual exclusion. Tellingly, the HLP explained that, in its meetings, "people living in poverty told us how powerless they felt because their jobs and livelihoods were precarious."[88] Governments from the Global South, by contrast, were more sensitive to the social and systemic dimensions of poverty. While the China–Indonesia–Kazakhstan troika recognized the MDGs' contribution to poverty reduction, it also argued that "what is truly missing in the equation is an integrated approach, which gives due weight to economic development."[89] For its part, Benin, like many other poor states, linked poverty with "the structural challenges faced by the developing countries."[90]

Inequality was also a key theme of ideological struggle. The importance of this theme was captured by the OHCHR, which pointed out that "[i]t is not only poverty that matters, it is also where we are in relation to each other and how wide the gaps are between us."[91] There was intense debate between those focusing on inequality of opportunities and those emphasizing inequality of outcomes. The US and Israel, for example, argued that "[w]hile we may all be born with the same rights, we have not always been born with the same opportunity, and that needs to change."[92] The priority given to inequality of opportunities was typically justified by "the need to provide incentives to accumulate human and physical capital."[93] Inequality of outcomes was most often highlighted by NGOs. Oxfam, for instance, noted that "[b]y concentrating wealth and power in the hands of the few, inequality robs the poorest people of even the minimal support they need to improve their lives, and means that, increasingly, their voices go unheard."[94] Among states, Brazil was perhaps the most ardent defender of the need to address inequality of outcomes. Condemning "excessive wealth accumulation," Brazil questioned "the legitimacy or even legality of such highly accumulated wealth."[95]

In addition, inequality was the source of a stark disagreement over the significance for sustainable development of the North–South divide. Diplomats from developed and developing countries had profoundly

---

[88] High-Level Panel of Eminent Persons on the Post-2015 Development Agenda 2013, 2.

[89] China, Indonesia, and Kazakhstan 2014a, 1.   [90] Benin 2015, 2.

[91] UN Office of the High Commissioner for Human Rights 2014.

[92] United States of America and Israel 2014, 1.   [93] World Bank 2016, 71.

[94] Oxfam 2014b.   [95] Brazil 2015a, 4.

differing views. The United Kingdom emphasized the "need . . . to move away from talking north-south."[96] Similarly, Germany proposed a "paradigm shift to move beyond traditional North-South thinking," arguing that "with regard to sustainable development we are all developing countries."[97] These stances generated strong resistance from developing countries. Starting in Rio, China asserted that "the global process of sustainable development is not balanced. The gap between the North and the South is widening."[98] India, for its part, coined a potent catchphrase: "North-South is not a divide, it is a fact."[99] Overall, the position of developing states was close to the prevalent view in civil society, which often emphasizes the distinction between the Global North and the Global South.[100] At the same time, developing countries remained more conservative than the small but audible minority among NGOs who argued that the real issue was "our current model of development."[101]

2.2 What Are the Ends?

As far as end goals are concerned, the SDGs were made possible thanks to a convergence of values around two issues. First, sustainable development was unanimously accepted as a global project. Taking into consideration the economic, social, and environmental dimensions of development, sustainable development provided a convenient "overarching framework" for tackling poverty.[102] To a large extent, convergence around sustainable development can be seen as the silver bullet of the 2030 Agenda.

A second element of normative consensus developed around the idea that global poverty must be eradicated and that, in this process, no one should be left behind. Coined by the HLP, the phrase "leave no one behind" was mentioned several times in the 2030 Agenda. In a particularly strong passage of the agreement, the world's leaders even pledged to "endeavour to reach the furthest behind first."[103] The "leave no one behind" slogan led to an impressive rapprochement

---

[96] United Kingdom 2015b, 1.
[97] See Germany 2015a, 4; and Germany 2015b, 1.   [98] China 2012, 1.
[99] India 2015b, 4.
[100] See Reflection Group on the 2030 Agenda for Sustainable Development 2016.
[101] Pillay 2013, 2.   [102] Italy, Spain and Turkey 2013, 2.
[103] UN General Assembly 2015, para. 4.

between states and civil society. A group of NGOs enthusiastically summarized the dominant mood as follows: "Globally, civil society is delighted that Leave No One Behind is recognised as the rallying cry of the Post 2015 development agenda. We see it as representing a transformative shift in terms of how we view and do development."[104]

Beyond these points of convergence, however, the debate over how to eradicate poverty led to several ideological conflicts. First, the consensus on sustainable development turned out to be an ambiguous one. Several participants – primarily but not only from the Global North – attempted to add a more political element to the economic, social, and environmental dimensions of poverty reduction and sustainable development. Italy, for example, wanted to recognize "the emergence of a 'further transversal dimension' of sustainable development, encompassing peace, rule of law, promotion of human rights and effective governance and institutions, as an essential pillar for the construction of a sustainable future for all."[105] In the same spirit, NGOs stressed that "a post-2015 framework should incorporate just governance as an essential foundation stone for sustainable development."[106] This approach was contested by several countries from the Global South, like Brazil and Nicaragua, who were "simply not convinced that peace and governance can be targeted and measured in ways that are consensual and that reflect the democratic plurality of nations."[107] In seeking to resolve these tensions, Agenda 2030 seemed to pull itself in different directions as it paid lip service to democracy without modifying the tridimensional definition of sustainable development.

A parallel normative battle had to do with the way in which the various dimensions of sustainable development were to be "balanced and integrated."[108] Like most developing countries, Bhutan, Thailand, and Vietnam presented economic growth as "the necessary precondition for the realization of any and all other goals."[109] This viewpoint was in tune with the assessment of the World Bank, which argued that "[d]ecades of experience have taught us that economic growth is the primary driver of increased personal income and poverty reduction."[110] According to India, Pakistan, and Sri Lanka, it was only natural that developing states' growth should be prioritized over

---

[104] Jones 2015, 1.   [105] Italy 2015, 3.   [106] Beyond 2015 2013, 19.
[107] Brazil and Nicaragua 2014, 3.   [108] UN General Assembly 2015, para. 2.
[109] Bhutan, Thailand, and Vietnam 2014, 1.   [110] Kim 2015, 3.

environmental concerns given that "the battle against unsustainable patterns of consumption will be won or lost in the developed countries."[111] Conversely, countries from the Global North systematically stressed the complementarity of sustainable development objectives. While the Poland–Romania duo maintained that "[p]overty eradication and environment protection should be mutually supportive,"[112] the France–Germany–Switzerland troika argued that the quest for "sustainability has ... positive impacts on economic growth."[113] The contributions of the business and NGO communities to this debate stood in stark contrast to one another. While the Business and Industry Major Group declared its enthusiasm for "playing a role in expanding productive capacity and being part of structural transformation worldwide," NGOs put forward the distinctly critical view that "there are limits to the growth paradigm."[114] In the end, the resolution of these differences was left to "mankind's capacity for innovation"[115] – in other words, deferred to some hopeful future.

Another axis of value cleavages concerned the architecture of global governance. Referring to quite distinct arguments, developing countries and civil society groups regularly emphasized the need to reform the key institutions of the global economic system, a concern that did not resonate well with governments of the Global North. Egypt, for instance, drew attention to "the need to address the systemic issues, including reform of the global economic and financial institutions."[116] Members of the Caribbean Community (CARICOM) called for "global trade reforms,"[117] and Sri Lanka pleaded in favor of "reforming global financial institutions for the benefit of a larger proportion of the global population."[118] In a similar vein, the Beyond 2015 Coalition argued that the post-2015 agenda should include "a framework for profound reforms of global governance."[119]

Yet, the convergence between developing states and civil society was subject to important limitations. The former primarily justified their

---

[111] India, Pakistan, and Lanka 2014, 2.   [112] Poland and Romania 2013, 2.
[113] France, Germany, and Switzerland 2014, 2.
[114] Business and Industry Major Group 2013, 4; International Federation of Red Cross and Red Crescent Societies 2013.
[115] High-Level Panel of Eminent Persons on the Post-2015 Development Agenda 2013, 8.
[116] Egypt 2015, 1.   [117] CARICOM 2015a, 3.   [118] Sri Lanka 2013, 4.
[119] Beyond 2015, 2013, 18.

call for changes in the architecture of global governance by pointing to the need to enlarge the policy space in which they operate and to increase their voice and representation in global institutions. For its part, the NGO Committee on Financing for Development (Finance and Trade Cluster) argued that global governance reform was a precondition for the strengthening of human rights.[120] Such nuances, however, remained secondary to the developed countries' firm refusal to entertain any discussion on systemic issues. Although the US–Canada–Israel troika did recognize that global institutions could be modernized, it was clear that the post-2015 forum was not the right context to do so: "We do not think ... that global governance should be a major focus of our effort at this stage. We have many venues and processes in which to discuss those issues, and we do have concern that discussions of global governance will distract us from the issues we believe require our immediate attention."[121]

The normative tensions around global governance paralleled another North–South conflict over the relationship between the right to development and other human rights. Bangladesh, for instance, emphasized the right to development by arguing that it "encompasses all [other] human rights."[122] In debating the right to development, the China–Indonesia–Kazakhstan troika was particularly straightforward: "We should ... avoid overemphasizing human rights or coupling multilateral and bilateral development assistance with human rights indicators, democracy and good governance."[123] Predictably, developed countries had a different position. While the US argued that "[t]he right to development lacks agreed international understanding,"[124] European countries were more explicit yet: "it is important to be clear that [the right to development] is not on an equal footing with the Universal Declaration of Human Rights."[125] Given such a deep cleavage, IOs' and NGOs' stance that human rights were indivisible and interdependent seemed out of touch with reality.

These divergent perspectives on global governance eventually led to differences of opinion on the Global Partnership for Development, which is at the heart of SDG 17. The debate centered on the role of states and the private sector, and it was packaged in the rhetoric of

[120] NGO Committee on Financing for Development 2013.
[121] United States of America, Canada, and Israel 2013c, 2.
[122] Bangladesh 2015, 1.   [123] China, Indonesia, and Kazakhstan 2013, 1–2.
[124] United States of America 2015, 3.   [125] European Union 2015a, 3.

multistakeholderism. Canada, for instance, explained that development depended on "the active and full engagement of all key stakeholders—governments, parliaments, civil society, private sector, academics, scientists, researchers, and above all the poorest and most vulnerable."[126] For its part, Croatia argued that "[b]y involving all stakeholders ... we can create a win-win situation for everyone."[127] However, the Global North's approach to the Global Partnership was often seen as a Trojan horse to favor the private sector. And indeed, several developed countries connected multistakeholder rhetoric with the idea that "[t]he private sector remains the key driver of inclusive and sustainable growth."[128] Not surprisingly, this stance was shared by the International Chamber of Commerce, which maintained that "[n]ow more than ever, sustainable development depends on the solutions, capabilities, contributions and engagement of business."[129] Skeptical on this point, the NGO Major Group condemned what it saw as "the abuse and misuse of the 'stakeholder' language and its pretence to domesticate and reconcile the difference between private and public interests."[130] Many countries from the Global South were even more suspicious and downplayed multistakeholderism to stress the fact that the Global Partnership for Development should rest on "intergovernmental processes."[131] For instance, while the China–Indonesia–Kazakhastan troika praised the active engagement of all development actors, it also noted that such participation "should be complementary to the G-to-G [government-to-government] partnerships, and not to be considered as a substitute."[132]

2.3 By What Means?

Negotiation on the ways and means of implementing the 2030 Agenda led to an unprecedented consensus around the principle of universality. The final document thus describes the SDGs as "universal goals and targets which involve the entire world, developed and developing countries."[133] India insisted that "the SDGs need to be truly

---

[126] Canada 2015, 1.   [127] Croatia 2012, 7.
[128] European Commission 2014, 14.
[129] International Chamber of Commerce 2015, 2.
[130] NGO Major Group 2015, 1.   [131] G77 and China 2015b, 3.
[132] China, Indonesia, and Kazakhstan 2014b, 2.
[133] UN General Assembly 2015, para. 5.

universal,"[134] a statement with which the US–Canada–Israel troika seemed very much to concur: "we fully agree that goals need to be universal, they need to be relevant to all of us, we all need to have a stake."[135] Diplomats and activists alike hailed the introduction of the universality principle in the 2030 Agenda as a victory against the traditional development model based on development assistance. In many ways, universality was the most innovative normative aspect of the SDGs compared to the MDGs.

A second element of this international consensus was the necessity to submit the making and monitoring of the 2030 Agenda to democratic procedures. This effort at inclusion was in large part due to recurring criticism that the MDGs were created in a top-down way. Starting with the first session of the OWG, the Australia–Netherlands–UK troika insisted that a "wide group of stakeholders should be involved in the design of the post-2015 development agenda,"[136] while Germany called for "effective and innovative participation mechanisms."[137] The G77, meanwhile, pleaded in favor of a process that would be "inclusive, open and transparent."[138] More firmly yet, the NGO Major Group argued that "[t]he processes of SDG agenda-setting, implementation, evaluation and accountability should be rooted in authentic social inclusion of those most marginalized."[139] The final agreement reflected these values by promising that the follow-up process "will be open, inclusive, participatory and transparent for all people and will support reporting by all relevant stakeholders."[140] It seemed obvious to all that democratizing the making and monitoring of the 2030 Agenda would bestow greater legitimacy upon the SDGs.

And yet, this apparent consensus was in fact riddled with misunderstandings. Significantly, the definition of universality never was universal. For countries from the Global North, it primarily implied domestic duties for all national governments, whereas for countries from the Global South, it meant global responsibilities for the international community as a whole. Differences of opinion on the issue were particularly stark during debates on the norm of "common but differentiated responsibilities" (CBDR). Elaborated during the 1992 Rio Earth Summit in an effort to meet the needs of the Global

---

[134] India 2014, 2.   [135] United States of America, Canada, and Israel 2013b, 2.
[136] Australia, Netherlands, and United Kingdom 2013, 3.
[137] Germany 2013, 4.   [138] G77 and China 2013, 1.
[139] NGO Major Group 2013, 1.   [140] UN General Assembly 2015, para. 74(d).

South, the CBDR norm recognized that global environmental challenges should lead to national obligations that were tailored to states' level of development. But CBDR, which was already controversial in environmental negotiations, became the object of even more contestation as developing states attempted to enlarge it to the sphere of development more broadly.

From the beginning of the negotiations, the G77 stressed that "the development and implementation of SDGs must be based on the [CBDR] principle."[141] India justified this approach with reference to the animating spirit behind sustainable development: "Environmental action is not a silo anymore, it underpins the entire agenda. Ipso facto, it is only natural that this principle [CBDR] is equally valid for the entire agenda too."[142] More succinctly, Brazil stated that "[u]niversality is not the same as equal responsibilities."[143] Civil society generally supported extending CBDR beyond environmental issues, but developed countries firmly rejected the idea. The United Kingdom explained bluntly: "We do not accept that CBDR applies as an overarching principle to the post-2015 development agenda and do not understand why it should be singled out from other Rio principles."[144] Japan summarized its position even more sharply: "One problem of CBDR is that it is based on the assumption of the traditional divide of the North and South."[145] By reaffirming the CBDR principle as it was defined in the Rio Declaration, the 2030 Agenda left the debate open, thus suggesting that the normative cleavage around CBDR is not about to disappear anytime soon.

The battle over CBDR concealed a deeper ideological conflict over how the responsibilities for promoting development should be shared. Developed countries sought to limit their obligations in two ways. First, they consistently stressed "the central place of domestic action and policies."[146] For governments from the Global North, it was essential to acknowledge that "each country has primary responsibility for its own economic and social development."[147] Second, developed countries also argued that the SDGs could only be implemented if "other partners—including new and emerging actors—contribute[d] their fair share."[148] Coming from a different perspective, states from

---

[141] G77 and China 2013, 3.   [142] India 2015a, 3.   [143] Brazil 2015b, 3.
[144] United Kingdom 2015a, 2.   [145] Japan 2015, 2.
[146] European Union 2015c, 3.   [147] Ibid.   [148] European Union 2015b, 2.

the Global South instead stressed the need to "correct the inequities that have long plagued the international system to the disadvantage of developing countries."[149] To reach this goal, they invoked the values of cooperation and sovereignty. Burkina Faso, for instance, stated that the pursuit of sustainable development required the creation of "new lines of solidarity between nations."[150] And China called on the international community to "respect the independent choice of path of sustainable development made by countries with different histories, cultures, religious beliefs and social systems."[151]

Finally, the debate on the best ways and means of implementing the 2030 Agenda revealed different views on how the SDG process could promote social inclusion. The technocratic approach of the Global North clashed with the more political approaches defended by the Global South and civil society. Aligned with the practice of benchmarking, developed countries gave pride of place to experts. Australia supported an agenda "with targets that are quantified and measurable and at least consistent with existing commitments and latest technical evidence."[152] While the US–Canada–Israel troika invoked "cutting-edge knowledge, science, and practice from all corners of the globe,"[153] the US specified that "[w]e should and must make decisions based on research and scientific evidence about what works."[154]

Developing countries, on the other hand, proposed a version of inclusion that reflected a distrust of experts and instead emphasized greater state involvement. CARICOM countries underlined that "the development process is context specific with multiple variables at play that may not be easily controlled for robust scientific analysis or replication at a global scale."[155] Speaking for the Global South, the G77 stressed autonomy and national ownership: "Accordingly there should be no indicators at [the] national level. National governments should implement the Post-2015 Development Agenda according to their national circumstances, capability and development stages, on [a] voluntary basis."[156] In this debate, civil society representatives once again articulated a distinct position by arguing that the SDGs' success would depend on the "full participation in the decision-making processes at all

---

[149] UN Secretary-General 2014, para. 95.   [150] Burkina Faso 2012, 7.
[151] China 2012, 2.   [152] Australia 2015, 2.
[153] United States of America, Canada, and Israel 2013a, 2.
[154] United States of America 2012, 1.   [155] CARICOM 2015b, 2.
[156] G77 and China 2015a, 3.

levels of all people."[157] Even though the 2030 Agenda attempted to reconcile these different views on inclusion, it arguably gave preeminence to the technocratic approach over other perspectives.

In sum, Agenda 2030, which is often depicted as a pioneering political compromise, is best understood as a normative bricolage that conceals deep value cleavages. As participants sought to defend their views with reference to the common good, the final push toward agreement required a great deal of improvisation. Very clearly, the scenario was not written down ahead of time. Among other things, the chairs' political leadership, both at the OWG and the IGN, proved decisive. Indeed, the final outcome has been described as "a textbook example of the [chairs] retaining the pen from beginning to end."[158] Inclined to practice creative innovation, the diplomats in charge managed to propose language that was sufficiently polysemous to paper over deep-seated disagreements on the way to an otherwise consensual adoption of the policy.

Ultimately, the value debates that pervaded SDG negotiations should be viewed in the context of broader political struggles over development policies. It is fair to say that the outcome of these debates has reinforced global social market policies at the expense of neoliberal, social-democratic, and neomercantilist alternatives.[159] More specifically, the elaboration of the SDGs has reinforced the position that development requires "corrective action" by the state as well as civil society, while granting a larger role to the market-based development model.[160] At the same time, the diversity of views expressed throughout the policymaking process demonstrates that the current dominance of global social market policies is far from irrevocable, faced as it is with much contestation from both the Left and the Right. One of the most striking aspects of this ideological competition consists in the prevalence of the idiom of universal values as the discursive infrastructure through which contemporary global policymaking takes place.

Conclusion

Our analysis of the SDGs illustrates that global governance may be usefully understood as a contingent bricolage of practices and values.

---

[157] International Federation of Red Cross and Red Crescent Societies 2013, 6.
[158] Dodds, Donoghue, and Leiva Roesch 2016, 76.
[159] Scholte and Söderbaum 2017.   [160] Ibid., 9.

While practices capture the material and active dimensions of global policymaking, values express ways of thinking that encapsulate its normative dimension. Taken together, the focus on practices and values allows us to explore two central questions about global governance: How does it work? And how do global governors think that it should work? Global public policies are best analyzed as convoluted answers to these questions, emerging out of deeply political processes that often unfold haphazardly.

The example of the SDGs also shows that when it comes to the making of public policies, global governance practices are far from politically neutral. On the contrary, these practices, whether established or innovative, generate dynamics of inclusion and exclusion that shape the global governance playing field. In this sense, the structuring practices of SDGs as a public policy have clearly reinforced the legitimacy of the technocratic approach to international development, at the expense of alternatives based on sovereignty or democracy. In addition, our case study demonstrates that global policymaking is structured around competing value systems that embody contrasting rationalities. Global governors may all speak the same language of universal values, yet their use of different dialects reflects enduring and deep-seated ideological conflicts. Agenda 2030 thus remains full of ambiguities and polysemous formulations that barely paper over a wealth of normative cleavages that are too easily dismissed by recourse to the notion of "public goods."

Above all, our analysis of the SDGs helps show why and how global governance forms a patchwork, the outcome of which could not be predetermined. This stands in sharp contrast to rational design approaches. Focusing on the global governance practices and value struggles that led to the adoption of SDGs shows the improvisatory nature of global public policymaking. In fact, some of the methods used to negotiate the SDGs, including the use of global surveys, would not even have been thinkable two decades ago. Similarly, given the strong value clashes that prefigured the adoption of Agenda 2030, unprecedented political compromises had to be found even if deep ideological cleavages remained. Taken together, these observations offer a useful reminder of how contingent the future of global governance actually is. They also suggest that process-centered explanations provide a unique way to make sense of the inescapably social nature of global policies.

4 | The Human Rights Council
Institution-Building by Doing

The Commission on Human Rights (CHR) was created in 1946 as a subsidiary body of the Economic and Social Council (ECOSOC). By the turn of the millennium, the body experienced a deep crisis of legitimacy after countries known to commit human rights abuses, such as Sudan and Libya, were elected to the Commission. The resulting uproar, felt in many corners of the UN – including the Secretariat, the American mission, and several human rights NGOs[1] – was concomitant with the preparations for the UN's World Summit of 2005. The World Summit Outcome eventually led to the creation of the Human Rights Council (HRC).

In this chapter, we argue that the making of the HRC is best understood as a bricolage of values and practices. Far from a rational design, the body is in fact a perpetual work in progress. In terms of policymaking practices, particularly striking is the level of open-endedness and the role of trial and error in the process (from 2004 to this day). The original institutional package was negotiated by diplomats in Geneva, based on a broad request emanating from the 2005 World Summit, in a string of improvisations. Since then, it has been submitted to virtually continuous internal revision, through various kinds of self-review practices. The HRC is testimony to the prevalence of bricolage in global public policymaking: even its anchoring practice, the Universal Periodic Review (UPR), is subject to unending revisions.

In terms of value debates, this chapter shows how the consensus against the politicization of human rights, which originally led to the demise of the CHR, actually hides deep cleavages over universality, equal treatment, and dialogue. A lot of these debates pit the North against the South, although the lines demarcating these two camps are

---

[1] "Annan says rights body harming UN," *BBC* News, April 7, 2005. See also Lauren 2007, 328.

often blurred. Countries disagree over the role of experts, the significance of sovereignty, and the meaning of selectivity in the HRC's deliberations, and especially in the UPR process. Throughout the negotiations, diplomats clashed over what elements from the CHR should be maintained in the HRC, as well as over the proper division of labor between states, NGOs, and international civil servants when it comes to the promotion of human rights. Overall, the chapter demonstrates that almost two decades after its creation, the HRC still rests on polysemous normative compromises.

1 The Making of the HRC: A Perpetual Work in Progress

This section analyzes the key practices that have structured the making and the functioning of the HRC. We explain how open-ended the policymaking has been, from inception up to the present. This is an exemplary case of incremental institution-building in global governance. Enlarging upon a very broad mandate obtained from the 2005 World Summit, country representatives in New York and Geneva have invented a set of procedures that remain under constant review.

1.1 Continuous Institutional Development

The institutional development of the HRC is part of a complex political process. For the sake of clarity, we divide it chronologically into three phases: (1) the run-up to the 2005 World Summit; (2) the institution-building package of 2007; and (3) the internal revisions made since by the HRC itself, including continuous reforms and formal self-reviews. Table 4.1 summarizes the key practices that have structured this process so far.

1.1.1 The Run-Up to the World Summit (2004–05)
In the first phase of the HRC's development, world leaders managed to agree on the creation of a new Council but put off all substantive decisions for later, offloading the responsibility to country delegates attached to the General Assembly and the HRC. While this approach was by no means unprecedented in global governance, it was nonetheless unusual. From a rational design perspective, such a leap of faith on the part of decision makers is surprising. As one observer explains,

Table 4.1 *Key practices in the making of the HRC*

Practices	Instances	Political effects
Forming a panel of experts	High-Level Panel on Threats, Challenges, and Change (2004–5)	Puts experts in control of agenda-setting; favors national consultations
Reporting by international civil servants	Secretary-General's Report and Explanatory Note (2005) OHCHR Plan of Action (2005)	Introduces a key role for bureaucratic actors
Holding intergovernmental negotiations	CHR negotiations (2005) World Summit (2005) General Assembly Informal Consultations of the Plenary (2005–6)	Places member states and their diplomats at the helm
Issuing an NGO joint statement	Joint letters (November 2005; January 2006) Opportunities for Strengthening and Leveraging HRC Membership report (2019)	Allows civil society to weigh in from the margins
Holding an informal workshop	Annual Glion dialogues (Geneva) Lausanne workshop (and dozens more) Pre-Working Group Meetings (2009–10) Universal Rights Group report (2015) *Strengthening the UN Human Rights Council from the Ground Up* (Geneva, 2018)	Facilitates contact between like-minded partners of all stripes
Launching a formal review	2011 HRC and General Assembly reviews Forthcoming review (2021–6)	Maintains state prerogative over institution-building
Holding organizational sessions	Annual December meetings (HRC) Efficiency process (2018)	Allows more flexibility for diplomats on site
Issuing presidential statements	A/HRC/OM/L.1 (2008) A/HRC/DEC/17/118 (2011) A/HRC/PRST/OS/12/1 (2018)	Enables institutional initiatives
Universal Periodic Review (anchoring)	Three cycles completed since 2006	Centers the process around states while allowing some input from IOs and civil society

"this very thin proposal [the Outcome Document of the 2005 World Summit] was sent as a working basis to diplomats in New York and Geneva, who did their best to make something out of it. The result is certainly totally different from what was initially expected."[2] We argue that the story of the HRC, by allowing us to see how the sausage is made, as it were, exemplifies the patchwork nature of global policymaking.

In the aftermath of the Iraq crisis, the UN faced mounting criticisms on a variety of counts, including the ineptness of its CHR. Resorting to a common practice, Secretary-General Kofi Annan put together the High-Level Panel on Threats, Challenges and Change in late 2003 in order to address this widespread negativity. The group of sixteen experts, coming from as many countries and chaired by Anand Panyarachun of Thailand, published its report in December 2004.[3] One of its key recommendations was to replace the CHR with a new body, the HRC, which was to become a principal organ of the UN with universal state membership. In another revolutionary twist, the panel also recommended that countries be represented on the Council not by professional diplomats, as per tradition, but by human rights experts.

In tune with UN practice, Secretary-General Annan took stock of the report in March 2005.[4] While supportive of the creation of the HRC, he opposed universal membership, suggesting instead that the body be subsidiary to the General Assembly rather than to ECOSOC, as was the case with the CHR. Under pressure from Washington, in April, the Secretary-General issued an "Explanatory Note" detailing his proposal ahead of the World Summit planned for September 2005.[5] In this document, he insisted that the HRC should have a smaller membership than the CHR, that its members should be elected by the entire UN membership, and that the Council should possess a new "peer review function."[6] He also called on the Office of the High Commissioner for Human Rights (OHCHR) to participate in determining the mandate, function, composition, size, and status of the new Council.

---

[2] De Frouville 2011, 244.   [3] UN General Assembly 2004.

[4] UN General Assembly 2005d.

[5] Explanatory note by Secretary-General Kofi Annan on the Human Rights Council, initially transmitted to the President of the General Assembly on April 14, 2005, and later published as an addendum to "In Larger Freedom," see UN General Assembly 2005c.

[6] Ibid., para. 6.

The debate soon moved to the CHR in Geneva, which, although considered moribund by most stakeholders, continued to function at the time. This kind of institutional overhaul, in which an existing body presides over its own dismemberment, seems unprecedented in global governance. Between April and June 2005, about fifty member states and a dozen NGOs met informally in Geneva to express their views on the best way forward.[7] High Commissioner Louise Arbour also presented her desire for greater country engagement, a closer partnership between civil society and UN agencies, and a stronger leadership role for her office (the OHCHR).[8] At around the same time, the Canadian delegation tabled a nonpaper about the peer-review mechanism put forward by Annan and supported by Arbour. This nonpaper outlined the mechanism's basic principles and modality, and explained the process for its use, including periodicity and follow-up.[9] Endorsed by the CHR chair, Manuel Rodriguez Cuadros of Peru, the proposition was informally discussed in intergovernmental channels. And in June, in preparation for the World Summit, a summary of the Geneva consultations was sent to the President of the General Assembly in New York.[10]

Building on the precedent of the Millennium Summit, the World Summit was held in September 2005 and brought world leaders together in a celebration of the UN's sixtieth anniversary. Wide-ranging in scope, the summit's Outcome Document – which was adopted by the entire UN membership – contains four paragraphs about the soon-to-be-created HRC.[11] In a rather vague call, world leaders tasked the President of the General Assembly with "conduct [ing] open, transparent and inclusive negotiations, to be completed as soon as possible during the sixtieth session, with the aim of establishing the mandate, modalities, functions, size, composition, membership, working methods and procedures of the Council." By delegating the critical work of institution-building to diplomats, decision makers yielded an "incomplete agreement" whose political ambiguities persist to this day. As one observer explains, "[o]ne must remember the prevailing atmosphere at that time. A conflictual consensus had

---

[7] Rizvi 2005.   [8] UN General Assembly 2005e.
[9] Interview with Henri-Paul Normandin, former Deputy Permanent Representative of Canada to the UN, June 2020. See Canada 2005.
[10] United Nations 2005a.
[11] UN General Assembly 2005a, para. 157–60. See Ghanea 2008, 703.

emerged. For different reasons, sometimes for totally opposing reasons, nearly all States demanded the end of the Human Rights Commission."[12] At its launch, in sum, the future of the HRC remained quite undefined.

1.1.2 Toward the 2007 Institution-Building Package

Pursuant to the Outcome Document, Jan Eliasson, the President of the General Assembly, convened a series of Informal Consultations of the Plenary in October and November 2005. Cochaired by South Africa and Panama, the negotiations addressed the mandate, functions, status, and composition of the HRC, as well as the rules of procedure and the transitional arrangements by which it would operate. In early November, the cochairs tabled an "options paper,"[13] a typical document at the UN containing the key proposals under consideration and highlighting those areas in need of agreement. Already accepted was the notion of a "universal periodic review;"[14] more contentious were the Council's size and the mode of election of its members. The draft agreement submitted in December 2005[15] led to "five months of protracted negotiations"[16] at the General Assembly. In order to break the deadlock, Eliasson held intensive consultations with member states (so-called "confessionals") in February 2006.[17]

It is worth noting that throughout this phase of institutional development, NGOs were largely kept to the side. In order to be heard, coalitions issued two joint letters containing a series of recommendations on the creation of the HRC. In November 2005, a group of forty NGOs provided a list of "indispensable" features for the future body, including principal organ status and "a level of participation by NGOs at least as high as that at the Commission on Human Rights."[18] Then, in January 2006, 160 NGOs sent a joint letter to Foreign Ministers and UN representatives calling for the election of HRC members via a two-thirds majority of the General Assembly; they also asked that regional groups be required to put forward more than one candidate per seat

---

[12] De Frouville 2011, 242.   [13] United Nations 2005b.
[14] Notice the slight terminological change from Annan's original proposal.
[15] See UN Human Rights Council 2005. Portions of the text remain in bold and brackets.
[16] Abraham 2007, 7.   [17] United Nations 2006.
[18] Joint Letter on the UN Human Rights Council 2005.

(*contra* the so-called "clean slates" practice). The NGOs also advocated the maintenance of a simple majority in votes on country-specific resolutions.[19]

Back in the General Assembly, following Eliasson's bilateral consultations with country delegations, a new draft resolution on the creation of the HRC was put to a vote on March 15, with 170 ballots in favor, four opposed (Israel, the Marshall Islands, Palau, and the US), and three abstentions (Belarus, Iran, and Venezuela).[20] The adoption of Resolution 60/251 created a Council that is subsidiary to the General Assembly and comprised of forty-seven states. Members are to be elected individually,[21] by a two-thirds majority, and in consideration of geographical distribution and human rights records and pledges. NGO participation follows the rules of ECOSOC, to which the new HRC is to report.[22] Moreover, the resolution's text establishes a UPR, maintains the so-called Special Procedures, sets up an Advisory Committee composed of experts, and provides for technical assistance and capacity-building. In typical UN language, the resolution states that the new HRC "shall be guided by the principles of universality, impartiality, objectivity and non-selectivity, constructive international dialogue and cooperation."[23] The resolution also calls for a formal review of the body in 2011 (more on this below). After holding elections in May 2006 (and with some staggered membership inherited from the CHR), the HRC held its first meeting in Geneva the following month. But the intense negotiations leading to this outcome were not over yet.

In a way reminiscent of the World Summit Outcome Document, Resolution 60/251 had left many loose ends, calling on the new Council to review its "mandates, mechanisms, functions and responsibilities ... within one year after the holding of its first session."[24] Once again, this form of institutional development is typical of bricolage and incremental institution-building. As one observer writes, "[t]he year of 'institution-building' [following the creation of the HRC] therefore began without an agreed blueprint. It was entirely dependent on States but also other stakeholders to articulate their vision of the new Council and its

---

[19] 160 NGOs Identify Essential Elements of a U.N. Human Rights Council 2006.
[20] UN General Assembly 2006b. Although it had initiated the reform process, the US ended voting against Resolution 60/251 due to alleged "deficiencies" in the document, see Nedeva 2006.
[21] Although in practice regional groupings remain salient, see Ramcharan 2015, 2.
[22] UN General Assembly 2006b.   [23] Ibid., para. 4.   [24] Ibid., para. 6.

institutions."[25] At its first session, in order to transition away from the CHR, the Council created three "intersessional working groups" dealing respectively with the UPR,[26] the Special Procedures and Complaint Procedure, and working methods and agenda. Primarily intergovernmental in nature, the Geneva negotiations, held in 2005–6 within the framework of the CHR, also involved a few major NGOs, including Human Rights Watch, Amnesty International, and International Service for Human Rights.[27]

In parallel to this formal process, Switzerland held a series of open workshops in Lausanne between May and August 2006. Delegates from 140 countries attended the meetings, together with human rights experts and NGOs, to discuss the first year's work program, the general procedure, and the new UPR.[28] The newly elected President of the HRC (Luis de Alba of Mexico) and representatives from the OHCHR, were also present.[29] These side practices expanded the level of participation in the policymaking process, although decision-making remained strictly in member states' hands.

Intergovernmental negotiations stalled for several months, primarily due to disagreement over the proposed review period: "In the months that preceded the final adoption, it looked extremely unlikely that the Council would be able to resolve all the pending issues and/or that it could do so without the package being put to a vote."[30] Faced with an approaching deadline, in June 2007, the President of the HRC decided to release a draft text, and he "made it clear that any attempt to amend any part of his document would lead to its withdrawal."[31] In a heated meeting on June 18 (the very last day before membership was due to change and just ahead of the deadline fixed by the General Assembly in its resolution), members had "to break up into smaller consultations as there was no agreement on the final text." What followed was quite dramatic:

Some say just before the stroke of midnight, others say a minute past, the President announced that agreement had been reached on the institution-building package, which would be formally adopted the next morning.... [The new Council President Costea] asked the Council to vote on his ruling

[25] Abraham 2007, 45.   [26] UN Human Rights Council 2006b.
[27] See Child Rights International Network 2006; Council Monitor 2006.
[28] Switzerland 2006a.   [29] Gaer 2007, 115.   [30] Abraham 2007, 43.
[31] Ibid., 10.

that the package had been agreed by consensus. Some regard this as a clever procedural manoeuver, and others describe [it] as an "aggressive Orwellian move." The Council voted 46 to 1 in favor of the new President's interpretation of events.[32]

The degree of improvisation and muddling through involved in the adoption of Resolution 5/1 – the HRC's 2007 institutional-building package – is nothing short of remarkable. As Abraham remarks, "[t]he rabbit was pulled out of the hat at the last minute and the package was perhaps the best political outcome that could be expected considering the membership of the Council and the positions that had been adopted by various States throughout the year."[33]

Resolution 5/1 features all the key elements that structure the work of the HRC. It contains rules of procedure and organization and establishes a Secretariat and a Presidency. It describes the Complaint Procedure and sets up an Advisory Committee composed of eighteen human rights experts elected by member states but acting in a personal capacity. The resolution also maintains the system of Special Procedures, which already existed under the CHR. Finally, and most importantly, the institution-building package provides organizational details for the new UPR mechanism centered on state-to-state dialogue. We will explore the modalities of this key practice in the next section. For now, it is sufficient to note that Resolution 5/1 created a heavily intergovernmental body, with some limited overtures to civil society along established ECOSOC rules.

1.1.3 Internal Revisions by the HRC (2008–20)

One intriguing characteristic of the making of the HRC is its continuity over time. Even after the institution-building package was adopted, in June 2007, the body has continued to develop through several self-reviews and low-key reforms. Recall that General Assembly Resolution 60/251, adopted in 2005, required that the Council "review its work and functioning five years after its establishment and report [its findings] to the General Assembly."[34] This kind of clause, not so frequent among IOs, reveals once again the provisional and open-ended nature

---

[32] Ibid., 11. Canada voted against the president's ruling because of a dispute over the Israel–Palestine question. Technically, the resolution is considered to have been adopted without a vote.
[33] Ibid.   [34] UN General Assembly 2006b, art.16.

of the HRC's institutional development – a feature further accentuated by other internal review practices. The 2011 review was also meant to give the General Assembly a chance to reconsider the HRC's status as a subsidiary organ.

In the run-up to the 2011 review, the HRC established a dedicated working group in 2009 chaired by its President.[35] Preparations took the form of six workshops in as many cities gathering member states and UN-recognized NGOs to discuss items such as the UPR, the Complaint Procedure, and the body's working methods and rules of procedure. Various documents came out of this process. The working group then met in Geneva from October 2010 to February 2011, producing in that time a 172-page report.[36] The review outcome was soon thereafter adopted by the HRC and the General Assembly in turn.[37] Overall, the review did not lead to big changes, as major proposals for reform (e.g., involving NGOs in early stages of the UPR and upholding more stringent criteria for membership) failed to garner sufficient support: "'Western states' were pushing in the direction of what developing countries, represented by the Non-Aligned Movement ..., interpreted as a 'reform' of the Human Rights Council, which involved instituting certain new tasks, whereas developing countries advocated a limited fine-tuning of existing mechanisms."[38] This last-minute drama and improvisation was reminiscent of the adoption of the 2007 institution-building package.

Reviews of the HRC are not over. Adopted on June 17, 2011, General Assembly Resolution A/65/281 provided for another review of the Council's status "at a time no sooner than ten years and no later than fifteen years" (art. 3). Narrower than the 2011 mandate, this second formal review does not explicitly call on the HRC to examine itself. At the time of writing, preparations had yet to begin in either Geneva or New York, although high-level practitioners, including the HRC's President and the High Commissioner for Human Rights, have already started to discuss the process. For example, at the 2019 Glion Human Rights Dialogue, an informal annual gathering co-organized by Switzerland and the NGO Universal Rights Group, participants from several permanent missions in Geneva disagreed on

---

[35] UN Human Rights Council 2009.   [36] UN Human Rights Council 2011.
[37] UN General Assembly 2011b; UN General Assembly 2011c.
[38] Cowan and Billaud 2015, 1183.

the opportunity for the Council to examine its procedures and work once again, and instead proposed that the General Assembly take the lead on the review.[39]

Indeed, in parallel to formal reviews, the HRC has continuously sought to reform its procedures since its launch, although in a more low-key manner. A central means of incremental institution-building has been the holding of "organizational sessions," usually in December in preparation for the next annual session of the Council. This is an opportunity for member states to discuss working methods and consider new mechanisms to improve the body's efficiency. For instance, in 2011, a new Office of the President was created with augmented staff and budget.[40] Through the yearly December organizational sessions, the Council also revised its financing and timeline in 2018 by adopting a presidential statement.[41] The document emerged from a yearlong series of informal consultations moderated by then President Vojislav Suc. Dubbed the "Efficiency Process," this institutional revision entailed contributions from member states, nonmember observer states, and NGOs, and concerned a variety of procedural matters, ranging from the annual work program to rules and procedures through to the integration of new technologies.

In a less structured fashion, finally, the Council has continued to specify, step by step, the workings of its flagship practice, the UPR (more on this below). For instance, in February 2008, the HRC adopted a new procedure to select the so-called troika. Based on "informal 'informal' discussions," the measure took the shape of a presidential statement. Organized by regions, the draw allows the country under review to substitute one of the names for a fourth pick should it so desire.[42] Further "modalities and practices for the universal periodic review" were hashed out in April 2008 through another presidential statement.[43] In subsequent years, Resolution 17/119 (July 2011) provided for the submission of documents by NGOs and other UPR-related procedures, while a September 2013 resolution addressed state compliance with UPR recommendations.[44] Overall, it seems fair to conclude that even after 2007, the Council has continued to reform its process incrementally, including when it comes to its anchoring practice: the UPR.

---

[39] Universal Rights Group 2019.   [40] UN General Assembly 2011a.
[41] E.g., UN General Assembly 2018c.   [42] UN Human Rights Council 2008b.
[43] UN Human Rights Council 2008a.   [44] UN General Assembly 2013a.

1.2 Anchoring Human Rights in the Universal Periodic Review

According to most observers, the UPR is "the 'flagship' of the Council, its most visible innovation."[45] We explained earlier how the idea was first proposed by Kofi Annan in his 2005 report, then refined by Canada, and finally hotly debated by diplomats from a plethora of countries in the aftermath of the World Summit. While innovative, the notion of "peer review" was not unprecedented in global governance, having been pioneered by the OECD in a wide range of economic and social policy areas. One OECD staffer describes the practice as "the systematic examination and assessment of the performance of a state by other states, ... with the ultimate goal of helping the reviewed state improve its policy making, adopt best practices and comply with established standards and principles."[46] Outside of the OECD, peer-review mechanisms have also been used by the European Union and African Union.

As stated in Resolution 5/1 (2007), the UPR is "an intergovernmental process, United Nations Member-driven." It offers an opportunity for member states to discuss their respective actions aimed at improving their human rights records, to share the best practices, and to provide technical assistance. Its basic principles include the universality, indivisibility, and interdependence of all human rights; cooperation and nonconfrontation; equal treatment of states; intergovernmentalism; and objectivity and transparency.[47] Led by a specific working group in the Council (composed of all forty-seven member states), UPR consists of an interactive discussion with individual member states, one after the other. Three states, selected by a drawing of lots and known as the Troika, serve as rapporteurs and lead the discussion. During the session, which lasts for three hours and thirty minutes, any state may comment or ask a question based on three key documents: (1) a national report produced by the state under review, (2) a compilation of documentation from experts and other UN entities (written by the OHCHR), and (3) documentation provided by national NGOs only. Throughout the UPR process, states must answer for any failures to live up to their human rights obligations derived from the UN Charter, the Universal Declaration, the treaties to which they are

---

[45] De Frouville 2011, 250.   [46] Pagani 2002, 15.
[47] UN Human Rights Council 2007b.

party, and various voluntary pledges. The review sessions of the UPR Working Group are public and transmitted online, with past webcasts archived by the OHCHR. Each UPR round lasts around four years; in mid-2017, UPR entered its third cycle, after all UN member states were reviewed in earlier rounds.

Once a review session is over, a report is prepared by the Troika and then discussed by the Working Group. The Working Group's report is later considered for final adoption in a regular HRC session. During that session, the country under review is given opportunities to comment but short of formal approval. In addition, NGOs may make statements. Resolution 5/1 states that each state is primarily responsible on an individual basis for implementation, although other "relevant stakeholders" may get involved "as appropriate." Accountability is expected to set in during the next UPR round, when countries have to report on their implementation of past recommendations. As one insider explains, "[t]here was opposition from some States to proposals for concrete follow-up mechanisms such [as] the appointment of a follow-up rapporteur or a requirement that the concerned State report to the Council on the implementation of the outcome." That said, she adds that "[o]ne of the most significant victories on the UPR is the provision that the Council can address, as appropriate, cases of persistent non-cooperation with the mechanism but only after exhausting all efforts to encourage a State to cooperate with the mechanism."[48]

While intergovernmental in nature, the UPR also involves some nonstate participation. Through its secretariat function, the OHCHR builds on the process to create training modules, administer funds, and mediate between states and civil society.[49] With help from law professors based in Switzerland and the UN's Department of Political Affairs,[50] the OHCHR also created a Universal Human Rights Index to compile all the recommendations made as part of the UPR. For their part, NGOs are involved at four levels. First, they may submit information pertaining to the facts on the ground to the OHCHR. Second, NGOs may take the floor at the very end of the plenary session during which the HRC adopts a country's final report. Third, they may get involved in the implementation of a given country's recommendations

[48] Abraham 2007, 41.
[49] UN Office of the High Commissioner for Human Rights 2013a.
[50] Switzerland 2006b.

as "relevant stakeholders" – a step requiring the consent of the concerned state, however. Fourth, NGOs may lobby friendly state delegations to draw their attention to specific issues they wish to have raised during the interactive dialogue. They may also assist in the formulation of recommendations that then make their way into the final report.[51]

How does the UPR "anchor" human rights policymaking at the UN? Because it "validates the international human rights norms promulgated by the United Nations,"[52] the practice is generally considered most central to the HRC's activities. Its effects on other political processes are visible in three ways. First, the report and recommendations that come out of the process are widely referenced. For instance, de Frouville notes that, "today, the treaty bodies and some special procedures are quoting 'accepted' recommendations by States during their UPR."[53] Ramcharan, for his part, argues that UPR reports "collectively amount to a world report on human rights."[54] Second, the UPR has transformed the ways in which human rights are monitored globally. Even though there still exist several bodies in charge of individual instruments, the HRC's regular review of all member states has become paramount, largely due to its universal, recursive, and public nature. As two experts conclude, "[t]he Universal Periodic Review process gives new flavor to the mix of human rights monitoring mechanisms."[55] Third, the UPR practice has reconfigured the political landscape of global human rights policymaking: "The UPR has revolutionized the human rights discourse.... Human rights are now openly broached in public exchanges between diplomats, government officials and members of civil society during national consultations."[56] The process draws a lot of public attention – for example, when it is featured in national media. In short, as Cowan explains, the UPR has substantially transformed the human rights regime:

The UPR has generated a political field which provides new spaces where things can be said and done, and enrolls existing categories of actors to speak and act in new ways. It has mobilised a wide range of actors, in different spaces, to respond to its requirements; it has generated new networks, invited the creation of new connections or the intensification of existing ones

---

[51] Cowan 2013.   [52] Ramcharan 2015, 50.   [53] De Frouville 2011, 252.
[54] Ramcharan 2015, 162.   [55] de la Vega and Lewis 2011, 384.
[56] Ibid., 377.

between networks, and prompted new kinds of collaborations. These actors have been enlisted into myriad practices either of audit itself or of making audit possible.[57]

A practice that generates such far-ranging effects, we argue, exerts a pull on the entire global policymaking process.

Another way the UPR acts as an anchoring practice at the UN is by taking human rights politics in certain directions and precluding others. More specifically, three aspects of this process need to be pointed out. First, the UPR operates in the spirit of a "learning forum," not unlike the UN Global Compact, for instance. As two experts put it, "[t]he mission of the UPR is best described as a forum where UN Member States consider the human rights records of peers and share best practices for human rights policies."[58] This cooperation-based mode of governance, often qualified as "soft,"[59] stands in opposition to more forceful practices such as regulation or third-party mandatory arbitration. That said, some critics argue that the practice does not depart significantly from earlier forums in which the Global North was able to exert its domination over the South: "The model of the UPR as a learning culture in which all countries 'have something to learn' has tremendous ethical appeal. Yet it is haunted by an older model of tutelage in which an enlightened West guides a backward non-West in its efforts to 'catch up' with the norms that the West has set."[60]

Second, UPR practices display an intriguing combination of transparency and opacity. On the one hand, the procedures strongly encourage publicity, by making documents and webcasts widely available: "The public nature of the reviews has been a key characteristic of the UPR which has lent to transparency of UN human rights surveillance."[61] That said, such a level of visibility – slightly unusual in global policymaking – also "elicits state performances.... This sometimes exciting – yet more often, rather dull – political theatre is the front-stage of the Geneva element of the UPR."[62] For instance, notes Cowan, "in the UPR's first cycle, states worked hard at impression management, mobilizing allies or even taking illicit control of the speaker's list of the interactive dialogue in order to ensure that 'friendly' states that

---

[57] Cowan 2015, 55.   [58] de la Vega and Lewis 2011, 362.
[59] Charlesworth and Larking 2015.   [60] Cowan and Billaud 2015, 1187–8.
[61] de la Vega and Lewis 2011, 376.   [62] Cowan 2013, 120.

could be counted on to offer praise and 'easy' recommendations spoke first."[63] Publicity, then, is no panacea.

On the other hand, significant parts of the UPR process take place in the shadows, as it "relies heavily on the less visible, back-stage work of the Secretariat."[64] This includes the drafting of the preparatory documents, which rests on "judgment and diplomacy. The team must be ready to defend its decisions to meddling states, who may accuse them of including information provided by an NGO."[65] This invisible work also involves collecting expert views on a country's human rights situation. According to one insider, "the most intense moments of the play take place off-stage, in the meeting rooms where drafters devise narrative strategies, in the corridors where diplomats bargain over recommendations with other state representatives and in the offices where UN civil servants tailor like craftsmen the paragraphs of a report reflecting the voices of 'civil society.'"[66] The significant role played by international bureaucracy is often contested by states, who decry the "fetish-like status"[67] of UPR reports. Others disagree with this view, arguing that "in the UPR, the UN Secretariat has a quieter presence. Its role is crucial yet symbolically muted and largely unremarked."[68]

Third, as a practice, the UPR reflects a certain normative discourse at the expense of plausible alternatives. Two scholars explain: "[The] UPR mechanism arose from the emerging ideology, taking shape in the new millennium, that the integral human rights record of each nation must form part of an international discourse on human rights."[69] For her part, Cowan locates UPR as part of an "audit culture" composed of "practices of oversight that include an important element of critical self-accounting."[70] Dominant in twenty-first-century global policymaking, this approach has significant political effects, including by transforming the meaning of sovereignty, which is so central to the practice: "the state has shifted from being the object of international supervision to being, also and primarily, a subject that self-reports."[71] By participating in the UPR mechanism, Cowan concludes, UN members join in "the community of rights-respecting states."[72]

Overall, in the making of the HRC, the roads not taken matter just as much as the options that were retained. The original proposal

[63] Ibid., 123.   [64] Ibid., 120.   [65] Ibid.   [66] Billaud 2015.
[67] Ibid. See also Abraham 2007, 38.   [68] Cowan 2013.
[69] de la Vega and Lewis 2011, 353.   [70] Cowan 2013, 104.   [71] Ibid., 124.
[72] Ibid., 118.

of having experts rather than state diplomats run the UPR would have revolutionized global governance, yet it was rejected by a majority of UN members. Similarly, universal participation in the Council, which had been considered during the early discussions, would have likely transformed the politics involved. Ultimately, the form of governance reflected in the UPR has set global human rights policies on a path that will persist for the foreseeable future.

2 Debating the Universality of Human Rights

In tune with what Soroos calls the "platitudes" of global public policymaking, the General Assembly resolution that sets up the HRC lists a patchwork of universal values that are as polysemous as they are potentially discordant. Among the key principles featured in the preamble and beyond, one finds universality, impartiality, objectivity, nonselectivity, constructive dialogue, cooperation, predictability, flexibility, transparency, accountability, balance, inclusiveness, comprehensiveness, gender equality, and national implementation. To make sense of this formidable list, we must reconstruct both the multifaceted cleavages that universal values seek to paper over and the clashing meanings that some of these values harbor on the global stage (see Table 4.2).

2.1 What Is the Problem?

The notion that the CHR had become defective achieved the status of a consensus assessment by the early years of the twenty-first century. Everyone seemed to agree that "politicization" was the key problem plaguing the flagship vehicle for human rights policymaking at the UN. In his Explanatory Note following the publication of *In Larger Freedom*, Kofi Annan expressed this view when he wrote that the CHR had been "undermined by the politicization of its sessions and the selectivity of its work."[73] Likewise, the General Assembly resolution creating the HRC recognizes "the importance of ensuring universality, objectivity, and non-selectivity in the consideration of human rights issues, and the elimination of double standards and politicization."[74] In a rare display of North–South agreement, the same diagnosis was offered by champions of the South, such as Pakistan, China, Cuba, and

[73] UN General Assembly 2005c.   [74] UN General Assembly 2006b, 2.

Table 4.2 *Main value debates in the making of the HRC*

	Value cleavages	Polysemous compromises
What is the problem?	Selectivity vs. cultural relativism	Politicization of human rights
What are the ends?	Equal treatment vs. uniform application of international human rights law	Universality
	Civil-political vs. social-economic rights	Indivisibility
By what means?	Expertise vs. state sovereignty	Improved institutional process
	Inclusive vs. restricted membership	Efficiency
	Capacity-building vs. publicity of abuses	Constructive dialogue

Kenya – the latter chastising the "selfish political agendas of Member States"[75] – as well as by countries from the North and major NGOs. For instance, Amnesty International denounced the "power politics and double standards" that plagued the Commission.[76]

Beneath this surface consensus, however, deep disagreements remained over what, exactly, politicization entailed. The rift may be summed up by describing two main positions. For many countries from the South, politicization meant "selectivity": the unbalanced targeting by the West of developing countries such as Cuba, Iran, Myanmar, and Venezuela. For instance, a representative from Sudan regretted that "[t]he Commission had ignored the flagrant human rights violations perpetrated by the major powers, but it readily considered and adopted resolutions condemning human rights situations in smaller countries."[77] Pakistan similarly denounced "the selective targeting of developing countries."[78] Perhaps most colorfully, the Cuban Ambassador opined that the Commission's "sinking was marked by its inconsistencies and the impunity enjoyed by a privileged few. . . .. It was not the poor and marginalized developing countries that

[75] Quoted in UN General Assembly 2006a.   [76] Amnesty International 2005, 5.
[77] Quoted in UN General Assembly 2006a.   [78] Quoted in ibid.

were responsible for this state of affairs. . . . Its legitimacy was under-mined by the membership of a superpower which trampled upon human rights and curtailed liberties."[79] Generally speaking, for many member states from the Global South, politicization essentially meant "selectivity and double standards."[80]

Meanwhile, other participants in the policymaking process, hailing mainly from the West, referred to something else when they talked about the politicization of the CHR: the games of coalition politics, especially along regional lines, as well as the temptation of cultural relativism that leads some countries to excuse human rights violations in the name of sovereignty and cultural difference. Quite amazingly, given his position as Secretary-General, Kofi Annan made his views very clear when he declared that "[i]t is no secret that governments get onto the Commission either to protect them-selves or to ensure that others are brought to the dock, as it were. And it has become so contentious; and groups form to ensure who is going to be castigated and who is not. In the process, the rights of the individual, and the human rights that they are there to protect, often get lost."[81] Human Rights Watch concurred that those who blocked the Commission in the name of sovereignty were part of the problem: "The crisis of credibility afflicting the commission stems partly from the membership on the commission of states with dismal human rights records."[82] Simply put, for some coun-tries, group politics, so prevalent at the UN, had come to structure policymaking.

Overall, then, everyone agreed that the problem to be fixed by the new HRC process was politicization. Yet, while many governments from the South chastised their northern counterparts for their selectiv-ity and double standards, several countries in the North, along with NGOs and even some UN bodies, denounced these political games for hampering human rights monitoring and compliance at the global level.

---

[79] Quoted in UN Office of the High Commissioner for Human Rights 2005a.
[80] Quoted in UN General Assembly 2006a.   [81] UN Secretary-General 2005.
[82] Peggy Hicks, Global Advocacy Director at the Human Rights Watch, paraphrased in Center for U.N. Reform Education 2005, 1. Note that the report was a rapporteur's summary of the participants' remarks, and therefore the comments provided may not be exact quotes.

2.2 *What Are the Ends?*

The consensus view on the solution to politicization was just as striking as the diagnosis posed by global policymakers: the new HRC had to give "equal treatment" to all countries and populations in the world. This is, indeed, the particular meaning of universality that features in most documents and that inspired the key innovation of the UPR. For Egypt, "all member states have the duty to interact with these mechanisms, without exception, [and] in tandem these mechanisms must be applied in a fair and equal manner on the basis of objectivity and impartiality."[83] The High Commissioner for Human Rights at the time of the creation of the HRC, Louise Arbour, similarly advocated a human rights system that operates "against a backdrop of universal scrutiny."[84] She later added that "[n]o country will be beyond scrutiny, and no longer will countries be able to use membership of the UN's premier human rights body to shield themselves or allies from criticism or censure for rights breaches."[85] In a rare display of consensus, China claimed that "[t]he proposed Universal Periodic Review should ensure that all countries, regardless of their sizes, are treated impartially and in a fair manner."[86] NGOs, too, called for "the universal coverage and the equal treatment of all States."[87] This principle was particularly central in the debate over the UPR. For example, Malaysia insisted that "[h]uman rights situations in all countries should be considered on an equal footing under the Universal Periodic Review mechanism."[88]

Beyond this consensus, though, a serious normative cleavage plagued the search for a solution in the realm of global human rights policymaking. For most developing countries, equal treatment means respect for sovereignty as well as for the specific national circumstances of each state, including its level of development. A leader of the Global South, Egypt claimed that "the sovereign equality of States" should be a basic principle for the new HRC.[89] Further specifying the dual meaning of this position, China added that "[t]he Council should refrain from interfering in the internal affairs of countries and it should

---

[83] Egypt 2012.
[84] UN Office of the High Commissioner for Human Rights 2005b.
[85] UN Office of the High Commissioner for Human Rights 2006, 1.
[86] China 2006; Gaer 2007, 132.   [87] UN Human Rights Council 2007a.
[88] Quoted in UN General Assembly 2007.   [89] UN General Assembly 2006a.

respect the development path chosen by the people of the concerned country."[90] Beijing also insisted that "all countries' historical, cultural and religious backgrounds and differences are [to be] equally respected."[91] On the one hand, then, equal-treatment-qua-respect-for-sovereignty entails the need for "consent of the country concerned,"[92] in Sri Lanka's words, as well as the rejection of any form of "coercion"[93] (Malaysia). On the other hand, it requires taking into account national circumstances with "respect [to] cultural and political differences, as well as the right to development"[94] (Sudan). Summing up this view, harbored primarily by governments from the Global South, former UN Deputy Secretary-General Louise Fréchette argued that "the world is composed of countries that have very different views on human rights."[95]

Standing against the dominant approach among developing countries, a position primarily defended by Western states held that equal treatment essentially meant universal compliance (that is, the absence of exception). For instance, Austria emphasized the need to "submit all to scrutiny, without exception," adding that it is "essential that the review had the possibility of further follow-up."[96] The European Union further specified that particular national circumstances should never serve as an excuse for violation, arguing that the new HRC should "ensure regular examination of the Human Rights record of each UN member state, without selectivity, on the basis of the same criteria and without consideration of the level of development other than in the outcome phase."[97] This view in favor of universal compliance was also echoed by a number of NGOs. For example, Alex Neve, Secretary-General of Amnesty International Canada, explained that the UPR gives the HRC "the means to promote human rights in all countries consistently."[98] Interestingly, this was also the position defended by Secretary-General Ban Ki-Moon: "No country, big or

[handwritten margin note: 2 definitions]

---

[90] UN Office of the High Commissioner for Human Rights 2017.
[91] China 2006; Gaer 2007, 132.   [92] Quoted in UN General Assembly 2007.
[93] Quoted in UN General Assembly 2010a.
[94] Omar Bashir Mohamed Manis quoted in UN General Assembly 2006a.
[95] Quoted in Terlingen 2007, 177.   [96] Quoted in UN General Assembly 2006a.
[97] European Union 2007.
[98] Alex Neve, Secretary General, Amnesty International Canada, testimony before the Canadian Standing Senate Committee on Human Rights, February 11, 2008, quoted in Canada 2008, 22–3.

small, will be immune from scrutiny,"[99] a principle that means that we have finally reached "the universality of human rights."[100]

It is worth noting how the polysemy of equal treatment made its way into the General Assembly resolution that led to the creation of the HRC in 2005. The document states that "while the significance of national and regional particularities and various historical, cultural and religious backgrounds must be borne in mind, all States, regardless of their political, economic and cultural systems, have the duty to promote and protect all human rights and fundamental freedoms."[101] As suggested by this ambiguous formulation, no clear position was found during the policymaking process, and the rift between those who seek respect for sovereignty versus universal compliance was barely papered over.

A second area of surface consensus, when it comes to resolving the politicization of human rights at the UN, concerns the idea of "indivisibility." This is another commonplace consistently brandished by a variety of global actors who otherwise think very differently about human rights. Addressing the Complaint Procedure, one HRC facilitator argued that the mechanism "covered all human rights, whether they were civil and political rights or economic, social and cultural rights."[102] This apparent agreement, however, hides a rather deep normative cleavage.

The dominant view is that indivisibility entails a better balance between economic and social rights on the one hand and political and civil rights on the other – a long-standing element of human rights discourse at the UN. This position was defended from the outset by the Secretary-General, who wrote in his 2005 Explanatory Note that the projected UPR "would give concrete expression to the principle that human rights are universal and indivisible. Equal attention will have to be given to civil, political, economic, social and cultural rights, as well as the right to development."[103] Zimbabwe's Ambassador asked that member states "look at all human rights as indivisible. This is because there has been a tendency by some members of the UN to put more emphasis on civil and political rights. But the developing countries have stuck together and said we want to include the Right to

---

[99] UN Secretary-General 2007.   [100] Ibid.
[101] UN General Assembly 2006b, 1.   [102] UN Human Rights Council 2006a.
[103] UN General Assembly 2005c, para. 6.

Development which should be given equal emphasis ... because you cannot talk about civil and political rights while people are refused the right to development."[104] A Chinese delegate concurred, saying that "the two main categories of human rights – economic, social and cultural, and civil and political – have not been treated in a balanced manner."[105] A similar view in favor of economic and social rights was aired by many countries from the Global South, including Egypt,[106] Myanmar,[107] and Nicaragua.[108]

By contrast, a number of actors coming from the North think that the indivisibility of human rights means that they must not be trumped by development issues. The conservative Heritage Foundation, for instance, goes so far as to lament the capture of the human rights agenda by developing countries: "One of the regrettable results of the Non-Aligned Movement's dominance in the U.N. system is the elevation of social and economic rights at the expense of civil and political rights."[109] The more mainstream view, however, is that the right to development should not be used as an excuse for noncompliance. There is a clear connection between this view and the belief in universal compliance (described above). According to an American Ambassador, "a lot of countries oppose the reforms that we're seeking because they fundamentally object to the scrutiny that the Human Rights Council can put on the conduct of individual governments."[110] Considering that the US has yet to ratify the International Covenant on Economic, Social and Cultural Rights, it appears that the indivisibility of human rights can be contorted to fit a rather distinctive understanding when used in favor of universal compliance.

2.3 By What Means?

In the same way that most actors agreed that the problem with global human rights policy is politicization, and that the solution is equal treatment, it is possible to identify a space of agreement when it comes to the means and ends by which this should be achieved: improving the institutional process. For example, Nicaragua stated that "the new institutional architecture would facilitate an evaluation process based

[104] Chidyausiku 2006. [105] China 2015.
[106] Quoted in UN General Assembly 2010a.
[107] Quoted in UN General Assembly 2007. [108] Quoted in ibid.
[109] Loconte 2005. [110] United States of America 2006.

on universality, objectivity and non-selectivity. This would ensure greater promotion of human rights."[111] But the hope placed in the design of a new institution, while widely shared, also took on a variety of clashing meanings.

For several actors, improving the institutional process essentially meant placing human rights experts in the driver's seat in an effort to increase the independence of policymaking. Recall that this was the original position taken by the High-Level Panel in 2004. Several Western governments expressed hopes for a more independent process. Referring to the Special Procedures, Latvia expressed concerns about "the non-cooperation or selective cooperation by States that under-mined human rights instruments."[112] France added that "experts had a primordial role to play; their expertise was the antenna by which the Council could 'listen in' to the real world."[113] This also happened to be the position of the UN itself, as conveyed by the Secretary-General, who lauded the Special Procedures and the OHCHR for providing "independent expertise and judgement, which is essential to effective human rights protection. They must not be politicized, or subjected to governmental control."[114]

Several NGOs also joined the chorus of voices expressing regret that experts, especially those working in the framework of the Special Procedures, often operate in the face of interference from member states. A Freedom House representative complained that the UPR guidelines placed too much emphasis on "intergovernmental consensus and inclu-siveness over rigorous standards and specificity."[115] Human Rights Watch concurred, lamenting the fact that "a number of governments have increasingly criticized the independence of special procedures and have sought to impose controls on the way Special Procedures interpret and implement their mandates. ... Any approach that puts governments in an oversight position over the special procedures would politicize and damage the effectiveness of the special procedures system."[116] Overall, the intrusion of intergovernmentalism into human rights policymaking was a common complaint among civil society organizations. A group of

---

[111] UN General Assembly 2007.
[112] Quoted in UN Human Rights Council 2017.
[113] Quoted in UN General Assembly 2007.   [114] UN Secretary-General 2006.
[115] Paula Schriefer, Director of Advocacy, Freedom House, testimony before the Committee, February 25, 2008, quoted in Canada 2008, 22.
[116] Human Rights Watch 2010, 17.

NGOs condemned "what appears to be a coordinated effort to intimi-
date Special Procedures, individually and collectively," reminding the
"fundamental requirement that States refrain from undermining the
independence of the Special Procedures mandate holders."[117]

Remarkably, many actors held the exact opposite view – that an
improved institutional process had to maintain states at the helm. For
example, China claimed that "[e]xperts of special mechanisms were
not judges of human rights and they had no right to fabricate cases of
reprisal in order to exert pressure on Member States."[118] For many
countries from the Global South, the primacy of intergovernmentalism
provides the necessary guarantee for sovereignty and state consent.
The Iranian Ambassador, for example, insisted that "[s]overeign states
were only accountable to their legal commitments and their voluntary
pledges."[119] For its part, Algeria suggested that the new HRC should
ensure that independent experts be kept under control by member
states: "It would be necessary for the Council to give a premium to
those Experts who were able to engage best in dialogue. Could the
Council think of a constructive way of expressing appreciation to
mandate holders who were able to engender dialogue?"[120] In this view,
sovereignty trumps independence in human rights policymaking.

Another key cleavage, once again tracking the North–South fault
line, had to do with whether membership in the Council should be
inclusive or selective. Those in favor of a more inclusive process felt
that any UN member state should be able to run for a Council seat,
thus opposing the notion of strenuous membership criteria based on
countries' human rights records, for example. One African
Ambassador claimed that "[y]ou cannot make qualifications for the
membership of that body. When you do come up with qualifications
and conditionalities for membership, who would determine the qualifications? Which standards are you going to use?"[121] An intermediate
view, which eventually triumphed, was expressed by Japan, which
called for "the submission of a written pledge by candidates seeking
membership, well in advance of the election, so that Member States
could examine it, and fully take it into account in casting their

---

[117] Open Letter to Member States of the Human Rights Council 2009.
[118] Quoted in UN Human Rights Council 2017.
[119] Quoted in UN General Assembly 2007.
[120] Quoted in UN Human Rights Council 2007a.   [121] Chidyausiku 2006.

votes."[122] Ultimately, the 2007 institution-building package also contained a suspension clause in case of a flagrant violation of human rights on the part of a member state. Several countries expressed doubts, however. An Egyptian delegate stated that "the suspension of the rights of membership, as stipulated in the text's operative paragraph 8 ... should be an exceptional application of the new body, only, and limited to, cases of gross and systematic human rights violations. Such a case, however, should not be a precedent or basis for the 'proliferation' of such a practice in other United Nations bodies."[123]

The dominant view at the UN, especially among developing countries, is that the existing membership criteria are too easily instrumentalized in favor of questionable political agendas. According to Cuba, "[i]f human rights are universal and are everybody's responsibility, why should the decision-making mechanism on these issues be limited? In fact, did not the High-level Panel recommend that, on these grounds, the new body should be one of universal membership?"[124] And that was indeed part of the original proposal by the HLP, as Gareth Evans recalled: "We did not go down the path of recommending tough criteria for the membership of the commission – taking the view that that would only lead to even more distracting political battles – but rather universal membership."[125] Some officials in the Secretariat also defended the view, here voiced by Shashi Tharoor, UN Under-Secretary-General for Communications and Public Information, that "[y]ou don't advance human rights by preaching only to the converted."[126] Interestingly, some civil society organizations, including in the West, agreed: "The presumption that a country is a violator of human rights is very subjective. If you want to create criteria ... that exclude certain countries, why not those that don't support trade liberalization or that don't implement foreign aid targets? The knife cuts both ways."[127] Ultimately, though, the option of broad membership did not win the day.

In the opposite camp stand a number of actors in favor of selective membership, to the point of excluding those countries that do not comply with human rights obligations. In his 2005 report, Kofi Annan set the tone when he wrote that "[t]hose elected to the Council should

---

[122] Quoted in UN General Assembly 2006a.   [123] Quoted in ibid.
[124] Quoted in Yeboah 2008, 81.   [125] Evans 2005.   [126] Loconte 2005.
[127] Schaefer 2006.

undertake to abide by the highest human rights standards."[128] The debate continued well after the passing of Resolution 60/251, in which restricted membership triumphed. Reflecting back on that text, the Chilean Ambassador said that he had hoped for "more clear-cut compliance with the highest human rights standards, when it came to the selection of Council members."[129] For its part, the US representative explained his negative ballot by claiming that "[t]he Council discredits, dishonors, and diminishes itself when the worst violators of human rights have a seat at its table. . . . Let there be no doubt: membership on the Human Rights Council should be earned through respect for human rights, not accorded to those who abuse them."[130] Israel concurred, regretting that "[t]he resolution contained worrying omissions, including the absence of sufficient benchmarks for membership."[131] In order to take action, Austria, speaking on behalf of the EU, declared that "[e]ach European Union member State committed itself not to cast its vote for a candidate that was under Security Council sanctions for human rights related reasons. No State guilty of gross and systematic human rights violations should serve on the Council."[132]

In the debate over inclusive versus restrictive membership, a key bone of contention concerned the highly prevalent practice of "clean slates" in UN elections, by which a regional group internally selects one candidate for a seat prior to voting at the General Assembly. As we saw above, this practice was countered in the new HRC, where member states are to be elected "individually." Yet, as Ramcharan notes, "[i]n practice, regional slates have continued without being so deemed."[133] This clash was already apparent in earlier debates. On one side, a group of NGOs led by Human Rights Watch explained that "'clean slates,' where the same number of candidates is presented as seats available in the region, undermine this principle and permit Council members to effectively be selected on the basis of rotation or reciprocal vote trading agreements. By contrast, competitive slates allow UN Member States to elect the best candidates proposed from each region of the world. We therefore support competitive slates in every region."[134] The opposite view was defended by the Pakistani

---

[128] UN General Assembly 2005d, para. 182.
[129] Quoted in UN General Assembly 2006a.
[130] United States of America 2011.
[131] Quoted in UN General Assembly 2006a.   [132] Quoted in ibid.
[133] Ramcharan 2015, 2.   [134] Human Rights Watch 2009.

Ambassador, who argued that "representatives of the new council should be selected on the basis of their neighbors' preferences, not strictly on their democratic credentials or their human rights records. 'It's peer selection. . . . If a majority of peers say "okay" despite the fact that you think Country X is a violator of human rights, we think they are still justified to be on the council. I think it would be artificial to try to exclude them.'"[135] This divide remains very much central to human rights policymaking to this day.

A third and final axis of conflict regarding the institutional process has to do with its confrontational versus cooperative nature. For a minority of actors, a better HRC had to target the worst violators and call them out publicly. For instance, the United States expressed concerns that an automatic and universal review system could detract attention from the critical situations highlighted through the system of Special Procedures: "We are not actually opposed to the peer review concept, as long as it does not divert time, attention and resources away from the more country specific, action-oriented plan."[136] Meanwhile, High Commissioner for Human Rights Zeid Ra'ad Al Hussein took a risky stance by embracing a more candid approach to human rights:

> I am often told in this chamber, in our debates, that I should not be "naming and shaming" member states. Somehow the naming is, or has become, the very shame itself. This is a disfigurement of the truth, which we must now reset. The shame comes not from the naming: it comes from the actions themselves, the conduct or violations, alleged with supporting evidence or proven. The greatest factory of shame is the blanket denial of human rights. . . . We name; the shame of States, where it exists, has already been self-inflicted. The loss of face for the affected countries has come well before OHCHR raises its independent voice.[137]

By contrast, a majority of stakeholders – first and foremost countries from the Global South – instead advocated a cooperative approach. Pakistan, speaking on behalf of the Organization of the Islamic Conference, similarly "rejected that practice of targeting developing countries, including Islamic countries, through country-specific

---

[135] Lynch 2006.
[136] Thomas Schweich, Chief of Staff at the United States Mission to the United Nations, paraphrased in Center for U.N. Reform Education 2005, 2.
[137] UN Office of the High Commissioner for Human Rights 2015.

resolutions. Those resolutions were often politically motivated."[138] The Pakistani diplomat also argued that the real solution rests with "promoting consensus and harmony."[139] There was a widespread fear that the "naming and shaming" that often prevailed at the CHR would be motivated by political reasons unrelated to human rights violations. For Zimbabwe's Ambassador, for example, country-specific resolutions should require "two-thirds of the membership to decide."[140] As he explained, "[t]his should be vetted and scrutinized to make sure that the aim of such a move is not to just to [sic] punish a country because of a bilateral dispute that has nothing to do with the issue of human rights at all."[141] In order to depoliticize human rights policy-making, then, only dialogue and cooperation should have currency at the new Council.

In practice, such cooperation would rest on the twin pillars of voluntary participation and capacity-building. Kofi Annan, for instance, insisted that the new review process would have to be "a process whereby States voluntarily enter into discussion."[142] A Chinese representative went further and chastised "heavy-handed interference in the internal affairs of States under the pretext of protecting human rights, naming and shaming and other confrontational approaches."[143] As a CARICOM representative added, "CARICOM sought the establishment of a Council which would be inclusive and open to the participation of all States and which would function as a cooperative mechanism for the promotion of human rights, serving as a vehicle for the promotion of genuine cooperation for capacity-building and for mutual assistance."[144] An improved institutional process had to guarantee fair treatment, including for poor or resource-deprived countries in need of assistance. India, for instance, feared that the new UPR and other human rights mechanisms within the UN increased the workload imposed on member states. As a result, it repeatedly demanded that "appropriate institutional capacities and financial resources [be made] available to the States in pursuit of their human rights commitments."[145] This view was echoed by the High Commissioner for Human Rights, who similarly argued that "[s]tate

---

[138] Quoted in UN Office of the High Commissioner for Human Rights 2005a.
[139] Quoted in ibid.   [140] Chidyausiku 2006.   [141] Ibid.
[142] UN General Assembly 2005c, para. 7.   [143] China 2015.
[144] Quoted in Yeboah 2008, 82.   [145] India 2016.

capacity should be strengthened and acknowledged."[146] The creation of the Trust Fund, which sought to encourage the participation of Least Developed Countries (LDCs) and Small Island Developing States (SIDS), was widely hailed as a key aspect of this cooperative endeavor – "an enabler for participation,"[147] to use the words of the Pakistani Ambassador.

Capacity-building was generally approved by the various stakeholders, although along different lines. For some, technical assistance was meant to reinforce sovereignty. Upon the adoption of the institution-building package, Brazil claimed that "[e]xperience showed that, as a rule, politicizing human rights tended to be counterproductive, if not accompanied by positive incentives, such as cooperation and capacity-building."[148] China also expressed concerns about "the politicization of technical assistance,"[149] while Sri Lanka warned against "intrusive monitoring."[150] For its part, Bolivia concurred that "[c]ooperation should not be used as a tool of interference."[151] Pakistan insisted that "[t]he varying degrees of development of states determines the incapacity, to focus on the magnitude and multitude of the issues they face.... The focus should be on strengthening national mechanisms and institutions for the protection, promotion and full realization of all human rights."[152] Referring back to the surface consensus discussed above, Tunisia, speaking on behalf of the African Group, argued that "[t]echnical cooperation should be anchored in the universality and indivisibility of all human rights."[153]

Other actors, especially countries and NGOs from the Global North, were more willing to tie capacity-building to human rights performance. For Austria, the new Council should "provide guidance and assistance to all countries to achieve the highest standards of human rights protection, through dialogue, cooperation and capacity-building."[154] This view was shared by several NGOs, for which technical assistance risked drawing attention away from gross violations.

---

[146] Quoted in UN Office of the High Commissioner for Human Rights 2005a.
[147] Pakistan 2017b.   [148] Quoted in UN General Assembly 2006a.
[149] UN Office of the High Commissioner for Human Rights 2017.
[150] Quoted in UN General Assembly 2007.
[151] UN Office of the High Commissioner for Human Rights 2017.
[152] Pakistan 2017a.
[153] Quoted in UN Office of the High Commissioner for Human Rights 2017.
[154] Quoted in UN General Assembly 2006a.

For Human Rights Watch, "[i]n the case of repressive governments that have no intention to reform, such as Uzbekistan, relying solely on technical assistance is a completely inadequate approach."[155]

All in all, there was both consensus and struggle over the norms that should guide the way forward in global human rights policymaking. Everybody seemed to agree on the need to improve the institutional process, including through capacity-building. However, for some, this involved selective membership, the naming and shaming of violators, and setting criteria for assistance. The opposite camp called for inclusive membership devoid of conditions, capacity-building in favor of sovereign participation, and a cooperative approach based on dialogue. These deep rifts in the normative underpinning of global public policymaking continue to structure the politics of human rights to this day.

Conclusion

The making of the HRC perfectly instantiates the patchwork nature of global policymaking. In what we have called "institution-building by doing," Council diplomats and a variety of other partners have as it were built the plane while flying it, as is often the case in global governance.[156] In a recent book taking stock of the body's development, Tistounet summarizes the policymaking process in the following terms:

There exist a vast array of practices, tools and mechanisms which have been progressively and patiently established by the Council.... [T]he Council developed its practices with a high level of flexibility. It used every possible entry point or sleight of hand in order to reach a goal which otherwise would not have been achieved.... [I]t did so with persistence and determination, adjusting its working methods, creating numerous new processes, envisaging multiple areas of development and working tirelessly on all matters which it had to tackle on a step-by-step strategy.... When improvements could not be agreed upon, new avenues were explored; when precedents could not be resorted to, it envisaged new ones; when no existing mechanism or tool was available, it simply created new ones.... [I]t did so in an extremely pragmatic manner, adopting decisions, resorting to practices initiated or proposed by

---

[155] Rory Mungoven, global advocacy director for Human Rights Watch, quoted in Human Rights Watch 2004.
[156] Pouliot 2021.

the successive Presidents and their Bureaux, and agreeing informally to setting up new procedures proposed by concerned stakeholders.[157]

Indeed, today's HRC forms an amazing bricolage of governance practices and universal values, one characterized by constant adaptation and constructive ambiguity. Without a doubt, in global governance, institutional design resembles Lindblom's "muddling through"[158] far more than any kind of rational optimization or even capture by the powerful. It is a patchwork of the many, and its coherence hinges precisely on that.

---

[157] Tistounet 2020, 2.   [158] Lindblom 1959.

5 | The Protection of Civilians
Policymaking by Fits and Starts

The protection of civilians in armed conflict (what we have earlier termed the PoC doctrine) has become a policy of major importance in twenty-first-century global governance. While the Security Council asserts that PoC has become "one of the core issues"[1] on its agenda, the Office for the Coordination of Humanitarian Affairs (OCHA) argues that recent years have seen the rise of "a culture of PoC ... across the United Nations and its membership."[2] In fact, PoC has become the primary goal of UN peace operations, replacing the old objective of creating a buffer zone between belligerents. Revealingly, in 2015, a panel of experts estimated that 98 percent of UN staff involved in peace operations operated under a PoC mandate.[3] In the words of two analysts, PoC has gradually established itself as "the most legitimate use of force on behalf of the international community."[4]

Like most global policies, PoC can be understood as a bricolage of practices and values, with improvisation once again playing a key role. This improvisation is especially apparent in the permanent conflict between the desire to make PoC a more consistent global policy and the goal of avoiding a one-size-fits-all approach. At the heart of this conflict is the fact that there is no common definition of PoC. As is often said, "everyone understands protection differently."[5] An operational challenge for PoC therefore consists in making continual trade-offs between the different visions of "protection," as well as between the various conceptions of PoC's proper place among UN priorities. In this context, rather than following a rational design, the history of PoC has been determined by the shifting balance of global power relations and the vagaries of international circumstances.

---

[1] UN Security Council 2015c, 1. See also UN Security Council 2018d, 1.
[2] UN Office for the Coordination of Humanitarian Affairs 2019, 7.
[3] High-level Independent Panel on United Nations Peace Operations 2015, 24.
[4] Willmot and Sheeran 2013, 529.   [5] Wynn-Pope 2013, 21.

Table 5.1 *Key practices in the making of PoC*

Practices	Instances	Political effects
Issuing a report by the Secretary-General	Regular Secretary-General reports on PoC since 1999; annual since 2016	Secretary-General summarizes the situation of PoC and proposes priorities of action
Holding an open debate at the Security Council	Annual open debates (since 1999)	Forum that is open to all UN member states who request to participate
Setting up a high-level panel	Brahimi (2000) HIPPO[1] (2015)	Experts put forward a set of political objectives and policy recommendations
Holding consultations between Security Council and NGOs	Arria formula meetings organized regularly	Expertise is sought from humanitarian experts in the field
Issuing a policy document	DPKO/DFS[2] (2010, 2015, 2019) OCHA aide-mémoire (seven editions between 2002 and 2018) Policy evaluations: OIOS[3] (2014), OCHA (2019)	Effort is made to provide concrete policy guidance for peace operations Agreed language from Security Council resolutions and presidential statements is summarized UN officials seek to identify the best practices and dysfunctions in the making and implementation of policy
Creating a Group of Friends	2007 (chaired by Switzerland)	Like-minded states join to facilitate consensus; provides a key platform for nonpermanent Security Council members

Creating an informal experts group	Informal experts group on PoC formed in 2009 at the initiative of the UK	Provides guidance before the renewal of UN peacekeeping mandates; China never attends; Russia attends sporadically
Meeting of a General Assembly committee	C34[4]	Debate on PoC is shifted from the Security Council to the General Assembly
Signing a declaration of Commitments	Kigali Principles (2015) Declaration on A4P[5] (2018)	States agree to a common set of objectives
NGOs organizing joint events	Red Cross-led workshops (1996–2000) PoC Week (2018)	NGOs cooperate with other stakeholders to influence global policy; uneven outreach to parts of global civil society
Voting Security Council resolutions (anchoring)	Dozens of resolutions adopted since 1999	Adoption of thematic and country-specific international plans of action; domination of the Security Council permanent members

[1] HIPPO = High-Level Panel on Peace Operations

[2] DPKO = Department of Peacekeeping Operations; DFS = Department of Field Support

[3] OIOS = Office of Internal Oversight Services

[4] C34 = Special Committee on Peacekeeping Operations

[5] A4P = Action for Peacekeeping Initiative

By exposing the bricolage of PoC by way of its practices and values, our analysis shows that it remains a global policy permeated by numerous ambiguities and contradictions. On the one hand, thanks to the enormous resources invested in PoC throughout the last twenty years, it has become a strongly institutionalized feature of world politics. On the other, PoC remains a highly contested policy, and this has given rise to repeated failures in terms of implementing it on the ground. Secretary-General António Guterres summed up PoC's development well when, in one of his recent reports on the subject, he asserted that "[t]here is no doubt that the Security Council's actions over the past 20 years have strengthened the framework for the protection of civilians in armed conflict and saved countless lives." Yet at the same time, he deplored the fact that "the state of the protection of civilians today is tragically similar to that of 20 years ago."[6] This chapter aims to make sense of this apparent paradox in global policymaking.

1 The Making of PoC: A Flexible Doctrine

The adoption of resolutions by the UN Security Council is undoubtedly the practice that has contributed the most to shaping the content of PoC as a global policy. That said, the Security Council's work must be understood as but one component in a complex web of practices involving a wide range of processes and actors. Before looking at the anchoring function of Security Council resolutions, it is important to explain how this web of practices took shape in the absence of any rational planning.

1.1 The Fits and Starts of PoC

Our narrative divides the transformation of PoC practices into three distinct phases: the emergence of the policy (1991–2005), the widening of the debate (2005–11), and the fragmentation of the agenda (2011–20). This periodization should not be understood rigidly, but as we will see, it does help us to clarify the politics behind PoC (Table 5.1).

---

[6] UN Security Council 2019b, 1 and 3.

1.1.1 The Emergence of PoC (1991–2005)

The birth of the PoC doctrine as a global policy is often dated to February 1999, when the Security Council held a first open debate and released a first presidential statement on the issue. The statement "strongly condemn[ed] the deliberate targeting by combatants of civilians in armed conflict and demand[ed] that all concerned put an end to such violations of international humanitarian and human rights law."[7] In addition, the statement requested the presentation, in September 1999, of a report by the Secretary-General containing recommendations to better protect civilians in armed conflicts. Without minimizing the historic nature of the initiatives taken by the Security Council in February 1999, it is nevertheless important to recognize that they did not happen *ex nihilo*. To this end, it first needs to be recalled that the origin of PoC is inseparable from the practical and doctrinal history of international humanitarian law. Moreover, it is quite possible that PoC would never have seen the light of day without the global awareness that followed the genocide in Rwanda in 1994 and the Srebrenica massacre in 1995. Finally, the development of PoC would undoubtedly have been very different without the creation, in 1991, of the UN Department of Humanitarian Affairs – the predecessor of the OCHA – and of its Inter-Agency Standing Committee, which brings together the heads of eighteen UN and non-UN organizations.[8]

The early development of PoC was largely the result of the leadership of nongovernmental actors. The dynamism of the International Committee of the Red Cross (ICRC) was particularly decisive. In 1993, the ICRC organized a major international conference on the Protection of War Victims, and from 1996, it coordinated a series of workshops at which human rights and humanitarian organizations gathered to discuss issues of civilian protection. A major outcome of the ICRC's work was the publication in 2001 of *Strengthening Protection in War*, whose definition of protection was adopted by the Inter-Agency Standing Committee.[9] Also noteworthy, in February 1997, the Security Council held its first ever consultation with NGOs when it hosted representatives of Oxfam International, CARE International, and Médecins Sans Frontières (MSF) for a briefing on

---

[7] UN Security Council 1999e, 2.
[8] Inter-Agency Standing Committee, https://interagencystandingcommittee.org.
[9] Giossi Caverzasio 2001.

the humanitarian situation in the Great Lakes region. One can easily assume that this meeting, which was organized in a framework that prefigured the future "Arria formula," inspired the report that Kofi Annan presented to the Security Council in 1998 on the situation in Africa, in which he declared that "providing assistance to the victims of conflict is a moral imperative."[10] In short, if it is true that the initiatives taken by the Security Council in 1999 enshrined PoC as a new global priority, these initiatives must also be seen as a response to a long chain of events.

After the presidential statement of February 1999, the Security Council exercised a quasimonopoly on the advancement of PoC, at least until 2005. In addition to acting as the engine for many doctrinal innovations through a series of thematic and country-specific resolutions, the Council also became the focal point of various practices that confirmed the importance of PoC in global governance.

In the wake of the Secretary-General's report, tabled in September 1999 at the request of the Security Council, the latter adopted a first resolution on PoC – Resolution 1265 – which established a link between PoC and the maintenance of international peace and security.[11] In doing so, Resolution 1265 effectively placed the new concept under the scope of Chapter VII of the Charter. The following month, the Council passed Resolution 1270, which for the first time ever authorized the use of force by a UN peace operation (the United Nations Mission in Sierra Leone) in order to protect civilians "under imminent threat of physical violence."[12] Then, in April 2000, Resolution 1296 brought additional legitimacy to the PoC doctrine by explicitly calling the targeting of civilians in armed conflict and the denial of humanitarian access a "threat to international peace and security."[13]

The Security Council strengthened its PoC leadership by instituting a series of practices to assist it in carrying out its own functions. For example, having served as a prelude to the presidential statement of February 1999, the organization by the Security Council of an open debate on PoC henceforth became a biannual practice. Likewise, the production of a report on PoC by the Secretary-General, as requested by the Security Council in February 1999, gave rise to a periodic

---

[10] UN Security Council 1998, 12.   [11] UN Security Council 1999c.
[12] UN Security Council 1999d, para. 14.
[13] UN Security Council 2000, para. 5.

procedure (this has since become annual). The open debates and the Secretary-General's reports certainly gave the Security Council a better understanding of the concerns of UN members and the UN bureaucracy about PoC.

The Security Council initiated another important practice in 2001 by asking the Secretary-General to prepare an aide-mémoire to assist the Council in its consideration of PoC issues. The first version of this document, the preparation of which had been delegated to OCHA, was adopted in March 2002.[14] The aide-mémoire does not outline a standard peacekeeping model, recognizing as it does that each operation must be considered on a case-by-case basis. However, it guides Security Council deliberations by systematically setting out the objectives of the Council in the field of PoC, and by providing a compendium of agreed terminology drawn from past Security Council resolutions and presidential statements on PoC matters. Updated periodically, the document is currently in its seventh edition and covers Security Council decisions up to August 31, 2018. Noting that the aide-mémoire has evolved from seven pages (S/PRST/2002/6) to several hundred pages in length (S/PRST/2018/18), OCHA has described it as "a testament to the relevance of the protection of civilians to the Security Council."[15]

The rise of PoC as a global policy could not have occurred with the same vigor were it not for the participation of NGOs in the work of the Security Council. Cooperation between NGOs and the Council was especially evident in meetings held within the framework of the Arria formula.[16] Since the meeting organized by two elected members of the Council – the Netherlands and Canada – with CARE, Oxfam, and MSF in April 2000, dozens of Arria meetings have taken place on PoC. NGOs have been particularly effective in drawing the international community's attention to the situation of children and women in armed conflicts. The NGOs' biggest achievement has arguably been the adoption of Resolution 1325 (on women, peace, and security) in October 2000. The resolution calls on all parties to conflict to respect international law by protecting women's rights and by limiting gender-based violence. Recognized as a turning point in PoC history, Resolution 1325 spurred subsequent resolutions condemning sexual

[14] UN Security Council 2002.
[15] OCHA, https://poc-aide-memoire.unocha.org/about.
[16] Security Council Report 2020.

violence as a tactic of war, as well as important institutional innovations such as the appointment of a Special Representative on Sexual Violence in Conflict and the establishment of a Team of Experts on the Rule of Law and Sexual Violence in Conflict.[17]

Other practices, less focused on the Security Council, have also shaped the emergence of PoC. In this regard, the creation of a panel of experts by the Secretary-General in 2000 deserves to be underlined. Coordinated by Lakhdar Brahimi, former Foreign Minister of Algeria, the panel's mandate covered all aspects of UN peace operations, including PoC.[18] The resulting Brahimi report concluded that "United Nations peacekeepers – troops or police – who witness violence against civilians should be presumed to be authorized to stop it, within their means, in support of basic United Nations principles."[19] At the same time, the report made clear that, in order to avoid disappointments in the implementation of PoC, UN peace operations needed additional resources. A practical consequence of the Brahimi report was a revision of the UN's rules of engagement. As a result, all UN missions were permitted to use force "up to, and including deadly force, to defend any civilian person who is in need of protection against a hostile act or hostile intent, when competent local authorities are not in a position to render immediate assistance."[20]

Finally, the emergence of PoC was reinforced by an appeal to the world's political leaders. The Millennium Summit and the 2005 World Summit definitely helped to legitimize the importance of PoC in global governance. The Millennium Declaration, for instance, pledged to "expand and strengthen the protection of civilians in complex emergencies, in conformity with international humanitarian law," while the 2005 World Summit Outcome paid special attention to the protection of women and children in armed conflicts.[21] Also introduced in the 2005 World Summit Outcome was the so-called Responsibility to Protect norm (or R2P). Yet, while R2P was originally conceived as a modern tool employed in the service of civilian populations, it would soon become a major source of distrust toward PoC. This political development is yet another reminder that PoC is a heavily improvised global policy.

[17] UN Security Council 2021.   [18] UN General Assembly 2000a.
[19] Ibid., x.
[20] UN Department of Peacekeeping Operations 2002, Rule 1.8, Attachment 1, 2.
[21] UN General Assembly 2000b, para. 26.

1.1.2 Widening the Debate (2005–11)

The political challenges raised by PoC steadily accumulated after 2005. The doctrine became the subject of extended debates, thus diluting the Security Council's control of the matter. And even though the institutionalization of PoC continued, the process took place in an atmosphere marked by uncertainty and constant tension.

To be sure, it should be acknowledged that the second half of the 2000s gave rise to some significant initiatives on the part of the Security Council. Adopted in 2008, for example, Resolution 1856 on the UN's Mission in the Democratic Republic of the Congo (MONUC) set a double precedent. On the one hand, it elevated PoC to the "highest priority" of the mission. On the other, it specified that civilians should be protected against violence "emanating from any of the parties engaged in the conflict," thus including government forces.[22] In 2009, marking the tenth anniversary of the PoC agenda, Resolution 1894 was another milestone. This document enshrined a broad conceptualization of protection by going beyond the strict protection from physical violence to embrace humanitarian access and a variety of accountability mechanisms. In addition, Resolution 1894 declared protection activities to be the priority in peacekeeping resource allocation. Interestingly, the resolution was the last with a comprehensive scope to be adopted before segmentation kicked in in the 2010s.[23]

Despite the importance of these doctrinal novelties, the enthusiasm that marked the Security Council's initial decisions on PoC gradually faded. For instance, Resolution 1674, which drew a connection between PoC and R2P in 2006, was adopted in the face of serious reservations from China, Russia, and Egypt.[24] Likewise, during the debate on Resolution 1856, mentioned above, China and Russia strongly opposed Western countries over the imposition of sanctions against perpetrators of attacks on civilians. And although the creation, in 2007, of an informal group of experts to brief the Security Council on protection issues could be seen as a reinforcement of PoC thinking, it should be noted that China has decided not to participate in the group's work, while Russia participates only rarely.[25]

More broadly, from 2005, PoC diplomacy was increasingly shaped by the engagement of member states outside the Security Council. One

---

[22] UN Security Council 2008, 4.   [23] UN Security Council 2009d.
[24] UN Security Council 2006.   [25] Foley 2017, 119; and Adamczyk 2019, 4.

key development was the creation of the Group of Friends of PoC in 2007. The group is made up largely of Western countries (including France and the UK) and includes only a handful of states from the Global South. Chaired by Switzerland, it aims to better coordinate the positions of its twenty-seven members in order to influence protection policies. The Group of Friends of PoC has been particularly helpful in garnering support from elected members on the Security Council.[26] Another important development came from the growing interest of the Special Committee on Peacekeeping Operations – the so-called C34 – in PoC issues. The C34, a large majority of which is composed of developing countries (unlike the Group of Friends), has served as a sounding board for concerns from troop-contributing countries (TCCs) regarding the use of force in peace operations. Incidentally, it is noteworthy that between 2009 – when the C34's annual report included the group's first references to PoC – and 2021, the number of paragraphs devoted to PoC in these reports increased from four to twenty-three.[27]

In addition to political negotiations at UN headquarters, field operations also had a major impact on PoC policymaking. In this regard, the well-documented reluctance of UN peacekeepers to use force proved to be one of the best indicators of the confusion surrounding the development of PoC as a global policy.[28] In turn, in 2009 and 2010, the Security Council and the C34 asked the Secretariat to dispel such confusion by providing a framework for comprehensive protection strategies.[29] These requests gave rise to meticulous analytical work on the part of the Department of Peacekeeping Operations [DPKO, now the Department of Peace Operations (DPO)] and the Department of Field Support (DFS).[30] However, the conclusions that resulted from this effort at policy guidance have been the object of contradictory interpretations that persist to this day.

---

[26] Adamczyk 2019, 4–5; UN Office for the Coordination of Humanitarian Affairs 2019, 13.

[27] Sharland 2019, 41; UN General Assembly 2021, 33–8.

[28] See Foley 2017, 112; and Rhoads and Welsh 2019, 610.

[29] UN Office for the Coordination of Humanitarian Affairs 2011, 1.

[30] UN Department of Peacekeeping Operations 2010a; UN Department of Peacekeeping Operations 2010b; See UN Office for the Coordination of Humanitarian Affairs 2011.

While recognizing that there was no common vision of PoC within the UN system, the policy documents produced by the Secretariat put forward an operational concept of the doctrine composed of three tiers: affording protection through the political process, providing protection from physical violence, and establishing a protective environment. Crucially, according to this conception of PoC, "there is no inherent hierarchy between the tiers."[31] Moreover, the Secretariat maintained that the whole PoC agenda – including protection from physical violence – should be implemented in accordance with UN peacekeeping principles: consent of the host government and the main parties to the conflict, impartiality, and the non-use of force except in self-defense and defense of the mandate. Formulated in 2010, the PoC approach jointly developed by the DPKO and the DFS has since proven rather enduring; indeed, it has maintained virtually the same form up to the DPO policy document released in 2019.[32] However, this approach has never succeeded in clarifying the nature of the connection between the political, humanitarian, and security dimensions of PoC. Furthermore, it has proved unable to specify the conditions under which the authorization of force should be put into practice.

The uncertainties over PoC turned into open mistrust in the spring of 2011 in the wake of Resolution 1973, which authorized UN military intervention in Libya. Officially justified under the need to protect civilians, the Libyan mission gave rise to an explosion of violence and a change of regime that fueled the concerns of many states regarding the possible slippages of PoC. After this episode, the institutionalization of PoC did continue, but it took place against a backdrop of increased "discursive and behavioral contestation."[33]

1.1.3 The Fragmentation of the Agenda (2011–20)

Over the past decade, PoC has been the subject of media headlines mostly because of its repeated shortcomings. Following the Libyan fiasco, the UN's failure to effectively protect civilians in Syria, Myanmar, and Yemen gave renewed impetus to those who would question the doctrine's credibility as a shared objective. Yet, as global

---

[31] UN Department of Peacekeeping Operations 2010b, 7.
[32] UN Department of Peace Operations 2019.
[33] Rhoads and Welsh 2019, 598.

policymaking is a complex and often contradictory process, PoC's recent evolution cannot be reduced merely to a series of setbacks.

Throughout the 2010s, the adoption of Security Council resolutions remained the dominant practice in PoC policymaking. In this regard, two country-specific resolutions deserve to be highlighted. First, in March 2013, the Council adopted Resolution 2098 to respond to the humanitarian crisis in the Democratic Republic of the Congo (DRC).[34] By establishing the so-called Force Intervention Brigade (FIB) within the United Nations Organization Stabilization Mission in the DR Congo (MONUSCO), the resolution authorized for the first time offensive military operations in support of PoC. Using diplomatic language, FIB was asked to "neutralize" the armed groups that posed a threat to civilians in eastern DRC. For Resolution 2098 to pass, however, the reservations of several members of the Security Council had to be overcome; this was done by specifying explicitly that it was adopted "on an exceptional basis and without creating a precedent." Of note here is the fact that the resolution also sparked resistance from various NGOs, who highlighted the concern that using offensive force to protect civilians could lead to an escalation of the existing conflict.[35]

Second, in May 2014, the Council adopted Resolution 2155 on South Sudan, which contained "one of the UN Security Council's strongest articulations of protection of civilians provisions in any peacekeeping mandate."[36] While recognizing that "the mandate of each peacekeeping mission is specific to the need and situation of the country concerned," this resolution essentially transformed the UN's Mission in South Sudan (UNMISS) mandate from peacekeeping and state-building to the task of PoC itself.[37] This was unanimously seen as "a radical departure from anything that the UN has attempted in nearly six decades of peacekeeping."[38] Another interesting development in Resolution 2155 was the disappearance of the qualifier "imminent" when describing the threats to civilians against which the mission intended to act (paragraph 4.ai). The change of wording, which was reproduced in resolutions concerning MONUSCO and the UN's Multidimensional Integrated Stabilization Mission in the Central African Republic (MINUSCA), was of course politically

---

[34] UN Security Council 2013c.   [35] Willmot and Sheeran 2013, 536.
[36] World Peace Foundation 2017, 3.   [37] UN Security Council 2014b, 1.
[38] Malan and Hunt 2014, 2.

motivated in that it was destined to increase peacekeepers' room for maneuver in the use of force.[39]

Despite the importance of these two country-specific resolutions, the quasilegislative work of the Security Council was above all marked by the adoption of a series of thematic resolutions that served to segment the PoC agenda. Resolutions were adopted on the protection of journalists (2015), medical personnel (2016), and persons with disabilities (2019). In 2018, another thematic resolution condemned the starving of civilians as a method of warfare.[40] For some, this fragmentation of the PoC agenda is hailed as a positive step that illustrates the degree to which the PoC doctrine has become increasingly specific. However, it is remarkable that the segmentation of the PoC agenda took place at the same time that the efforts to put PoC within a holistic approach were abandoned.

Periodical policy evaluation through the publication of reports is another practice that fueled discussions about PoC during the 2010s. In 2015, the High-Level Panel on Peace Operations (HIPPO) rehashed already well-known misunderstandings and frustrations regarding PoC. While arguing that "[u]narmed strategies must be at the forefront of UN efforts to protect civilians," the report maintained that the traditional norms of peacekeeping "should never be an excuse for [the] failure to protect civilians."[41] The HIPPO report also deplored the fact that the growth of resources devoted to PoC have "yet to transform reality on the ground, where it matters."[42] Three years later, the Santos Cruz report gave unprecedented weight to the TCCs' perspective on PoC. Coordinated by Carlos Alberto dos Santos Cruz, a Brazilian general who had served as MONUSCO's Force Commander, the report argued that by focusing on the protection of civilians, UN peace operations had failed to properly take into account the fact that "the blue helmet and flag ... are a target."[43] Accordingly, the Santos Cruz report argued that "[p]eacekeepers must adopt a proactive posture in self-defense."[44] Finally, in 2019, on the occasion of PoC's twentieth anniversary, OCHA presented an overall

---

[39] UN Department of Peacekeeping Operations 2015, 5, fn.14.

[40] UN Security Council 2015b; UN Security Council 2016c; UN Security Council 2018c; UN Security Council 2019c.

[41] High-level Independent Panel on United Nations Peace Operations 2015, 84 and x.

[42] Ibid., 22. [43] dos Santos Cruz, Phillips, and Cusimano 2017, 10. [44] Ibid.

assessment of the policy. While welcoming the gradual prioritization of PoC on the UN security agenda, OCHA criticized the trend of the 2010s by which a subthematic rather than a global approach to PoC was emphasized. "On the twentieth anniversary of PoC," the report concluded, "the Council might consider taking advantage of the momentum to take actions towards reunifying, or at least reaffirming, the unity of the PoC agenda."[45]

One final practice that has marked the recent history of PoC relates to the use of club diplomacy. Faced with the difficulties of establishing intergovernmental agreements on PoC, a group of like-minded states has circumvented the UN to elaborate a common protection strategy known as the Kigali Principles. As of 2020, this document had been endorsed by fifty states. The Kigali Principles are a set of nonbinding norms designed to strengthen the protection component of UN peacekeeping missions. One of the key pledges made by the signatories of the Kigali Principles is "[t]o seek to identify, as early as possible, potential threats to civilians and proactively take steps to mitigate such threats."[46] Spearheaded by Rwanda, the Netherlands, and the US, the Kigali Principles put forward a vision of PoC that is fairly similar to that defended by the P3 allies in the Security Council (France, Great Britain, and the US). It is little wonder, then, that China and Russia have not adhered to the Kigali Principles, and that the document has deeply divided the Non-Aligned members in the C34.[47] The jury is still out as to the long-term impact of the Kigali Principles on the implementation of PoC.

Our overview of PoC practices demonstrates that states, despite a growing openness toward NGOs and civil society, maintain a tight control over all major decisions concerning PoC. In fact, several national governments place PoC in the category of high politics and for this reason see the issue as their exclusive preserve. Within the community of states, the activism of the C34 and the Group of Friends has hardly affected the control that the Security Council and its permanent members enjoy over PoC. Over time, however, the latter body has been forced to confront an increasingly confrontational diplomatic context resulting from "the rebalancing of relations between states of the global North and the global South" in UN peace

---

[45] UN Office for the Coordination of Humanitarian Affairs 2019, 8.
[46] United Nations 2015b.   [47] Sharland 2018, 29.

operations.[48] While in its early days, PoC emerged as a relatively consensual global policy despite its Western origins, the reservations increasingly expressed by Russia and China – reflective of many developing countries' preoccupation with external intervention in their domestic affairs – created a less inclusive climate within the Council. To a large extent, the polarization of relations among the five permanent countries of the Security Council (P5) arguably explains why efforts to protect civilians in countries such as Syria, Libya, or Yemen have been such a failure.

1.2 Anchoring PoC in the Voting of Resolutions

When it comes to the making of PoC policy, the Security Council has indisputably played a leadership role, with significant political effects. As Richard Gowan argues, the Security Council can be described as the "driver of the PoC agenda."[49] The previous sections explained the Council's widespread influence over policy changes, characterized as it is by many fits and starts. We now want to show how the actual functioning of PoC is specifically structured around the intergovernmental practice of voting on resolutions, both thematic and country-specific. Thematic resolutions have set generic political priorities and steered the normative development of the PoC doctrine. For their part, country-specific resolutions, which tend to be reactive in nature, have organized and shaped the variety of PoC practices along the fault lines of global power relations. Both types of resolutions have led to the innovation of new tools and concepts, while inscribing PoC as part of the regular activities of the UN system. Although the bricolage of PoC clearly is a multiparty endeavor, overall it seems fair to say that Security Council resolutions have exerted a strong pulling effect on the behavior of all other actors.

As a practice, the voting of resolutions rests on a number of ways of doing things that characterize the everyday operation of the Security Council.[50] The key practice of "pen holding," for instance, has ensured

---

[48] Peter 2019, 8.   [49] Gowan 2019, 7.

[50] See Hurd 2002; Malone 2004; Prantl 2006; Gharekhan 2007; Cronin and Hurd 2008; Blavoukos and Bourantonis 2011; Ambrosetti 2012; Clark and Reus-Smit 2013; Schia 2013; Sievers and Daws 2015; Wiseman 2015; Pouliot 2016; Laatikainen 2017; Niemann 2018; von Einsiedel and Malone 2018; Gehring and Dörfler 2019; Recchia 2020; Pouliot 2021.

that some countries – especially the P3 – have remained the principal drivers of policymaking for the better part of the past two decades. That being said, in recent years, the Council has evolved a revised approach, referred to as "co-pen holding," which has allowed the body's ten elected members (E10) to play a larger role in the drafting and monitoring of PoC resolutions. Moreover, other Council practices such as the reliance on subsidiary committees, expert groups, and groups of friends have altered political dynamics and facilitated the creation of coalitions.[51] Finally, while the Security Council remains fairly closed off, some practices, like the Arria formula meetings, have allowed limited input from select civil society actors, such as major humanitarian NGOs.

The defining trait of anchoring practices is that they structure the whole policy field, meaning that policymakers more or less willingly orient their actions around them. In what follows, we identify two key indicators of the gravitational effects exerted over PoC by Security Council resolutions. First, these documents have served to define the "strategic and operational goals and specific tasks and responsibilities" of PoC mandates in peace operations.[52] As such, they have consistently generated the most significant inflections on the policy. As is well recognized, "the specific language used by the Security Council when mandating PoC in peacekeeping has evolved over the years and may vary between peacekeeping operations."[53] Identifying PoC as a "priority" in a peacekeeping operation or removing the word "imminent" when referring to threats of physical violence are prime examples of how Security Council resolutions have gradually delineated the manner in which PoC should be implemented. More generally, the inscription of PoC at the center of UN peace operations, as well as most policy innovations, results from successive Council resolutions. Other actors do influence the making of PoC from the margins, including UN agencies and departments or large NGOs, but in order to do so, they work through Security Council corridor negotiations and formal meetings.

It should come as no surprise that thematic resolutions build on one another, generating a cumulative doctrine over time. After all, one typical effect of anchoring practices is to give coherence and a sense

[51] Sharland 2018, 20–1.   [52] UN Department of Peace Operations 2020, 6.
[53] Ibid.

of direction to a global policy. For instance, Resolution 2474 (2019) on persons reported missing in armed conflict, referenced ten earlier resolutions adopted since 1999. As the PoC doctrine evolves, then, further Council resolutions construct their legitimacy on the basis of preceding ones. More intriguing, perhaps, is the fact that a similarly cumulative process seems to obtain from country-specific resolutions as well. For example, Resolution 2155, on South Sudan, adopted in 2014, refers to no fewer than twenty-seven country-specific or thematic resolutions. Given the value that the Council traditionally attaches to flexibility, such consolidation based on case-by-case management is striking – and goes a long way in making sense of the erratic evolution of a PoC doctrine. The simultaneous yet contradictory patterns of accumulation and improvisation form an intriguing paradox of global policymaking.

There is, then, a kind of precedent-setting logic to PoC Council resolutions.[54] Of course, one should not exaggerate the constraining effects of past decisions on Council activity, especially in the absence of any formal rule to this effect and given the reluctance of some members to follow such a logic. However, the development of PoC in peace operations is clearly owed to the fact that its main proponents (essentially the P3 and their allies on the Council) have consistently played a leading role in drafting resolutions, utilizing their institutional memory and well-staffed delegations. Needless to say, referring to past resolutions also helps preempt negative reactions and build momentum in favor of new action. And as cross-citations have multiplied over time, UN agencies have simultaneously reinforced the consolidation of PoC by offering ready-made language through the publication of an aide-mémoire and other policy documents.

A second indicator of the gravitational effects of Security Council resolutions is that they force other international actors to adjust and adapt to their changing content. Resolution 1894 (2009), for example, called on the Secretary-General to develop an operational concept for the protection of civilians. From then on, the different policy documents produced by various branches of the Secretariat over the years have made an increasing number of references to Security Council resolutions. Remarkably, whereas the 2010 concept note released by DPKO and DFS in the wake of Resolution 1894 referred to four

---

[54] Pouliot and Thérien 2015.

Security Council resolutions, the 2019 DPO Policy on the Protection of Civilians in Peacekeeping mentioned no less than thirty-three Security Council resolutions. In the refinement of PoC doctrine, then, UN agencies systematically rely on the "jurisprudence" of the Council.

When a voted resolution is not warranted, the Security Council can make use of presidential statements and letters in order to orient the work of other policymaking actors. The publication of the first aide-mémoire, for instance, was sparked by a request made in a 2001 letter to the Secretary-General. In addition, key institutional innovations initiated by the UN administration, such as those related to the protection of women and children, for instance, have followed from Council resolutions. The influence is also substantive: for example, major components of the PoC doctrine, including its location under Chapter VII [Resolution 1270 (1999)], its prioritization over other tasks [Resolution 1856 (2008)], and its forcefulness [Resolution 2098 (2013)], are easily traceable to specific resolutions. Finally, the content of open debates on PoC has often been directly influenced by Council resolutions. For example, the 2021 open debate on PoC focused on the implementation of Resolution 2286 (2016), on the protection of health-care personnel. Although some Council resolutions have admittedly reflected preoccupations expressed by other actors – such as the UN Secretary-General – it is fair to say that, overall, the global PoC agenda has been largely controlled by the Council.

The anchoring effect of Council resolutions on the PoC policy field may also be observed in the involvement of nonstate actors, especially those NGOs seeking to influence developments from the periphery. The stream of resolutions on women, peace, and security, for example, led to the creation of a dedicated NGO working group, which organized several debates on the matter and even intervened at the Council itself. In a similar way, the new concept of "force intervention brigade," developed in Resolution 2098 (2013), led a group of fourteen NGOs to send a letter to the Special Representative in order to express their concerns and suggest alternative modes of action.[55] Over the years, civil society groups have consistently focused on Council dynamics, whether informally, by working through friendly delegations, or more formally, by addressing the body under the Arria formula, in order to shape the development of PoC. Participation in

[55] O'Neill 2015, 117–8.

side events and initiatives – such as the recently established "PoC Week" – has arguably been another focus of NGOs' diplomacy, but resolutions have consistently remained the principal target of civil society advocacy activities.

Overall, the fact that the functioning of PoC is structured around Security Council resolutions has strongly influenced the policy's politics. Most obviously, the practice has led to exclusionary dynamics allowing a handful of states – primarily the permanent members – to monopolize large swaths of the policymaking process. Internal practices of pen holding and closed meetings have only reinforced the intergovernmental nature of the policy. As a result, compared to most global policies of our era, PoC is one of the most state-centric ones. To the extent that other actors such as UN agencies and humanitarian NGOs have been able to exert their influence, it has largely been at the request of (and with tight control from) Council members. The more informal days of the 1990s, when the Red Cross developed and operationalized the early concept of PoC, have long passed; instead, the more controversial the policy has become over the years, the stronger the Council's grip has grown.

Finally, perhaps the most important effect of PoC's anchoring in Security Council resolutions is that it has opened the door to inconsistency in the policy's implementation. This point is particularly meaningful in light of our larger claim about global policymaking as a patchwork of practices. Because Council dynamics reflect larger geopolitical interests and the political expediencies of the day, the body's output often seems to respond to multiple standards. Successive PoC resolutions may build on one another, but they also differ in significant ways. Some innovations, such as FIBs, disappeared from the radar screen almost as quickly as they had appeared. In a thinly veiled criticism, OCHA notes that "the Council's consistency can vary greatly between contexts, depending on Council dynamics and the degree of the situation's politicization, and an existing 'base line' of protection language has yet to be mainstreamed across all relevant protection contexts."[56] In short, the haphazard nature of the PoC policy can largely be attributed to its anchoring practice. Yet, as we show in the next section, normative ambiguity and cleavages are also key factors at work in this global bricolage.

[56] UN Office for the Coordination of Humanitarian Affairs 2019, 7.

2 Debating PoC Between Humanitarianism and Sovereignty

PoC has given rise to complex value debates for several reasons. First, as shown in the previous section, the development of PoC is an open-ended process that, far from cleaving to any particular rational design, evolves without any predetermined timetable or set of procedures. In addition, PoC has been shaped by different configurations of geopolitical interests, according to the armed conflicts that have shaken the international community. Finally, PoC is a global policy whose content has been defined by hundreds of international actors, including governments of large and small states, international agencies, and NGOs.

Like most global policies, PoC is a mixture of normative disagreements and polysemic compromises. To a large extent, the normative bricolage of PoC may be understood as a process whereby elements of consensus are emphasized and disagreement is minimized. By dissecting the ins and outs of this bricolage, our analysis will again show that global policies are marked by constant ambiguities and compromises.

PoC is based on the shared recognition that civilians have today become the main victims of armed conflicts. At the same time, PoC is characterized by a deep ideological cleavage between those who promote a liberal humanitarianism and those who fear that such humanitarianism could be used to justify interventionist policies. In general, this cleavage has pitted the Western countries against the countries of the Global South. Yet, one should also recognize that the divide between the so-called West and the Rest has never been set in stone, and has in fact been called into question periodically. In that respect, the sustained commitment of several African countries to PoC – through the Kigali Principles, for example – is a particularly striking phenomenon (Table 5.2).

Following our analytical framework, the debates about PoC will be examined according to the three questions posed elsewhere in this book. Our demonstration will help us to better understand that PoC remains a contested global policy resting on distinct visions of the common good.

2.1 *What Is the Problem?*

PoC grew out of an international consensus regarding the nature of a specific global problem. According to this consensus, which has

Table 5.2 *Main value debates in the making of PoC*

	Value cleavages	Polysemous compromises
What is the problem?	Developmental vs. security approach	Civilians have become the main victims of armed conflict (which threatens international peace and security)
What are the ends?	Expansive vs. restrictive interpretation of international law	Compliance with international (humanitarian) law
	Traditional peacekeeping principles (non-use of force/consent) vs. new principles (robustness/ partial consent)	PoC measures should be included in peace operations
	Leadership vs. assistance role of the UN	States have the primary responsibility
By what means?	Flexible vs. systematic application of PoC measures	More guidelines are needed/more consistency
	Political means vs. military means	Whole-of-mission approach
	National justice system vs. international justice system	End impunity

changed very little since 1999, civilians have become the main victims of armed conflict; this fact constitutes a threat to international security. In this regard, the first Security Council presidential statement on PoC, adopted in February 1999, was a major turning point. The statement expressed the Security Council's "grave concern at the growing civilian toll of armed conflict" and noted "with distress that civilians now account for the vast majority of casualties in armed conflict and are increasingly directly targeted by combatants and armed elements."[57] The 1999 presidential statement also drew attention to vulnerable

[57] UN Security Council 1999e, 1.

groups particularly affected by armed conflict – namely, women, children, refugees, and internally displaced persons.

In September 1999, the Security Council's stance was reinforced by a report from the Secretary-General arguing that "one feature of internal conflicts today is that the dividing line between civilians and combatants is frequently blurred."[58] The Secretary-General also deplored the fact that, in most contemporary armed conflicts, "civilians suffer disproportionately" because of "the deliberate targeting of non-combatants."[59] In the wake of the report, the Security Council unanimously adopted Resolution 1265, in which it argued that its interest in PoC flowed from its responsibility for maintaining international peace and security. In April 2000, the Council recognized more explicitly than ever that the targeting of civilians "may constitute a threat to international peace and security."[60]

The view shared by the Security Council and the Secretary-General received broad support from UN member states and civil society. Western countries have united behind the US position that "[f]ew are more likely to be the victims of mass atrocities than civilians caught in armed conflict. . . . The protection of civilians is a fundamental element of the Security Council's obligation to ensure international peace and security."[61] Beyond the West, Russia acknowledged that, "[i]n spite of efforts by the international community, conflicts continue to occur and to take the lives of many people, most of them civilians. It is therefore civilians who require our special protection, first and foremost women, children, older persons and the humanitarian staff who assist them."[62]

Several developing countries agreed with these analyses. For example, China deplored the fact that "[i]n too many places around the world, armed conflicts are still raging that not only endanger world peace and security and undermine regional development and stability, but also inflict terrible suffering on the civilians caught up in them. Vulnerable groups, including women and children, suffer the most in armed conflicts."[63] Noting that the percentage of civilian casualties in armed conflict had increased from 5 percent to 90 percent between the First World War and the 1990s, Brazil referred to "the unspeakable magnitude of the human disasters to which we bear witness

---

[58] UN Security Council 1999b, 2.   [59] Ibid.
[60] UN Security Council 2000, 3.   [61] UN Security Council 2013a, 13–4.
[62] UN Security Council 2009b, 15–6.   [63] UN Security Council 1999a, 21.

nowadays."[64] Tanzania observed that violence against civilians "constitutes a threat to international peace and security."[65] In this debate, the ICRC summed up the core of the international consensus by recalling that "[t]he undeniable reality is that civilians continue to be the main victims of armed conflict, due to indiscriminate attacks or targeted violence."[66]

This convergence of views, however, should not be exaggerated. Although, on the surface, the international community does seem to be united in recognizing the problem posed by the attacks against civilians in armed conflict, a clear divide remains in terms of how the problem is described. In short, the protection of civilians in armed conflict, while broadly shared as a general principle, has always comprised a security approach and a developmental approach. This opposition has rarely assumed a stark, black-and-white antagonism between two mutually exclusive worldviews, since the vast majority of international actors consider that armed conflicts have both military and socioeconomic dimensions. However, the difference in emphasis placed on these two dimensions has been significant.

The security approach to PoC infused the presidential statement of 1999, in which the Security Council questioned "the widening gap between the rules of international humanitarian law and their application."[67] In a similar perspective, the report presented by Kofi Annan the same year attributed the targeting of civilians to two factors: "the failure of parties to armed conflict to comply with the law on the one hand, and the lack of effective enforcement mechanisms on the other."[68] Over the years, the security approach has also been expressed through the will of influential Security Council members to preserve the political leadership of that body on the issue of PoC. In 2013, for example, the United States stressed that "[p]rotecting civilians in armed conflict is . . . a core function of the Security Council in carrying out its mandate to safeguard international peace and security."[69] For its part, France declared in 2014 that "[t]he protection of civilians is an issue that requires constant attention by the Security Council. It must be at the heart of its work."[70] Although primarily supported by Western countries, the security approach to PoC has also been

---

[64] Ibid., 11.   [65] UN Security Council 2005a, 25.
[66] International Committee of the Red Cross (ICRC) 2011.
[67] UN Security Council 1999e, 2.   [68] UN Security Council 1999b, 2.
[69] UN Security Council 2013a, 12.   [70] UN Security Council 2014a, 23.

championed by some developing countries, which have argued – like Burkina Faso – that weapons are "the root causes" of civil wars.[71] Perhaps the most radical version of the security approach was issued by Israel, which maintained that terrorism was the main source of violence against civilian populations.[72]

By contrast, several international actors – including most governments of the Global South – have sought to place PoC in a developmental rather than a security framework. According to a recurring argument, the developmental approach makes it possible to better understand the "root causes" of armed conflicts. Uganda, for example, has summarized the developmental approach in the following terms: "As we focus attention on addressing humanitarian crises, we should not forget to ask why there is conflict in the first place. In other words, the international community should address the root causes of conflicts, such as poverty and lack of democratic participation."[73] In more recent debates, the Egyptian government has voiced the same idea, saying that PoC "must address the root causes of conflict and take a more comprehensive approach that addresses the challenges of eradicating poverty and socioeconomic marginalization, while promoting the role of national institutions and mechanisms involved in preventing and managing conflicts."[74] For its part, Iraq has explicitly questioned "the inequitable and unbalanced international economic environment, which adversely affects the economies of developing countries,"[75] while China squarely pointed out that "most conflicts take place in the less developed areas of the world."[76] "To address the root causes of conflict," China also made clear, "we must take integrated measures, fully implement the 2030 Agenda for Sustainable Development [and] help countries in conflict achieve poverty reduction goals as soon as possible."[77]

Not surprisingly, UN humanitarian agencies and NGOs have also generally favored a developmental approach to PoC. In 1999, the Under-Secretary-General for Humanitarian Affairs and Emergency Relief Coordinator noted that "[t]he best way to protect civilians is . . . to prevent conflict, and in this context, development and combating poverty is an essential tool to achieve sustainable peace and

[71] UN Security Council 2009a, 24.   [72] UN Security Council 1999a, 4.
[73] UN Security Council 2005a, 3.   [74] UN Security Council 2019a, 83.
[75] UN Security Council 1999a, 7.   [76] UN Security Council 2009b, 25.
[77] China 2021.

stability in conflict and post-conflict areas."[78] Widely recognized for its efforts at fighting poverty and inequality, Oxfam has sought to focus on what it calls the "driving factors" of conflict. To this end, it has noted that "[c]ountries associated with violent conflicts and fragility typically have poor public services, weak and often corrupt or repressive forms of governance and justice, and politically and economically marginalized communities and groups."[79]

In short, the need to better insulate civilians from armed conflict is acknowledged almost unanimously by the international community. However, this consensus remains ambiguous to the extent that, on a more granular level, global governors do not share a common diagnosis of the problem.

2.2 What Are the Ends?

To a certain extent, PoC can be seen as a comprehensive solution to the problem of violence against civilians in armed conflicts. However, this rather trite observation deserves a more thorough analysis. As will be seen, PoC's normative meaning as a policy rests on at least three components, each of them based on a polysemous consensus.

A first polysemic consensus concerns the need for increased compliance with international law – most notably international humanitarian law – on the part of the parties to conflicts. This is one of the main guiding threads in the normative history of PoC – something to which states, UN agencies, and civil society actors have all apparently firmly adhered. In 2018, for example, the C34 report argued that "priority should continue to be given to the promotion of knowledge of [*sic*], respect for and observance by all States and other relevant actors, as appropriate, of their obligations under the Charter and other international law, including international human rights law, international refugee law and international humanitarian law."[80] In this architecture of legal standards, international humanitarian law has always appeared at the top. Thus, France defended PoC by arguing that "[t]he first priority is ensuring compliance with the relevant international conventions, foremost of which are the Geneva Conventions."[81] Similarly, the UN Secretary-General called for "strict compliance by parties to conflict

---

[78] UN Security Council 1999a, 10.   [79] Oxfam 2014a, 1.
[80] UN General Assembly 2018b, 64.   [81] UN Security Council 2019a, 21.

with international humanitarian law," insisting on "the principles of distinction and proportionality, and the requirement to take all feasible precautions in attack and defense."[82] The ICRC echoed the international consensus by saying that "compliance with international humanitarian law is critical to ensuring the protection of civilians."[83]

Yet, it should be noted that the need to strengthen compliance with international law was emphasized in very distinct ways by different actors. The most expansive version of the argument has been put forward by humanitarian organizations, which often draw attention to the objective of achieving a rights-based sustainable peace. Subscribing to this approach, Macedonia observed that "the prime concern of the Secretary-General and the Security Council should be the enforcement of the observance of human rights, and the well-being and dignity of civilians in danger," and that this should trump any "preoccupation with the observance of the principles of the sovereignty of States and of non-interference in internal affairs."[84] Countries like Canada and Chile have likewise voiced a broad conception of international law framed in the rhetoric of human security. Chile has thus advocated a policy "based on the promotion and protection of human security, defined as the right of people to live in freedom and dignity without fear of their overall development and human potential being threatened."[85]

Meanwhile, other states have relied on the UN Charter to defend a much more traditional approach to international law. In 2019, for example, Syria complained that "[s]ome Governments are erroneously interpreting the principles of the Charter and international law to justify military aggression and occupation under the pretext of protecting civilians."[86] Russia denounced "attempts to freely interpret the norms of international humanitarian law with regard to the protection of civilians in armed conflict," and supported a conception of PoC "founded on international law in its classic sense, without invented artificial concepts."[87] In the same spirit, China has constantly associated PoC with a state-centric conception of international law: "the protection of civilians in armed conflict must be strengthened in line with the Fourth Geneva Convention, international humanitarian law,

---

[82] UN Security Council 2009c, 6.   [83] UN Security Council 2016a, 5.
[84] UN Security Council 1999a, 14.   [85] UN Security Council 2019a, 74.
[86] Ibid., 31.
[87] UN Security Council 2018a, 26; and UN Security Council 2019a, 16.

So ... which IL!

and the principle of respect for State sovereignty, political independence, and territorial integrity as enshrined in the United Nations Charter."[88]

Debates on how to solve the humanitarian challenges of armed conflict have resulted in a second element of polysemic consensus: the need to "incorporat[e] measures aimed at enhancing the protection of civilians in the mandates of peacekeeping missions."[89] While a study done for OCHA noted that "[t]he link between the protection of civilians and peacekeeping mandates is central,"[90] Uruguay asserted that "peacekeeping operations are probably the most tangible tool that the Organization possesses to make [PoC] effective."[91] The African Union supported this view by claiming that "[t]he protection of civilians is central to the purpose and legitimacy of any peace operation."[92] Argentina, for its part, concurred with Africa's interpretation, stating that "[i]t is necessary to strengthen protection activities in the mandates of peacekeeping operations and to ensure that they have the resources necessary for their implementation."[93] And the United Kingdom reinforced the same idea by saying that "[p]riority should be given to the protection of civilians in mission planning assessments and the allocation of resources and in activities on the ground."[94]

We should recognize, however, that this seeming convergence does not preclude the evident tensions involved in the inclusion of PoC measures in peace operations. Many actors have insisted on the need to respect the traditional doctrine of peacekeeping. China and Russia, for instance, regularly express a common position when they argue that "[a]dhering to the three principles of the consent of the country concerned, impartiality and the non-use of force except in self-defense is the key to the success of peacekeeping operations. Any deviation from those basic principles will cause more conflicts and problems, even to the point of jeopardizing the success of the peacekeeping operation concerned, rather than help to protect civilians."[95] Held up by several TCCs, the traditional peacekeeping doctrine has also received support in the UN Secretariat. For instance, in 2009, the Under-Secretary-General for Humanitarian Affairs and Emergency

---

[88] UN Security Council 2010b, 24.
[89] International Committee of the Red Cross (ICRC) 2005.
[90] Holt, Taylor, and Kelly 2009, 3.   [91] UN Security Council 2009b, 16.
[92] UN Security Council 2019a, 69.   [93] Ibid., 142.
[94] UN Security Council 2014a, 11.   [95] UN Security Council 2010a, 28.

Reliefs Coordinator made clear that, "even when they have protection of civilians mandates under Chapter VII of the Charter, United Nations peacekeeping operations continue to be guided by the basic principles of peacekeeping. They are not peace-enforcement operations."[96] This point of view was reinforced by the DPKO in 2015: "Peacekeeping operations operate with the consent of the host state, are impartial in implementing their mandate, and use force only in self-defence and as otherwise authorized by the Security Council, including for the protection of civilians."[97]

Against this approach, other voices have insisted on the need to adapt the principles of peacekeeping to authorize the use of force to protect civilians. As early as 1999, the United Kingdom suggested that "the Council should not shy away – as perhaps we have done in the past – from more robust mandates if a force needs to act in enforcement mode, for example to protect civilians."[98] Fifteen years later, the United States argued that "we cannot ask extremist groups for their 'consent'; remain 'impartial' between legitimate governments and brutal militias; or restrict peacekeepers to using force in self-defense while mass atrocities are taking place."[99] Interestingly, and contrary to a widespread belief, Western governments have not been the only defenders of a robust definition of peacekeeping. The HIPPO report of 2015, for example, maintained that "[t]he United Nations must not stand by as civilians are threatened or killed: missions must demonstrate the determination to use every tool available to protect civilians under imminent threat."[100] For its part, Rwanda called "for a change in mindset" vis-à-vis peacekeeping. "This change," argued the Rwandan delegate at the C34, "is not for the faint of heart, for traditional peacekeeping will never adapt, let alone keep up with the needs of civilians."[101] In the spirit of the Kigali Principles, several NGOs have also supported the use of force and called for investment in "robust policies."[102]

---

[96] UN Security Council 2009a, 6.
[97] UN Department of Peacekeeping Operations 2015, 7.
[98] UN Security Council 1999a, 17.   [99] Power 2014.
[100] High-level Independent Panel on United Nations Peace Operations 2015, 39.
[101] UN General Assembly 2018a.
[102] Civil Society Statement on the Protection of Civilians in Armed Conflict 2021; see also Center for Civilians in Conflict 2019.

Finally, the quest for a solution to attacks against civilians in armed conflict has spurred a debate over the division of labor between governments of host countries and the UN. And here, again, the issue has given rise to a polysemous consensus. At first glance, the vast majority of international actors seem to agree that the primary responsibility for PoC lies with states. For the DPKO, this means that "[t]he host state always has the primary responsibility to protect civilians within its borders," and "this responsibility is not diminished when a peacekeeping mission with a PoC mandate is deployed."[103] Predictably, this point of view has been defended by anti-interventionist countries, most notably China and Russia. According to Russia, for example, "the Governments of States involved in conflicts bear the primary responsibility for protecting the population living on their territory."[104] But it is noteworthy that this principle has also been widely supported by governments within the Global North and South, as well as by civil society representatives. Thus, while Japan agreed with the notion that "the primary responsibility for the protection of civilians rests with the host country,"[105] Thailand proposed to make that norm a "universal guiding principle."[106] The ICRC added to the apparent consensus by stating that "[s]tates are primarily responsible for protecting individuals within their jurisdiction."[107]

A closer examination of the issue, however, shows that the emphasis on individual states' responsibility for PoC was accompanied by very different views about the extent of the UN's responsibilities toward civilians. Supporting an active UN engagement in favor of PoC, the UN's Office of Internal Oversight Services (OIOS) summed up a disputed interpretation as follows: "While the primary responsibility for protecting civilians lies with their own Government, the international community has a crucial role to play when that Government is unable or unwilling to do so."[108] France has also stressed that PoC could not be left solely to host states: "The responsibility to protect civilians belongs first, we all know, to national Governments. But when they do not fulfil that duty, and when serious violations of international

---

[103] UN Department of Peacekeeping Operations 2015, 6.
[104] UN Security Council 2011a, 9.   [105] UN Security Council 2016b, 19.
[106] UN Security Council 2015a, 40.
[107] International Committee of the Red Cross (ICRC) 2010.
[108] UN General Assembly 2014a, 20.

humanitarian law and human rights – war crimes, crimes against humanity – are planned or committed, it is then the duty of the Security Council to intervene to protect civilian populations."[109] In the same vein, the US delegate to the Security Council explained in 2016 that "when civilians come under threat, the Council must consider every appropriate action at its disposal. We may disagree on what the perfect tool is, but we must agree that we need to open up the toolbox and try to put as many tools in place as have a chance at achieving influence."[110]

This proactive approach has not been shared by the entire international community. Several states, indeed, have insisted that the UN should avoid taking a leadership role in PoC. Speaking on behalf of the Non-Aligned countries, Iran explained that "United Nations peacekeeping missions with [PoC] mandates should conduct their tasks without prejudice to the primary responsibility of the host Government to protect civilians. Efforts of the United Nations must be in support of and not in substitution for those of national authorities."[111] China has repeated several times that "the international community can assist in the protection of civilians, but such assistance should not substitute for the responsibilities and obligations of the national Government concerned."[112] Similarly, Russia emphasized that "international institutions and mechanisms should perform a subsidiary role, assisting national efforts in that area."[113] And governments from the Global South specified that the UN's primary responsibility was to "support the building up of the relevant national capacities and enhancing synergy among the various national actors on the protection imperative."[114]

As a solution to a global problem, PoC rests on elusive agreements about the need to respect international law, to better integrate PoC into UN peace operations, and to grant states a priority role in the implementation of such policies. However, each of these points, while enjoying some agreement, is pervaded by differences of interpretation that clearly show that PoC remains the object of marked tension among states.

---

[109] UN Security Council 2011b, 19.   [110] UN Security Council 2016a, 20.
[111] UN Security Council 2016b, 75.   [112] UN Security Council 2018a, 16.
[113] UN Security Council 2012, 22.   [114] UN Security Council 2015a, 51.

2.3 By What Means?

Debates on how to implement PoC have revealed three points of polysemous compromise. The first one refers to the need to consider PoC as a multidimensional endeavor that requires a whole-of-mission approach. This point of view was expressed with particular force in the Secretary-General's report released on the tenth anniversary of the first PoC resolution: "Protection of civilians is not a military task alone. All components of a mission, including police, humanitarian affairs, human rights, child protection, mine action, gender, political and civil affairs, public information, rule of law and security sector reform, can and must contribute to discharging the mission's protection mandate."[115] Many states have also emphasized the multifaceted nature of PoC, as well as the need to address PoC from an integrated approach. South Africa eloquently spoke of PoC as "a complex effort requiring coordinated efforts from all parts of the United Nations system and the wider international community," and claimed that it "should be approached from a holistic point of view."[116] Hinting at the delicate balance that such a policy would require, the United Kingdom observed that "[p]rotecting civilians requires a holistic approach that will sometimes stray into areas that are sensitive for some Governments."[117] For its part, Russia expressed its desire "to combine efforts on every front."[118] This relative unanimity was also supported by civil society, which called on the UN to "take a comprehensive and whole-of-mission approach to protection."[119]

Taken at face value, such statements would seem to obscure the perennial conflict between states over the correct balance between political and military means. While the UN has at times seemed divided on the issue, developing countries and NGOs have generally supported a more political approach. This point of view was summarized by the HIPPO report: "Unarmed strategies must be at the forefront of United Nations efforts to protect civilians."[120] In line with this perspective, Nepal underlined "the primacy of politics, and particularly inclusive

---

[115] UN Security Council 2009c, 11.   [116] UN Security Council 2009b, 40.
[117] Ibid., 12.   [118] UN Security Council 2018b, 4.
[119] Center for Civilians in Conflict 2019.
[120] High-level Independent Panel on United Nations Peace Operations 2015, 37; UN Security Council 2019a, 36.

politics and constant dialogue,"[121] while Benin explained that "the best way to protect civilians from armed conflict is to engage in effective preventive diplomacy, which can prevent the outbreak of conflicts, with their unforeseeable consequences for human dignity."[122] For its part, China noted that "[o]nly by actively promoting a political solution by peaceful means through dialogue and negotiation can civilian casualties be minimized. Military means are not an effective answer to these issues."[123] Finally, as its name suggests, the Nonviolent Peaceforce federation has championed an approach that "relies solely on dialogue with the armed actors themselves to help them behave in ways that will reduce violence and protect civilians."[124]

While admitting the need for political action, some international actors – especially the P3 governments – have clearly put more emphasis on the military dimension of PoC. In 1999, the United States asked the Security Council to "act to strengthen United Nations capacity to plan and deploy more rapidly military and civilian police personnel, as well as to consider deployment in certain cases of a preventive peacekeeping operation."[125] Moreover, the US government has often recalled that it "invests significantly in peacekeeper training."[126] Also in favor of the establishment of a rapid intervention force, the United Kingdom has for its part noted that "United Nations rapid reaction and planning capabilities have to be improved."[127] And France declared its commitment "to ensuring that the protection of humanitarian and health staff is integrated into military operations, starting at the schedule course."[128] Although the military dimension of PoC has been of great concern to Western powers, it is not surprising that TCCs from the developing world have also been very sensitive to this issue. Senegal, for example, emphasized that "[i]t is also important to bear in mind the importance of providing missions with appropriate equipment in order to strengthen peacekeepers' operational capabilities and thereby enable them to maintain superiority amid negative forces."[129]

A second element of polysemic consensus relates to the need for clearer guidelines for PoC. This has arisen from the notoriously vague character of PoC mandates. In 2009, Secretary-General Ban Ki-moon

---

[121] UN Security Council 2019a, 36.   [122] UN Security Council 2009b, 50.
[123] UN Security Council 2011a, 21.   [124] Nonviolent Peaceforce .
[125] UN Security Council 1999a, 13.   [126] UN Security Council 2013a, 13.
[127] UN Security Council 1999a, 17.   [128] UN Security Council 2019a, 21.
[129] Ibid., 88.

summed up the situation in no uncertain terms: "Currently, there remains a disconnect between mandates, intentions, expectations, interpretations and real implementation capacity.... This means that the 'protection of civilians' mandate in peacekeeping missions remains largely undefined as both a military task and as a mission-wide task."[130] A few years later, the OIOS report called for the formulation of policy guidance "that clearly lays down the actions expected in particular scenarios appropriate to each mission's circumstances in order to prevent, minimize or deal with threats to civilians."[131] And while Ecuador called for clearer PoC mandates in order to "avoid possible interpretations based on political motivations,"[132] France highlighted the need to give peacekeepers "a common and unambiguous understanding of their obligations."[133] Even Russia supported the objective of defining more precise guidelines: "Of course, operational mandates must be clear, realistic and situation-appropriate, and each peacekeeping operation should have a clear political goal, stabilization strategy and command."[134]

Although widely shared, the desire for clearer PoC mandates once again concealed a recurring divide between supporters of a systematic application of PoC and those advocating a more flexible approach. In 1999, the Under-Secretary-General for Humanitarian Affairs and Emergency Relief Coordinator summed up the former perspective in a succinct formulation: "We should treat all conflict situations around the world equally."[135] Twenty years later, OCHA used the notion of "consistency" to echo the same preoccupation: "Consistency . . . is important to achieve clarity of standards and predictability of expectations, and thereby an overall stronger and more coherent PoC agenda."[136] Meanwhile, several actors have denounced the international community's double standard on PoC. Pakistan, for example, noted that, "[i]n some situations, there is a quick and even robust response; in others, the perpetrators enjoy virtual impunity at both the national and the international levels."[137] A similar sense of frustration underpinned Oxfam's analysis in 2010: "the way the international community decides who to prioritize, who to protect, is very arbitrary."[138]

---

[130] UN Security Council 2009c, 11.   [131] UN General Assembly 2014a, 22.
[132] UN General Assembly 2016.   [133] UN Security Council 2009b, 15.
[134] UN Security Council 2014a, 15.   [135] UN Security Council 1999a, 10.
[136] UN Office for the Coordination of Humanitarian Affairs 2019, 63.
[137] UN Security Council 2005a, 14.   [138] Oxfam 2011.

Against the proponents of a more systematic approach to PoC, the great powers have demonstrated a convergence of views, arguing for the need to approach PoC with flexibility. The United States contended, for example, that, "[d]iffering in scope and dimension, the problems each mission [faces] must be assessed individually. There [is] no 'one-size-fits-all' model for United Nations peacekeeping missions."[139] Russia likewise rejected a uniform approach to PoC, arguing instead for the "need to take into account the economic, social, historical, religious, cultural and other specific aspects of countries and regions, as well as the nature of each conflict, its root causes and options for finding a settlement.... We call on all members of the international community to eschew indiscriminate, unilateral approaches to the issue of the protection of civilians."[140] This was a view with which China concurred: "Giving a United Nations peacekeeping mission a mandate to protect civilians is a decision to be made by the Council on a case-by-case basis."[141] While the great powers' position has always been justified in terms of the common good, it is clear that the flexibility they have requested directly serves their foreign policy interests.

A final polysemous consensus concerns the widely recognized need to end the impunity enjoyed by those who have committed attacks against civilians. MSF put this in unequivocal terms when it argued that "[i]mpunity must end."[142] Sharing the same objective, the United Kingdom argued that "tackling impunity and strengthening accountability for serious violations of international humanitarian law and human-rights law must be a central element of international efforts to protect civilians."[143] Poland, too, called for firmer international action on the issue: "As [UN] Member States, we must do our utmost to end impunity for any violation of international humanitarian law."[144] The Netherlands expressed the same goal in a more theatrical manner: "And yes, perpetrators should be afraid, aware that they will be called to account. They should be lying awake at night in the knowledge that one day they will face justice."[145] Finally, speaking on behalf of the Non-Aligned countries, Venezuela underlined "the importance of ensuring that those responsible [for attacks and threats against civilian

---

[139] UN General Assembly 2005b.   [140] UN Security Council 2012, 22.
[141] UN Security Council 2010a, 28.   [142] Médecins Sans Frontières 2016.
[143] UN Security Council 2013b, 14.   [144] UN Security Council 2019a, 18.
[145] Ibid., 27.

populations] are held accountable before the law, in order to break cycles of impunity and send a clear and united message of zero tolerance for such despicable acts."[146]

And yet, in spite of this apparent unanimity, the call for an end to impunity has nonetheless divided the international community between those who encourage the use of the international justice system and those who are firmly in favor of engaging national legal mechanisms. The European countries certainly figure among the staunchest defenders of the former approach. In 2013, the United Kingdom explained that

[e]nsuring accountability for the most serious crimes of international concern lies at the heart of protecting civilians and is key to delivering global justice. The International Criminal Court is an essential tool in promoting and ensuring such accountability. The United Kingdom also stresses the importance of international commissions of inquiry and fact-finding missions to verify and investigate allegations of serious violations of international human rights and humanitarian law. The Security Council must support such mechanisms. Justice must be delivered.[147]

More recently, the European Union delegate repeated the same message on behalf of the whole continent: "The EU also maintains strong support for international justice and accountability, including the work of the International Criminal Court, and urges all UN Members to do the same."[148] Chad was one of the few developing countries to share this point of view; it claimed that "the role of the International Criminal Court in the fight against impunity is a vital instrument, and one that must be strengthened and promoted."[149]

By contrast, Russia, along with the vast majority of governments from the Global South, has favored a national approach to the fight against impunity. Russia has expressed the view that "the efforts of the international community should be aimed first and foremost at strengthening national efforts in this area."[150] In equally clear terms, China explained that, "[w]ith regard to combating impunity, we are in favor of letting the domestic judicial systems of the countries concerned play the role of principal channel."[151] While emphasizing the need for an end to impunity, Tanzania called for "priority [to] be placed on

---

[146] Ibid., 46.   [147] UN Security Council 2013a, 15.
[148] UN Security Council 2019a, 62.   [149] UN Security Council 2014a, 23.
[150] UN Security Council 2010a, 17.   [151] Ibid., 28.

assistance in the restoration of national judicial systems in countries emerging from conflict."[152] A comparable emphasis on the need to rely on national justice mechanisms was also formulated by Indonesia: "Only through this avenue can we, the international community, prevent the emergence of atrocities committed against civilians. Should local institutions fail to discharge their duty in the first instance, no amount of international assistance and effort can bring long-term results."[153]

On the surface, again, we see a degree of consensus around the notions that the implementation of PoC requires a whole-of-mission approach, clearer mandates, and a firm commitment to fight impunity. But as we have explained, these areas of general agreement have nonetheless given rise to important divisions, showing yet again that PoC remains a fragile global policy.

Conclusion

While PoC as a global policy has grown in importance over the past two decades, its evolution has been marked by profound political ambiguities. On the one hand, PoC has become highly institutionalized thanks to the mobilization of enormous human and financial resources by the UN, member states, and the NGO community. But on the other hand, as a policy, PoC has developed as a succession of improvised or ad hoc decisions.

In terms of practices, PoC has been defined mainly through Security Council resolutions. Indeed, since 1999, the Council has had the final say on the policy's multiple thematic and geographic priorities. At the same time, Security Council resolutions have taken shape within a web of contradictory practices, with some actors seeking to strengthen PoC and others moving to constrain it. At the normative level, PoC has helped to bring about a polysemous consensus around the notion that the norms of international humanitarian law are both universal and peremptory. In reality, however, these norms have often been blocked by recourse to the principles of sovereignty and nonintervention.

While PoC is certainly here to stay as a central objective of UN peace operations, the future of this global policy remains highly uncertain. In the current context, it would be surprising to see a renewal of the

[152] UN Security Council 2005a, 25.   [153] UN Security Council 2009b, 34.

momentum of the 1990s anytime soon. With the rise of China and the ongoing reconfiguration of the global order, it seems more likely that the coming years will give way to a growing contestation of PoC, at the level of both practice and discourse. And as this political bricolage continues to evolve, the principle of sovereignty will probably take systematic precedence over the defense of human rights.

6 Key Trends in the Making of Global Policies

A Comparative Synthesis

Building on our comparative analysis of the three cases examined in Chapters 3–5, the present chapter aims to identify key trends in contemporary global policymaking. The results of such an ambitious task are admittedly bound to be tentative, for a variety of reasons. First, the global policymaking processes analyzed in this book are all centered on the same political site, the United Nations. While significant on several planes, this sample obviously cannot capture the full constellation of possible cases. Second, every global policy is somewhat idiosyncratic, in the sense that it is the product of a specific set of power relations and bureaucratic rules – the product, in short, of a complex ecosystem in which a multitude of actors interact. Due to this multiplicity and contingency, any analysis of the common features that may be observed across global policies is necessarily circumscribed. Third, comparing global policies is a complex endeavor because global governance processes are permanently "in the making." In addition to being subject to rival interpretations, the history of any single policy – whether global or not – rarely comes to an end.

These considerations aside, we nonetheless believe that the comparison proposed in this chapter is empirically well-grounded and theoretically important. First, thanks to its parsimonious and portable nature, our analytical framework, based as it is on practices and values, can be transposed onto any form of global policymaking. In addition, the diversity of cases examined in this book provides a solid basis for a number of analytically open-ended claims about global policymaking. Finally, and most fundamentally, we believe that the comparative approach deserves much more attention from students of global policies insofar as it is one of the best ways to reach analytical generality.

This chapter identifies ten trends that we feel capture key dynamics of global policymaking in the early twenty-first century: the clash of sovereignties, the growing focus on individuals, the universalization of aspirations, the promotion of a holistic narrative, the orchestrating role of international organizations, the pursuit of inclusion, increasing codification, the emphasis on expertise, the resilience of the North–South divide, and Western hegemony. While each of these dynamics may be understood to embody a combination of practices and values, their arrangement obviously differs across issue areas. More importantly perhaps, the trends we identify arguably do not carry the same political weight or meaning. They have different historical backgrounds, and their structuring power varies considerably. For instance, few would deny that sovereignty shapes global policies in a more profound way than the growing demand for expertise. We nevertheless argue that today, most of these ten trends are observable in pretty much any instance of global policymaking.

In the following synthesis, we first focus on how each of our ten trends is reflected in the practices and the value debates related to the adoption of the SDGs, the creation of the HRC, and the making of the PoC doctrine. Subsequently, we assess their broader significance for global policymaking in general. The ultimate goal of this comparative exercise is to determine whether there are (1) practices that recur more often than others and (2) worldviews that seem to regularly triumph over others. The key points of comparison are summarized in Tables 6.1 and 6.2.

1 Sovereignty as Centerpiece

Sovereignty is the cardinal concern in global public policymaking. For many an IR theorist, this will come as no surprise: despite the rise of nonstate actors over the past few decades, states remain in the driver's seat of global governance, delegating some of their prerogatives only when it suits their interests. For others, though, the persistence of sovereignty will seem like an anomaly in a world that faces an increasing number of "problems without passports."[1] Building on our case studies, we claim that sovereignty remains a centerpiece of global policymaking, though perhaps not exactly in the way that one might expect. In principle as in practice, sovereignty has become far more plastic a concept than was previously understood – an evolution that helps explain its longevity as a fundamental institution of international society.[2]

---

[1] Weiss 2014. [2] Bull 1977.

Table 6.1 *Ten trends in global policymaking practices (with case illustrations)*

Trends	SDGs	HRC	PoC
Sovereignty as centerpiece	Initiation and completion of policymaking by the General Assembly	Heads of state initiate; Geneva diplomats tie up the loose ends	Key role of Security Council negotiations and resolutions
Targeting individuals	Goals focused on individuals' needs; consultation through worldwide survey	Complaint Procedure and Special Procedures focus on individuals	UN peace operations become people-centered
Universalization of aspirations	All countries are invited to submit regular reviews of progress	UPR seeks to evaluate the human rights situation in every country	Secretary-General reports on all aspects of peace and security
Holistic approach	Involvement of actors from peace, development, and environment sectors	UPR covers civil, political, social, economic, and cultural rights	Civilian protection defined as a component of sustainable peace; PoC mandates seek to integrate military, police, and civilian activities in peace operations
Orchestration by IOs	UN Task Team plays a preponderant role	OHCHR plays a key supportive/administrative role	Security Council filters most policy inputs
Inclusive policymaking	UN Development Group organizes public consultations in nearly 100 countries; General Assembly Open Working Group has universal membership	Informal consultations in plenary format (General Assembly); a broad variety of stakeholders consulted as part of UPR	Arria formula meetings allow NGO input; open debates broaden consultations

Growing codification	SDGs include seventeen goals, 169 targets, and 231 indicators	UPR helps share the best practices; series of reports structure tightly scheduled UPR	Security Council resolutions accumulate to form PoC doctrine; aide-mémoire; numerous policy documents
Centrality of experts	High-Level Panel of Eminent Persons runs worldwide consultations; Statistical Commission/Sustainable Development Solutions Network in charge of operationalization	High-Level Panel on Threats, Challenges and Change puts the issue on the agenda	Panel of experts effect changes in doctrine (Brahimi; HIPPO); Security Council relies on subsidiary committees; increased role of mission advisers and experts
Resilience of North–South cleavage	Functioning of SDG OWG follows strict North–South boundaries; nominations to leadership positions seek to bridge the development gap	Troika system meant to soften structural clashes (UPR)	Secretary-General reports, policy documents prepared by agencies and open debates seek to aggregate contending views
Western hegemony	Soft commitments from rich countries	Western conception of human rights preeminent	Robust peace operations

Table 6.2 *Ten trends in global value debates (with case illustrations)*

Trends	SDGs	HRC	PoC
Sovereignty as centerpiece	National responsibility takes precedence over international solidarity	Sovereign equality tends to prevail over human rights law	State autonomy in the balance of multilateral intervention
Targeting individuals	Poverty defined as individual exclusion ("no one left behind")	Civil-political rights emphasized over social-economic rights	End impunity (human rights as part of security)
Universalization of aspirations	Sustainable development conceived as a common concern for countries rich and poor	Universal applicability of human rights	Global reach of international humanitarian law
Holistic approach	Sustainable development covers social, economic, and environmental dimensions	Indivisibility of human rights	Whole-of-mission mandate
Orchestration by IOs	UN promotes sustainable development compromise	HRC spearheads dialogue with international and domestic actors (UPR); OHCHR provides administrative support	UN seeks to take on a leadership role in conflict situations
Inclusive policymaking	Partnership approach to development	Willingness to hear domestic actors through UPR; constructive dialogue approach	All-around compliance with international humanitarian law

Growing codification	Benchmarks facilitate measurement and comparisons of performance	Consensus in favor of a scripted institutional process (UPR; three-year cycles)	Consistency principle vs. case-by-case approach; PoC mandates need to include increasingly detailed guidance
Centrality of experts	Technical approach to development	Policy advice from OHCHR and NGOs is welcome (UPR)	PoC requires coordination between military officers and mission experts on children, women, justice, and human rights
Resilience of North–South cleavage	Distinct views on the sources of inequality (domestic vs. international)	Mutual suspicions of selectivity; universality contested in the name of cultural difference	Sovereignty as responsibility challenges noninterference; security vs. developmental approach to civil conflict
Western hegemony	Refusal to discuss reform of international institutions	Western countries portray themselves as role models	P3 succeeds in making PoC a core issue on SC agenda

Indeed, sovereignty is a persistent theme in all three of our cases. In value debates, it is particularly salient when we consider the means of implementation and the end goals that actors promote. For example, in the making of the SDGs, sovereignty differentiates between two loci of responsibility for development (national vs. global). It also shows in polysemous compromises favoring inclusivity. When it comes to PoC, sovereignty is central to distinguishing between competing levels of justice (national vs. international), and even more visibly so in the appearance of consensus that formed around the notion that states bear the primary responsibility when it comes to protecting civilians. Finally, sovereignty is critical in countering several positions concerning the making of the HRC, including the role of experts (as opposed to country diplomats), a more expansive membership (vs. a small body), and the nature of reviews (to be performed either by lawyers and international civil servants or by state officials). As a key polysemous compromise in the making of the HRC, the principle of equal treatment also embodies the centrality of sovereignty in human rights policy.

With regard to practices, we observe a similar prominence for sovereignty. In the making of the SDGs, intergovernmental practices such as General Assembly sessions played a central role at the initiation and decision stages. Because it is softer in nature than most of its alternatives, the anchoring practice of goal-setting also provides states with ample room to maneuver. As to PoC, the priority given to Security Council resolutions offers a stark reminder of the state-driven nature of this instance of policymaking. International summits and UN committees such as the C34, central to PoC policymaking, are equally dominated by the principle of sovereignty. Finally, the making of the HRC similarly saw pride of place given to practices that privilege sovereignty over other concerns, including informal consultations in Geneva and various working groups and sessions of the General Assembly. The anchoring practice of peer review, performed by and for states, with nonmandatory recommendations, also reaffirms sovereignty's position at the center of contemporary global policymaking.

It is easy to see how sovereignty also retains its central position beyond our three cases. In the global governance of the environment, for instance, states remain in charge of the UN's Framework Convention on Climate Change (UNFCCC) process, despite the obvious limits of annual Conferences of Parties (CoPs) and other intergovernmental processes. Multilateral trade negotiations have been at a stalemate for decades because of the consensus rule at the WTO, which protects state sovereignty. In the cyber domain, the plethora of nonstate initiatives pale in comparison to ongoing intergovernmental discussions about extending international law to this new set of questions.

Beyond its pervasiveness, the most striking aspect about sovereignty in contemporary global policymaking concerns its plasticity. Indeed, as a single referent, it is often used to justify opposite positions. The case of PoC is particularly telling here. On the one hand, sovereignty is invoked by opponents of ever-more intrusive international interventions. This traditional view in favor of noninterference stands in contrast to a more heterodox understanding, which interprets sovereignty as compatible with PoC-justified intervention through the concept of consent. Host governments are now able to mobilize peace operations to support their sovereign efforts to protect their civilians (and/or quell their opponents). Similar contradictions show at the HRC, where equal treatment is taken to mean nonselectivity (i.e., sovereign equality) for some, and universal compliance (i.e., human rights trump sovereignty) for others. The SDGs are likewise traversed by the competing demands to let states control their development efforts and to ensure that each state is responsible for meeting its targets. In sum, once a defensive principle, sovereignty is now being used to justify ever-increasing layers of global governance.

2 Targeting Individuals

The adoption of the SDGs, the creation of the HRC, and the protection of civilians in peace operations all reflect global policymakers' growing preoccupation with individuals. This trend helps illuminate a deep-seated change in the international environment, since global policies were traditionally much more state-centric than they are today. While states arguably remain the principal actors in world politics, our cases show that, partly thanks to the pressure exerted by civil society, they are no longer the sole subjects in global policymaking. As Dingwerth et al. observe, "'the people' have become a central reference point in the legitimation of international organizations."[3] Historically, the

---

[3] Dingwerth et al. 2019b, 21.

targeting of individuals in global policymaking has been considerably accelerated by the development of the human rights regime after the Second World War.[4] Conceptually, it has relied on the idea that individual human beings are "the ultimate units of the great society of all mankind."[5]

Individuals are the explicit focus of PoC. From its very beginnings, the policy has been justified by way of a polysemous compromise in which civilians have come to be recognized as the main victims of armed conflict. Security Council resolutions have repeatedly drawn attention to the dramatic situation of women, children, and other vulnerable groups. While the Council has been unable to solve the tensions between restrictive and expansive interpretations of international law, it has regularly urged all combatting parties to comply with international humanitarian, human rights, and refugee law. The increased emphasis on individuals is also visible at the HRC, the making of which has clearly reinforced the institutional basis of the international individual rights system (deep value cleavages concerning compliance and the specific nature of these rights notwithstanding).[6] In addition, the HRC has strengthened the notion that individual rights are indivisible. As to the SDGs, they embody a conception of development that is much less state-centric than the dominant view of previous decades. In particular, the eradication of poverty and hunger and the promotion of gender equality are indicators of a rebalancing between economic growth and individual dignity.

While governance practices generally fall short of the lofty rhetoric of universal values (expressed in phrases like "we the people"[7]), some political innovations are worth mentioning. One groundbreaking pattern of action was the global survey (My World) conducted in the course of the SDG process. The millions of respondents to the survey added a popular voice that is rarely heard in global governance. The scale of public consultations and the involvement of civil society in the negotiation process have also played an important role in moving the traditional interstate framework. By and large, NGOs remain the main transmission belts between governments and peoples. With respect to PoC, NGOs have been particularly adept at mobilizing public attention with campaigns like #NotaTarget and the "Children,

[4] Normand and Zaidi 2008; Forsythe 2017; Ramcharan 2020.
[5] Bull 1977, 21.   [6] Reus-Smit 2013.   [7] UN General Assembly 2005d.

Not Soldiers" initiative. In a less publicized manner, civil society organizations took part in Security Council debates through procedures like the Arria formula, in addition to being actively involved in policy evaluation. In the context of the HRC, NGOs have played a major advocacy role through joint statements and the organization of workshops and seminars. Moreover, the functions assigned to NGOs and experts in the UPR ensure input from civil society in the effort to spotlight vulnerable individuals and communities.

The preoccupation with individuals that can be observed in the SDGs, the HRC, and PoC is relatively new. As an emerging norm, it arguably remains quite weak in comparison with the principle of sovereignty. After all, Agenda 2030 is an intergovernmental agreement; the HRC's UPR is a state-driven process; and state consent remains key in most peace operations. That said, the growing focus on individuals is probably here to stay. From a broad perspective, the individualization of the international realm can be understood as a result of the influence of liberal values within the world order.[8] Critics interpret the hold exerted by these values as an expression of market ideology or an attempt at social control, while civil society and other proponents of liberalism see the individualization of the international as a positive change that expands citizens' freedom and power.[9] In any event, it is clear that the human rights ethos now permeates the activities of most international institutions. At the UN, in particular, the promotion of human rights has gradually become one of the organization's defining missions, along with peace and development. Unsurprisingly, certain contexts – the rise of the human development and the human security agendas being textbook examples – have led to a joining of forces between the UN and NGOs in favor of a "people turn" in global policies.[10]

Today, few issue areas remain immune to the individualization of global policies. Quite predictably, human rights law has been especially willing to pay more attention to individuals in global policies. In recent years, various conventions and declarations have sought to address the needs of vulnerable groups such as women, indigenous

---

[8] Forsythe 2017.   [9] Jaeger 2010; Sikkink 2017; Moyn 2018.
[10] Haq 1995; MacFarlane and Khong 2006; Thérien 2012a, 2012b; Martin and Owen 2014.

peoples, and the disabled. For their part, the IMF and the World Bank have toned down their historic emphasis on macroeconomic discipline to put more focus on poverty reduction. Finally, multilateral negotiations on climate change are increasingly concerned with environmentally displaced persons, while the Global Compact on Migration has drawn attention to migrants' rights. Although each of these policies has faced stiff resistance from some quarters, their continued salience suggests that demands for a humanization of global policies are likely to impact global governance more and more.

3 The Universalization of Aspirations

The global policies analyzed in this book all express universal aspirations as formulated through polysemous compromises. In principle, the SDGs, the HRC's objectives, and PoC norms should apply everywhere, without any geographical restrictions. References to global aspirations might not be so surprising for policies that pretend to be "global," but this type of rhetoric is clearly more common today than before. It derives directly from the universalist assumptions of the liberal world ordering.[11] In addition to illustrating the centrality of a universalizing language, our case studies show how global policies' universal aspirations are obstructed by the persistence of normative conflicts and the role they play in structuring political practices.

The creation of the HRC was essentially the result of a shallow consensus – the notion that the former Commission was too politicized to achieve the UN's official objective of "all human rights for all." Indeed, the 2006 General Assembly resolution establishing the HRC states that "the Council is responsible for promoting universal respect for the protection of all human rights and fundamental freedoms for all, without distinction of any kind and in a fair and equal manner."[12] Universality and nonselectivity were explicitly designated as guiding principles of the new institution. In a similar vein, the SDGs were presented as a universal solution. More specifically, the preamble of Agenda 2030 describes the SDGs as "a new universal Agenda," and explains that "all countries and all stakeholders" are called upon to

---

[11] Bull and Watson 1984; Russett and Oneal 2001; Dunne and Reus-Smit 2017; Ikenberry 2018.
[12] UN General Assembly 2006b, 2.

implement it.[13] This quest for universality was well summarized in the SDGs' key promise that "no one will be left behind." And although PoC has often been portrayed as an ad hoc and highly politicized enterprise, it has also been permeated by universal aspirations. Indeed, not only is it founded on the universal thrust of international humanitarian law, but repeated calls to end impunity also illustrate a rhetorical consensus on the need to bring to justice all perpetrators of crimes against civilians.

Although universal aspirations were reflected in all sorts of practices, the effects of these practices have been structurally limited. In order to leave no one behind, for example, the SDGs have given way to a detailed plan of action comprising seventeen objectives, 169 targets, and more than 200 indicators. To this day, however, this huge job of goal-setting continues to divide supporters of international solidarity and proponents of national responsibility. At the HRC, the UPR formally ensures equal treatment for each state, but its recommendations remain nonbinding. In other words, universality is constrained by a value debate concerning the question of whether compliance should be obligatory or voluntary. Finally, while the Security Council regularly supports the use of force to implement its universal aspirations, PoC continues to face consistency problems. On the one hand, in the field, the Council's robust mandates have not been applied uniformly. On the other hand, it is worth repeating that Council decisions "can vary greatly between contexts, depending on Council's dynamics and the degree of the situation's politicization."[14]

References to universality in the SDGs, the HRC, and PoC have sometimes been portrayed as the natural consequence of a march toward progress or the advancement of civilization. By naturalizing appeals to universal aspirations, however, this approach glosses over the political nature of these appeals, as well as the practical obstacles that hinder the real-world application of any universal value. Thus, agreement on universality can hardly account for the fact that poverty is unlikely to be eradicated by 2030, that human rights are not respected in many parts of the world, or that civilians keep being killed in armed conflicts. To a large extent, the reference to universal aspirations stems from a desire to increase the legitimacy of the SDGs, the

---

[13] UN General Assembly 2015, 1.
[14] UN Office for the Coordination of Humanitarian Affairs 2019, 7.

HRC, and PoC. Through universal aspirations, these policies have sought to mobilize political support among governments and the public at large. Yet, while the discourse of universality has provided a political resource to expand consensus, it has overlooked the normative disagreements surrounding competing aspirations, as well as the disconnect between aspirations and implementation.

Although increasingly challenged by the need to better recognize the importance of cultural diversity,[15] the narrative of universality has strongly permeated global governance in recent decades.[16] Universal aspirations have thus informed a wide range of global policies beyond our three cases. In the security realm, it is often assumed that all peoples have a right to peace. In the world economy, the WTO and the IMF justify their promarket policies on the basis that these policies provide the best means of ensuring the prosperity of all nations. With respect to social matters, the United Nations Educational, Scientific and Cultural Organization (UNESCO)'s and the International Labour Organisation (ILO)'s policies have referred to "education for all" or "decent work for all." Finally, in environmental negotiations, global policies are regularly defended in the name of intergenerational equity. In these fields of activity as in the SDGs, the HRC, and PoC, universal aspirations allow actors to maintain the illusion that they are "above politics." And yet, they are constantly held up by practices that are shaped by conflicts between competing interests and various power asymmetries.

4 A Holistic Approach

Our three global policies showcase similar efforts to offer a holistic (i.e., comprehensive and integrated) perspective on global governance. Although each policy focuses on a specific issue area, all three attempt to make connections beyond their immediate silos. Our cases thus suggest that coherence between a given global policy and global governance as a whole is a powerful source of legitimation in contemporary world politics. The push for a holistic approach in global policymaking echoes the process of "complex interdependence" by

---

[15] Acharya 2018; Reus-Smit 2018.
[16] Kennedy 2008; Jolly, Emmerij, and Weiss 2009; Pahuja 2011; Thérien and Joly 2014.

which domestic and international issues "impinge on one another."[17] Importantly, although complex interdependence has grown along with globalization, it is far from new. Already in 1919, for instance, a holistic approach was exposed in the ILO's constitution, which stated that "universal and lasting peace can be established only if it is based upon social justice."[18] More recently, the need for a comprehensive and integrated perspective on global policymaking has been eloquently articulated by Kofi Annan: "We will not enjoy development without security, we will not enjoy security without development, and we will not enjoy either without respect for human rights. Unless all these causes are advanced, none will succeed."[19]

The SDGs exemplify particularly well the need to link global policies to a wider perspective on global governance. Indeed, the concept of sustainable development, which seeks to reconcile "humanity and the planet," offers an extremely broad intellectual framework in which to think about international development.[20] Moreover, the developmental objectives of the SDGs are linked to security goals, to the extent that Agenda 2030 maintains that "sustainable development cannot be realized without peace and security," and that "peace and security will be at risk without sustainable development."[21] PoC, for its part, has been construed as a policy that goes beyond traditional peacekeeping to connect the UN's security operations with its human rights work. Additionally, PoC fits into a long-term approach whereby the objective of "sustaining peace" parallels the social and economic objectives of sustainable development. Finally, PoC is one of the key challenges of the Agenda for Humanity submitted to the 2016 World Humanitarian Forum by former UN Secretary-General Ban Ki-moon. The creation of the HRC provides another example of how global policies systematically seek to ensconce themselves in an all-encompassing vision of global governance. The resolution that established the HRC referred to such a grand narrative when it explained that "peace and security, development and human rights are the pillars of the United Nations system," and that "development, peace and security and human rights are interlinked and mutually reinforcing."[22] Further reflecting the intention to assign a global mission to the HRC, the resolution also

---

[17] Keohane and Nye 1989, 26.
[18] International Labour Organization (ILO) 1919, preamble.
[19] UN General Assembly 2005d, para. 17.   [20] UN General Assembly 2015, 1.
[21] Ibid., 9.   [22] UN General Assembly 2006b, 1.

maintained that the creation of the HRC would strengthen the dialogue between civilizations, cultures, and religions.

In terms of practices, the SDGs' holistic approach was apparent in the adoption of hundreds of targets and indicators that sought to integrate the economic, social, and environmental dimensions of development. It also stood out from the creation of the UN Task Team, in which sixty agencies combined their expertise to provide a multidimensional perspective on development issues. In PoC, the introduction of the "whole-of-mission" concept signaled a desire to better coordinate the military, political, economic, and social components of peace operations. Meanwhile, yearly Secretary-General reports have widened the scope of PoC to include issues such as sexual violence, refugees, human trafficking, flows of small arms, and natural resources.[23] Finally, the HRC's work has consistently promoted the idea that human rights are indivisible and interdependent. Following this line of reasoning, civil, political, economic, social, and cultural rights – including the right to development – constitute a comprehensive whole, one that touches upon all aspects of social relations.

Efforts to embed global policies in an integrated global governance script derive primarily from dominant actors' inclination to demonstrate that the disparate pieces of global governance "hang together." Coherence clearly is one of the universal values that are most treasured in contemporary global policymaking. Interestingly, the contestation of global policies also has coherence as a goal, as it is usually founded on contrasting perspectives regarding what global governance should entail. In the SDGs, the HRC, and PoC, a large proportion of the debates involve conflicts between worldviews centered either on sovereignty or on human rights. Of course, one may question whether the grand narratives that are mobilized in global policymaking are nothing more than rhetorical devices. Yet, the fact remains that most global policies seek to establish ideological and practical bridges between an array of issue areas.[24]

Over the years, scholars have documented a range of interactions between the fields of security, development, trade, the environment, migration, and human rights.[25] Not surprisingly, appeals to a holistic

---

[23] UN Security Council 2005b.   [24] Holthaus and Steffek 2020.
[25] Sampson 2000; Duffield 2007; Hestermeyer 2008; Joseph 2013; Drezner, Farrell, and Newman 2021.

perspective may thus be observed in all fields of global policymaking. Following a standard practice, international agreements often begin with a preamble that explains how a given policy is intertwined with other international agreements or policy objectives. More specifically, multilateral initiatives in favor of peace – such as disarmament agreements – are typically justified by reference to the idea that peace is a prerequisite for development. Conversely, the WTO and the IMF argue that, as their policies foster economic growth, they also contribute to world peace. In environmental negotiations, a link has been made between climate change mitigation and sustainable development, poverty eradication, and intergenerational equity. Reference to a grand narrative can also be observed in areas as technical as civil aviation. For instance, the 1944 Chicago Convention states that the development of civil aviation "can greatly help to create and preserve friendship and understanding among the nations and peoples of the world."[26] In short, the majority of global policies seek to increase their legitimacy by highlighting their contribution to global governance as a whole.

5 Orchestration by IOs

Several scholars emphasize the growing collaborative role that IOs play in global policymaking. As "orchestrators,"[27] IOs coordinate a plethora of actors – including states, NGOs, private corporations, and other policy networks – in the service of achieving common goals. While the functional benefits of this model have been theorized, it seems equally important to document exactly how, through practices and debates, IOs have become such key platforms of global policymaking. This is partly the result of IO autonomy,[28] but we also observe that it is increasingly driven by interagency collaboration as well.

The orchestrating role of IOs shows in each of our three case studies. Concerning the SDGs, the creation of the UN Task Team, composed of sixty agencies, as well as the public hearings held by the UN Development Group in about 100 countries and the establishment of the Inter-Agency Expert Group that presided over the definition of development goals are key examples of the sort of coordination role

[26] International Civil Aviation Organization (ICAO) 2006, 1.
[27] Abbott and Snidal 2010.   [28] Barnett and Finnemore 2004.

that IOs can play. When it comes to the making of PoC, annual reports by the Secretary-General and the intensive involvement of agencies such as OCHA and DPO in the development of guidelines demonstrate the centrality of the Secretariat, even in a deeply intergovernmental process. Finally, the UPR practice, which anchors HRC policymaking, is significantly informed by input from OHCHR, which provides administrative and logistical support for the state-led body. Integrated into the UN Secretariat, the OHCHR was also quite influential in shaping the new institution between 2004 and 2006.

Although less evident, the orchestration role of IOs also informs value debates, especially when it comes to determining the means of implementation. On the SDGs, some actors favor a strong international input, primarily in the form of technical advice and support administered by international agencies. On PoC, the view that justice should be administered internationally, or that interventions should be depoliticized and run according to strict guidelines, also gives pride of place to IO involvement and leadership. Finally, when it comes to the HRC, the extent of the advice and capacity-building to be provided by the UN and other agencies is central to the debate over the most effective means of implementing a given policy.

The orchestrating role of IOs is obvious across the entire range of global public policies. A growing number of global initiatives take the form of partnerships in which the UN coordinates the work of like-minded governments, NGOs, and private corporations. In the sphere of international development, the World Bank increasingly positions itself as a global convener, organizing collaborative networks composed of other international agencies, donor and recipient states, private corporations, and civil society organizations. The same logic applies to the field of health governance, where the WHO sits atop a complex structure of partnerships, including the type of multistakeholder partnerships explored earlier in this book.[29]

The fast-growing phenomenon of orchestration is increasingly documented in global governance studies. That said, it is often analyzed in terms of institutional design, emphasizing functionality and Pareto-optimization. What our comparative analysis further illuminates is the political nature of orchestration. On the one hand, IOs often face off against one another and jockey for the position of orchestrator.

---

[29] Hanrieder 2015a.

This new form of competition is likely to transform global governance. On the other hand, orchestration increasingly takes place in the form of direct, peer-to-peer coordination between IOs. This phenomenon enables these organizations to partially bypass intergovernmental practices while building and defending their authority. In sum, orchestration by IOs yields new political dynamics – of both the competitive and collaborative types – that are yet to be fully understood.

6 Inclusive Policymaking

Global policymaking is far more inclusive today than it ever was – undemocratic as it may be by some standards.[30] A more numerous and diverse cast of participants are now involved, whether based on their claimed "stake" in the issue, on normative pressure toward democratization, or on the failings of traditional intergovernmentalism. Our comparative analysis shows that this trend toward inclusivity overwhelmingly takes the form of loose associations based on limited formality. By implication, we also observe critical forms of exclusion.[31]

The narrative of inclusiveness was critical in the making of all three global policies analyzed above. From the get-go, the SDGs were meant to be the most inclusive development policy ever created. For one thing, the SDG process was an offshoot of the 2012 Rio Conference on the Environment, which was celebrated as the most participatory conference in history. Furthermore, the objective of "leaving no one behind" imposed a moral duty to ensure that the negotiations were as open as possible. The making of the HRC was also informed by the notion of inclusiveness. Based on the 2004 High-Level Panel report, debates over the number of member states to be included, or the role of experts and UN specialized agencies in the peer-review process, saw the proponents of different views clash over who should be part of the policymaking process. Finally, PoC has also seen a push for more inclusivity, despite the fact that the policy has thus far remained largely under the control of the Security Council. By its very nature, PoC intends to broaden the array of international legal subjects beyond states to include private citizens.

The drive for inclusivity is equally visible at the level of practice. The SDGs gave way to some of the most participatory policymaking

---

[30] Scholte 2011b.   [31] Pouliot and Thérien 2018a.

practices ever enacted on the global stage, including worldwide online surveys and a variety of interactive dialogues with civil society constituents in various countries. Inclusivity is also reflected in the practice of benchmarking, which targets a variety of population segments in need of particular assistance. Overall, calls for inclusiveness met greater resistance in the case of the HRC. In establishing the peer-review mechanism, state diplomats made sure to retain control over the procedure and successfully relegated nonstate actors to a secondary role. Nonetheless, the process remained far more inclusive than traditional intergovernmentalism. Finally, for a global policy spearheaded by the Security Council, PoC is also comparatively inclusive. Initiated by civil society, especially humanitarian organizations such as the Red Cross, PoC continues to be influenced by nonstate actors, whether through parallel practices (e.g., policy networks composed of think tanks and institutes) or direct involvement at the UN (e.g., Arria formula meetings involving NGOs).

Global policymaking is witnessing a similar increase in inclusivity in all of its subfields.[32] The global governance of the environment certainly is the clearest case here: while the IPCCC process remains primarily intergovernmental, it is increasingly being sidelined by parallel initiatives spearheaded by hybrid or private actors.[33] In the security sphere, pressing issues such as the rise of private military and security companies are handled through multistakeholder partnerships – the Montreux Code of Conduct being a good example – in which a variety of policymakers interact on a more or less equal footing.[34]

While our comparative analysis substantiates the claim of a growing inclusiveness in global policymaking, it is equally important to point out the persistent limitations of this trend. Put differently, while it is undeniable that more experts and NGOs are involved in global policymaking than ever before, it is equally clear that some social groups, especially the most marginalized ones, have not yet benefited from this opening. The political limitations of civil society participation in global forums have been well-documented. Also striking is the fact that in terms of determining exactly what counts as a state – let alone defining the broader category of public actor – the rules of participation are as

---

[32] Pouliot and Thérien 2015; Viola 2020. [33] Hoffmann 2011.
[34] Avant 2016.

strict as ever. For example, it remains nearly impossible for substate actors, diasporas, or stateless societies to play a significant role in global policymaking. In other words, inclusivity may be growing but in a selective way that is far from benefiting every citizen of the world equally.

7 Growing Codification

The global policies analyzed in this book demonstrate the growing codification of global governance. Increasingly, politics are inscribed in texts, operationalized in data, and formalized in categories. While the general pattern is clear, the movement toward codification should not be equated with "legalization,"[35] as it describes a much broader and variegated trend. What is more, our empirical observations suggest that fierce debates continue between advocates of flexibility and those supporting prescription in global policymaking, and that recent codification practices, such as the development of numerical indicators[36] or the spread of contracting across different forms of organizations,[37] do not entail the same kind of obligation as international law.

Codification practices are pervasive across all three of our global policies. In the making of PoC, the anchoring practice – adopting Security Council resolutions – has grown increasingly specific, detailed, and prescriptive. The texts, some of which were adopted under Chapter 7 of the UN Charter (and thus carry legal force), now deal with particular categories of civilians, such as journalists, humanitarians, or women, refining the list of international obligations under international humanitarian law. In addition, the production of an "aide-mémoire" by OCHA and other UN agencies reflects the flexible codification (so to speak) of a PoC doctrine. With regard to the SDGs, here as well, the anchoring practice, goal-setting, attests to the growing significance of operationalization and formalization in global policymaking. At the HRC, the endless production of a variety of documents (such as the annual reports of Special Procedures mandate holders) and the many materials supportive of the peer-review mechanism (such as national

---

[35] Abbott et al. 2000.
[36] Broome and Quirk 2015; Cooley and Snyder 2015; Kelley and Simmons 2015; Baele, Balzacq, and Bourbeau 2018.
[37] Cooley 2010; Seabrooke and Sending 2020.

reports and country evaluations by the OHCHR) further confirms the centrality of inscription practices.

In terms of normative debates, the issue of codification is also key. A major axis of contention over PoC is whether the guidelines found in Council resolutions or in OCHA aide-mémoire should be applied in a systematic or more of an ad hoc way. Everyone agrees on the need for consistency, but what this entails in practice, at the level of case-by-case differentiation, remains hotly contested. Interestingly, in the case of the SDGs, the main debate pitted advocates of soft codification against those calling for a more hardline approach. The choice to base the policy on targets and indicators came at the expense of stronger regulation – for instance, in the form of redistributive policies. Finally, codification was framed as the solution to the main problem that had plagued the HRC's ancestor – namely, politicization. While there has been much debate around the issue of compliance – obligatory versus voluntary – overall, the production and circulation of written documents and reports are meant to ensure equal treatment under human rights law.

The trend toward codification applies across the different subfields of global governance. On environmental issues, the Paris Agreement presents similar features to the SDGs, with country-specific targets and the self-reporting by nations of activities and outcomes. When it comes to combatting terrorism and the spread of weapons of mass destruction, the Security Council has arrogated to itself the role of global legislator, creating new international legal obligations for member states and operating a complex system of individualized sanctions. Finally, on the issue of mass migration, states have sought to coordinate their responses through a new multilateral agreement in the framework of the United Nations, while pursuing other forms of cooperation at the bilateral and regional levels.

While our observation of an increase in codification is not a particularly novel point, the trend is nonetheless worthy of further scrutiny. For one thing, codification admits a variety of practices, ranging from legalization to self-reporting through the development of targets and the production of guidelines. In other words, critical as international law may be to contemporary global governance, it coexists with several other forms of textual inscription. For another thing, at the normative level, codification remains a contested topic. While calls for consistency cut across the board, the precise meaning of this ideal gives way to certain persistent cleavages. Advocates of flexibility, for instance, draw attention to the dangers of any "one-size-fits-all" solution and call for case-by-case adaptability. Their counterparts decry such ad hoc applications and call instead for more exhaustive and systematic codes and reports. All in all, the trend toward codification, far from depoliticizing global policymaking, has become a major axis of debate.

8 The Centrality of Experts

It is widely recognized in global governance studies that the past few decades have witnessed the rise of the expert, whether economists, lawyers, or a plethora of technicians from various other fields – to the point that global governance may be construed as "a system of professional competition."[38] This phenomenon obviously owes much to the bureaucratization of global politics,[39] but it actually extends beyond that. State diplomats now interact with a variety of (self-described) experts on a daily basis, receiving support from, say, technocrats in different line ministries or from representatives of domestic NGOs.[40] Our comparative analysis contributes to this literature by documenting the paths by which expertise enters into global policymaking – and illuminating how these dynamics remain contentious to this day.

Several value debates observable in our three global policies demonstrate the centrality of the expert. Beginning with PoC, the whole policy is based on a legal ethos superimposed on security dynamics. Normatively, the policy requires compliance with international humanitarian law to trump military objectives. It also raises the profile of legal experts in UN peace operations. The making of the HRC was similarly based on the need to put human rights law above politics. The peer-review process is based on the provision of technical advice to help countries solve their problems. Finally, the SDGs illustrate particularly well the new domination of experts over development policy. Far from a struggle against structural injustice, the fight against

---

[38] Sending 2015, 128. See also Leander and Aalberts 2013; Best 2014; Nay 2014; Seabrooke 2014; Nuñez-Mietz 2016; Littoz-Monnet 2017; Niederberger 2020; Sondarjee 2021a; Steffek 2021.
[39] Barnett and Finnemore 2004; Weaver 2008.
[40] Sending, Pouliot, and Neumann 2015.

poverty is now primarily focused on technical deliberation among experts in order to refine measures and facilitate the spread of so-called best practices.

Turning to practices, we also observe the penetration of expertise in global policymaking. The PoC policymaking process, to begin with, gives pride of place to expert committees, including those composed of state diplomats specialized in the issue. The large role played by the Secretariat – for instance, in preparing stock-taking documents – also increases the weight of technical knowledge. As for the HRC, the body also enhances the position of expertise by integrating expert assessments into the peer-review process, and even more so by granting the OHCHR a prominent role in terms of advice and capacity-building. Finally, the making of the SDGs was structured around several expert-based practices, ranging from bureaucratized interagency coordination, and panels of eminent persons, and statistical committees.

The growing mantle of expertise has left no sphere of global governance untouched. We can easily see the trend in well-established institutions such as the IPCCC in environmental matters. But it is also apparent in the field of security, with the ever-expanding influence of lawyers and jurists in warfare and peace operations. Development has similarly become an economist-dominated field of practice, as the World Bank's policies attest. Even trade, despite its recent politicization, continues to maintain a central place for legal experts on account of the unprecedented level of technicality that characterizes its dynamics.

Clearly, experts are here to stay in global policymaking. However, more research is needed to understand the exact role that they play. The specific practices by which they enter the policymaking process do not yield the same amount of influence. Equally important is the fact that, as experts get involved, other segments of the global constituency also vie for representation, potentially balancing technical knowledge with other forms of political interest. As Shapiro puts it, "these processes are largely invisible to and uncontrolled by electorates; more governance may well mean less democracy."[41] Finally, our comparative analysis helps capture the shifting terms of global debates over the place of expertise. Current trends remain quite contentious and the nuanced distinctions that actors make, in terms of exactly how experts should be brought into the process, suggest further evolutions ahead.

[41] Shapiro 2001, 376.

9 The Resilience of the North–South Cleavage

The rise of emerging countries and the multiple changes brought about by globalization are often perceived as indicators of the obsolescence of the North–South cleavage.[42] However, our detailed study reveals that the SDGs, the HRC, and PoC have all been marked by major tensions between developed and developing states. Despite shifting fault lines and the occasional appearance of surprising coalitions, the North–South cleavage – sometimes summarized in the phrase "the West and the Rest" – remains a decisive political axis in global policymaking.

North–South value debates were particularly conspicuous in the SDG negotiations, for example. Rich and poor countries disagreed over the meaning of poverty, the sources of inequality, the priority to be given to growth, and the need to reform global institutions. And while the North defended the principle of national responsibility, the South insisted on international solidarity. In the establishment of the HRC, North–South tensions primarily concerned the scope of the rights to be covered. Developed countries promoted a universalist approach that emphasized civil and political rights. Advocating a more relativist view, developing countries were more preoccupied with social and economic rights. In PoC debates, the North–South division has been fuzzier. Depending on the circumstances, North–South convergence has occurred over such issues as the need for diplomatic solutions or the use of force.[43] Overall, however, northern countries have been the chief proponents of including PoC measures in peace operations, whereas southern countries have been the most reluctant. Moreover, contra traditional peacekeeping principles – which include the nonuse of force – supported by developing countries, developed countries have been much more open to robust peace operations undertaken without consent.

In terms of practices, both the composition and the functioning of the Open Working Group that defined the SDGs demonstrate the extent to which North–South dynamics continue to infuse

[42] Thérien 1999; Malone and Hagman 2002; Payne 2005; Mahbubani 2013; Farias 2019; Horner 2020.
[43] See Rotmann, Kurtz, and Brockmeier 2014, 370–2.

intergovernmental procedures. Duos and troikas of negotiating parties clearly reflected the proclivity of states to hang with their peers. Also telling is the fact that at several key junctures, the negotiating process was entrusted to pairs of diplomats representing both the developed and the developing world. At the HRC, the North–South opposition has been most evident in the functioning of the UPR process. The adoption of a peer-review mechanism, which was inspired by OECD practices, was a clear gain for the developed countries, while the upholding of a state-centric approach as well as the nonbinding nature of the peer-review reports can be seen as gains for the developing countries. In PoC, country-specific Security Council resolutions have led to fierce battles between North and South. Developing countries have often been worried about PoC becoming an instrument of neoimperial interventionism, while developed countries have tended to see PoC as a step forward in favor of human rights. An important aspect of this polarized dynamic is that developing countries have striven to shift PoC discussions toward broader UN forums, while developed countries have preferred to keep the decision-making process under the control of the Security Council, where they generally hold the pen.

Our analysis of the SDGs, the HRC, and PoC shows that the North–South divide still remains one of the main sources of political tensions in global governance. Of course, this opposition is not carved in stone. In PoC, Security Council decisions have required unanimity among the P5 countries, which of course includes China. Moreover, the Kigali Principles, adopted in 2015 to promote good peacekeeping practices, have illustrated the possibility of new forms of cooperation between developed and developing countries. In the SDG process, developing countries were far from unanimous on their evaluation of environmental priorities. And at the HRC, a number of governments from the Global South defended a universalist approach to human rights. Yet, overall, North–South dynamics remained prevalent in our three cases because of historical and institutional factors. While the North benefits from a long tradition of leadership in world affairs, the South shares a common past of political subordination that fuels a widespread mistrust of the values and practices championed by the developed countries. Institutionally, the North–South divide has perpetuated itself thanks to the UN system of bloc coordination and voting.

The North–South cleavage permeates a large number of global policies beyond our cases.[44] The most telling examples concern the international economy and the environment. Almost all decisions taken by the WTO and international financial institutions – whether on tariffs, intellectual property rights, investment rules, or financial assistance – are based on patterns of give-and-take between developed and developing countries. In climate diplomacy, CBDR ("common but differentiated responsibilities") has crystallized the differences between the two groups. While the countries of the North strive to limit the use of the CBDR norm, those in the South – including big greenhouse gas emitters – keep criticizing the developed countries for betraying their promise to lead the way against climate change. Aside from economic and environmental matters, the North–South cleavage has impacted a wide range of international negotiations regarding disarmament, the Internet, or corruption. Although the North–South cleavage has become fuzzier in recent years, it still pervades large portions of global policymaking.

10 Western Hegemony

The North–South dynamics discussed above are inextricably linked to what neo-Gramscians call "Western hegemony." According to this line of thinking, hegemony refers to a form of power relations in which coercion and consent intermingle.[45] This definition provides a useful framework for understanding the formulation of the SDGs, the creation of the HRC, and the evolution of PoC. Indeed, our three case studies show that the North–South cleavage often materializes in social patterns whereby Western states (the Global North) dominate the developing world. Yet, this domination does not rely on the use of brute force; indeed, it can give way to compromises in order to accommodate subaltern governments and elites. In recent years, such compromise has arguably been more and more frequent. In fact, despite remaining a distinctive feature of global policymaking today, Western hegemony – which has been embodied by the global dominance of the

[44] Soederberg 2006; Alden, Morphet, and Vieira 2010; Hurrell and Sengupta 2012; United Nations Development Program (UNDP) 2013; Singh 2017; Farias 2019; Timossi 2019.

[45] Cox 1983; Gill 1993; Puchala 2005; Sinclair 2012; Dutkiewicz, Casier, and Scholte 2021.

US since the Second World War – is increasingly challenged by states such as China and Russia, which push for alternative values and practices.

The protection of civilians offers a prime example of Western hegemony in global policymaking. Western countries have been the staunchest proponents of making PoC "one of the core issues" on the Security Council's agenda.[46] Their active mobilization has made it possible to transform traditional peacekeeping principles so as to broaden the permissible criteria for robust interventions in postcolonial states. With the establishment of the HRC, the West has further legitimized the view that human rights should be universal and that they should be monitored more closely, both by the international community and by human rights experts. Moreover, Western countries have been able to maintain more or less intact the international human rights culture that dates back to the postwar era, and that emphasizes individual over collective rights. In the SDGs case, Western states have successfully mounted a tour de force aimed at enshrining sustainable development as the new development paradigm. Within this new model, every country can now pretend to be "developing." Western governments also succeeded in limiting the negotiations around the SDGs to a framework wherein sustainable development objectives were strictly separated from any talk of reforming international institutions.

With respect to practices, the influence of Western states on PoC stems from the political power that they wield within UN agencies in charge of peace operations and humanitarian decision making (e.g., the Security Council, DPO, OCHA). Their role as penholders at the Security Council and chairs of expert groups has been particularly decisive. Moreover, Western NGOs have been at the forefront of PoC policy evaluation. In HRC negotiations, Western governments kept the upper hand thanks to the size and expertise of their diplomatic corps, their inner knowledge of the peer-review system, their close connections with human rights NGOs, and their financial leverage over developing countries' capacity-building programs. Finally, with respect to the SDGs, Western states have used their technical and scientific knowledge to shape the content of the goals, and to exert leadership in the various expert groups.

---

[46] UN Security Council 2018d.

Although it remains strong, Western hegemony also has limits, however – something that our three case studies help illustrate. In PoC, for instance, Western countries have faced various forms of discursive and behavioral contestation.[47] In particular, non-Western states have used the C34 forum to reaffirm their preference for political over military solutions, while the use of force on the ground has been "routinely avoided as an option by peacekeeping operations."[48] At the HRC, the West had to accept that its human rights standards could not be enforced against the will of sovereign states, and that the outcome reports stemming from the UPR process would consist solely of recommendations. And in SDG discussions, Western states could not impose a preestablished agenda in the same way they had done with the formulation of the MDGs in 2000. All these accommodations feed into the argument that Western hegemony is no longer as solid as it used to be.

Notwithstanding its relative weakening, though, it is undeniable that the West has profoundly shaped global policymaking over the past two centuries in a variety of ways.[49] Those who have heralded Western hegemony's imminent demise have been a bit too quick.[50] At the United Nations, Western powers hold three of the five permanent seats on the Security Council. In the field of security, Western states continue to exert considerable global influence through NATO. With respect to global economic policies, Western hegemony is reflected in major WTO agreements – or the lack thereof, as the case may be – as well as in the programs of the IMF and the World Bank, two financial institutions where the US enjoys veto power over major decisions. In addition, the ambitions of the OECD, which serves as the intellectual core of Western hegemony, have become more and more global with respect to a range of economic and social issues. Even soft policy areas like public health or education have been profoundly fashioned by Western states' interests and vision. History tells us that hegemony is a transient state of affairs, and Western hegemony is unlikely to be an exception to this rule. However, Chomsky rightfully points out that "despite America's decline, in the foreseeable future there is no competitor for global hegemonic power."[51] While Western hegemony is

---

[47] Rhoads and Welsh 2019, 597.   [48] UN General Assembly 2014a, 1.
[49] Keohane 1984; Wallerstein 1991; Fieldhouse 1999; Ikenberry 2001; Cox and Schechter 2002; Puchala 2005; Kupchan 2012.
[50] Strange 1987; Knight 2013.   [51] Chomsky 2011.

increasingly an object of contestation, "counter-hegemonic"[52] alternatives have had only a limited impact on policymaking so far. In other words, while Western countries' power in global governance is clearly being diluted, it is unlikely to be replaced anytime soon.

Conclusion

In this chapter, we have sought to capture a set of common patterns in global policymaking today. The ten contemporary trends discussed here certainly do not have the same salience across all policies, but they do cut across subfields and organizations. More importantly, perhaps, we have used a comparative analysis to draw attention to some of the more intriguing specificities of each trend. For instance, sovereignty remains central to global governance, but this can be expressed in highly heterodox ways. Codification is a much more diverse process than legalization. Orchestration is as much about cooperation as it is about competition and collusion. North–South politics can give way to unexpected alignments. And sometimes Western hegemony is successfully contested, even if, overall, global governance continues to play out on a highly unlevel playing field.

Beyond common trends, our comparative analysis also yields insights into the rich complexity of global policymaking today. Particularly striking, in our view, is the coexistence of multiple if overlapping logics of governance, or, as Barnett, Pevehouse, and Raustiala put it, "modes of global governance."[53] The three anchoring practices that we identify in our policies differ from one another, especially in terms of the alternatives that they served to suppress. In the case of the SDGs, goal-setting sidelines topdown rulemaking, which has been a key mode of global governance for decades. At the HRC, UPR and its learning mechanism surpass legal adjudication and human rights compliance. Finally, the ad hoc accumulation of Security Council resolutions that comprise the PoC doctrine substitutes for alternative forms of legal consolidation, including multilateral treaty-making. As Fioretos aptly sums it up, "global governance has gradually become characterized by many more types of governance

---

[52] Cox and Schechter 2002, 105.   [53] Barnett, Pevehouse, and Raustiala 2022b.

arrangements, including a variety of hybrid arrangements that have widened the color palette with time."[54]

However distinct, these anchoring practices nonetheless share a couple of fundamental traits. First, they tend to be more flexible than their alternatives. Implementation is generally more supple and open to case-by-case variation. The trend toward "soft governance," through mechanisms such as voluntary pledges and the adherence to best practices, continues, shifting global policymaking from hierarchical to market and network modes,[55] while also reflecting continued American dominance. Second, these practices appear to be more participatory, by breaking out of the intergovernmental monopoly to a certain extent. States maintain their prerogative over final decision making, but they now have to contend with more heteronomy than before. Needless to say, we remain very far from anything remotely resembling global democracy. Overall, then, comparison helps us understand where global governance currently stands, and it suggests some clues about the movement of history. Intricate and complex as it is, global policymaking does exhibit a changing structure over time.

---

[54] Fioretos 2022, 361.   [55] Barnett, Pevehouse, and Raustiala 2022a.

Conclusion

Grasping the Patchwork of Global Governance

The past half-century has witnessed an unprecedented expansion of governance instruments that apply to jurisdictions and constituencies of a planetary scope.[1]

The key point we hope readers – whether scholars and students or practitioners on the ground – will take from this book is that it is past time that we move away from the notion that there is a set of technical or rational solutions by which we can resolve global problems once and for all. Global policymaking is fundamentally political: the assumption that "if only people could agree, then we would live in a better world" makes for a deeply problematic starting point for the analysis of global governance. Any collective course of action is bound to favor some groups more than others, and to embody a particular vision of the common good at the expense of alternative perspectives. Not only are costs and benefits never distributed equally in and across societies; values and worldviews, too, consistently clash and vary despite the many well-intentioned calls for consensus and harmony. Focusing on social conflict as the engine of global governance helps us to bring politics to the fore, not as a hindrance but as the natural condition of society – global or otherwise. In any policymaking process, power dynamics and unequal participation ultimately remain, however inclusive contemporary global practices claim to be. Likewise, the competing value systems and ideologies that structure global policymaking can never be fully arbitrated by objective and neutral means. Such, we believe, is the inherent backdrop of global governance.

This conclusion has two goals. The first is to summarize the objectives and the findings of our research. The second is to broaden the discussion in order to situate our analysis of global policymaking within the more general study of global governance.

---

[1] Scholte 2011a, 1.

1 Global Policies: A Bricolage of Practices and Values

We started this book with the rather mundane observation that, as citizens of the globe, we are all constrained by the politics of global governance. Following a growing stream of research, we then argued that the study of global policies offers an innovative perspective by which we can better understand how global governance actually works. In our view, the concept of global policymaking helps reconcile key insights of global governance scholarship regarding processes of fragmentation, orchestration, experimentation, and legitimation. In addition, it sheds new light on the exclusionary dynamics and the ideological conflicts that inform global governance.

Our main contribution to global governance debates has been to portray global policymaking as a form of bricolage. Borrowed from the writings of Claude Lévi-Strauss, our use of the bricolage concept offers a powerful metaphor by which to problematize assumptions that global governance is based on some rational design; it also allows us to capture the improvised nature of the policymaking process. While some instances of global policymaking are more scripted than others, overall it seems fair to say that all global policies result from the haphazard and combinatorial logic of bricolage. In this regard, the notion of bricolage has been particularly useful for exploring an idea repeated by many IR scholars – namely, that global governance forms a highly complex and contingent patchwork.

Anyone who makes a bricolage – a bricoleur – obviously must draw from a variety of materials. To describe the bricolage of global policies, we reduced the available materials to two categories: governance practices and value debates. Self-interested as they may be, global actors find themselves enmeshed in a normative and institutional structure that enables and constrains their variegated pursuits. Favoring a constitutive rather than a causal approach, we focused on how the global bricolage of practices and values has made it possible to open up the black box of global governance. Overall, the picture we paint significantly complicates the dominant view, according to which "[g]lobal governance is a response to collective action problems that transcend national boundaries."[2] This functionalist logic is certainly part of the story, but

[2] Stone and Moloney 2019, 3.

so are the political dynamics that involve hard work, struggle, and choice in the everyday "muddling through" of global policymaking.

Taken together, global governance practices and value debates help account for the material as well as the ideological dimensions of global governance. We conceived of practices as formal and informal ways of doing that shape the social configuration of the global sphere. We argued that policymaking practices, as a reflection of power relations, give shape to strategies of inclusion and exclusion that characterize the politics of global governance. We also maintained that the web of practices that characterizes global policies, far from being randomly organized, is structured by specific anchoring practices that guide other patterns of action. Value debates, for their part, were interpreted as processes of negotiation over the normative structures that inform the definition of global problems and global solutions. A key feature of these debates, we noted, is that they oppose values that are generally presented as universal and thus "beyond politics." We showed that value debates generally result in polysemous compromises that serve to paper over ideological cleavages that, notwithstanding claims to the contrary, remain intact.

We applied our theoretical framework to the study of three global policies drawn from recent UN activities: the adoption of the SDGs in 2015, the institutionalization of the HRC from 2005 onward, and the ongoing promotion of the protection of civilians in peace operations. In addition to the fact that the UN forms the organizational crucible of global governance today, we chose these three case studies for four basic reasons. First, by covering the fields of development, human rights, and security, they provide a fairly broad view of the main issue areas of global governance. Second, each of our cases has led to the introduction of significant changes in the functioning of the global order. Counterfactually, global governance would not look the same but for the global policies of the SDGs, the HRC, and PoC. Third, our cases span the so-called three United Nations, showing the density and complexity of global policy networks. Fourth and finally, they capture the variety of political forms and logics that preside over global policymaking in the twenty-first century.

We believe that the empirical analysis presented in Chapters 3–5 supplies ample confirmation of the usefulness of our analytical framework. Resulting from the unforeseen merger of the post-Rio and post-MDG processes, the SDGs offer a telling illustration of how the bricolage of global policies takes shape. At the same time, as it gave rise to an unprecedented participatory dynamic, the adoption of the SDGs was clearly dominated by states and statisticians. Moreover, the notion of sustainable development constituted a superficial consensus hiding deep normative disagreements over the obligations of governments in terms of international solidarity. The establishment of the HRC, meanwhile, provides a perfect example of what we call institution-building by doing insofar as the organization has from its very inception tried to adapt through a step-by-step approach. In this process, the respective roles of national diplomats, the international bureaucracy, civil society representatives, and experts have been subject to constant renegotiation. On the normative level, the official rhetoric concerning the need to depoliticize human rights has not precluded accusations from all sides that states do not respect their international commitments. Finally, the elaboration of the PoC doctrine also shows the improvisatory nature of global policy-making. Since the 1990s, PoC has developed through a succession of ad hoc decisions whereby the activism of the Western members of the Security Council and the NGO community has been hampered by the resistance of many countries from the Global South, who see the protection of civilians as a form of neoimperial interventionism. And despite the apparent consensus that PoC should be a global priority, the international community remains deeply divided over the use of force in peace operations.

Building on a comparison of these three case studies, the last chapter offered a reflection on the common characteristics of contemporary global policies. This comparative view allowed us to identify ten contemporary trends: the clash of sovereignties, the growing focus on individuals, the universalization of aspirations, the promotion of a holistic narrative, the orchestrating role of international organizations, the pursuit of inclusion, increasing codification, the emphasis on expertise, the resilience of the North–South divide, and Western hegemony. While these ten trends clearly have distinct historical foundations, they may be observed across policy domains. Although additional case studies would be necessary to assess more precisely the extent to which these dynamics actually shape global policies, they nonetheless appear to be widespread and powerful.

While in this book we refrained from offering policy advice, the real-world consequences of our analysis are far-reaching; indeed, as

Kennedy put it, "[i]f we understood the machinery by which inequalities and hierarchies of influence and wealth and knowledge are reproduced, we might begin to know how to make the world a better place."[3] The present account arrives at a similar conclusion: better understanding the manner in which global policies are made can help us to imagine how things may be improved, including the politics that such a process necessarily entails.

2 The Macropolitics of Global Governance

One way to broaden the discussion undertaken in this book is to look at how our cases can feed into the more general study of global governance. While global policymaking is certainly a useful entry point for analyzing global governance, global governance obviously cannot be reduced to global policymaking, no matter how that term is defined. One should not forget, for instance, that global governance has ramifications that run all the way to the intricacies of domestic politics. A compelling question, then, is how does global policymaking connect to the "big picture" of global politics? One method for assessing this connection is to examine how the main axes of contention that we documented in our case studies illustrate the deeper cleavages that shape the global agora. While such an examination can only be conducted here in a tentative and exploratory manner, it nonetheless suggests a new way of thinking about "what makes the world hang together."[4]

Consider first that our three global policies are characterized by the same basic cleavage between "globalists" who support a strengthened form of global governance, on the one hand, and "sovereigntists" who propose a more limited form, on the other. The two groups hold sharply contrasting understandings of how objectives of efficiency and democracy should be reconciled. Moreover, it is striking that actors' preferences over the reach of global governance – strengthened or limited, as the case may be – vary little across issues. In the making of the SDGs, the HRC, and PoC, nonstate actors and Western middle powers have generally sustained the strengthening of global governance, whereas developing countries and the great powers have shown more reluctance. Interestingly, the basic cleavage over the reach of

[3] Kennedy 2008, 828.   [4] Ruggie 1998.

global governance echoes the critical fault line that students of European integration have observed between those who support more regional governance and those who want less.[5] It is also in line with what Steffek identifies as the "fundamental tension of modern political life," springing from a struggle between competing ideals of "popular sovereignty" and "performance" that operate "both domestically and internationally."[6]

Cutting across the divide between globalists and sovereigntists, our three cases are also marked by issue-specific conflicts that, while unique in their particularities, nonetheless display major elements of convergence. The adoption of the SDGs pitted those wanting to maximize global solidarity against those insisting on liberalizing the world economy. The establishment of the HRC set advocates of social and economic rights against proponents of civil and political rights. And the making of the PoC doctrine has led to a confrontation between those favoring a developmental approach to the issue and those defending a security-centered framework. Beyond the specific nature of these thematic cleavages, obvious family resemblances may be observed. Indeed, developing countries and many NGOs, who generally emphasize the promotion of international solidarity, also tend to support economic and social rights as well as a developmental approach to PoC. For their part, Western countries and pro-business groups, who promote free markets, tend overall to support civil and political rights, in addition to a security approach to PoC.

Examined through the lens of their similarities, the issue-specific cleavages of our three global policies are highly reminiscent of the Left–Right opposition that structures social conflicts in many parts of the world. Considering that the Left is typically more concerned with questions of justice, equality, and social development, while the Right generally foregrounds issues of order, freedom, and economic prosperity, the issue-specific cleavages that we identify in our case studies seem consistent with the Left–Right spectrum. This is far from surprising. Although the Left–Right divide is both context-dependent and protean, it arguably stands out as "the most ubiquitous and encompassing" political cleavage that one can think of.[7] And indeed, there is a

---

[5] Gabel and Hix 2002; Hooghe, Marks, and Wilson 2002; Marks and Steenbergen 2004.
[6] Steffek 2021, 193.
[7] Noël and Thérien 2023, 250. See also Bobbio 1996; Noël and Thérien 2008.

relationship between Right-leaning positions centered on political free-dom (HRC), open markets (SDGs), and robust military action (PoC). The same may be said of Leftist value claims around global solidarity (SDGs), economic and social justice (HRC), and a development-based approach to security (PoC). It is also fair to say that Left-leaning actors favor inclusive and bottom-up political processes (e.g., global surveys, NGO consultations, local ownership), while those on the Right are attached to efficient and actionable institutions (e.g., club diplomacy, experts benchmarking, public–private partnerships).

In sum, the negotiations over the SDGs, the HRC, and PoC were shaped by two key cleavages – reach of global governance and Left–Right priorities – giving rise to four policy positions: Left-wing glob-alist, Right-wing globalist, Left-wing sovereigntist, and Right-wing sovereigntist. While the social groups that have defended these four policy positions have never been perfectly demarcated, their distinct ideas have exerted a profound influence on each of our case studies (Table 7.1).

Building on these observations, we suggest that the same configur-ation of cleavages that marked the making of the SDGs, the HRC, and PoC also permeates the bricolage of most global policies. Recent global policies such as the 2015 Paris Agreement on climate change; the 2018 Global Compact for Safe, Orderly and Regular Migration; and the 2020 COVAX Facility to fight COVID-19 have also been fash-ioned by conflicts over the reach of global governance and Left–Right orientations. In the making of these policies, a fundamental divide opposed those who supported a strengthening of multilateral cooper-ation and those who resisted it. Running through this divide, another cleavage pitted those emphasizing economic performance and security concerns against those stressing social justice.

In fact, it can be argued that most instances of global governance politics may be plotted along two orthogonal axes and modeled as a struggle among the four social groups identified above (see Figure 7.1). In this stylized depiction, the vertical axis represents the reach of global governance: it opposes globalists who favor more global governance to sovereigntists who prefer less. The horizontal axis, which refers to the objectives of global governance, opposes progressives on the Left and conservatives on the Right. While the resulting representation is of course an analytical simplification of a much more complex reality, it is nonetheless based on heuristic shortcuts that capture the main

Table 7.1 *Values and practices in the macropolitics of global governance*

Global policy position	Case	Key universal value claim	Preferred policymaking practice
Right-wing globalists	SDGs	Trade is better than aid	Public–private partnerships
	HRC	Political freedom for all	Legal action against violators
	PoC	Protection by all necessary means	Robust peacekeeping
Left-wing globalists	SDGs	Global solidarity	Global conferences with civil society
	HRC	All human rights for all	Naming and shaming by NGOs
	PoC	Human security	Civil society and humanitarian coalitions
Right-wing sovereigntists	SDGs	Good domestic governance	Technical expertise
	HRC	Rights are defined by national governments	Intergovernmental dialogue
	PoC	Case-by-case approach to intervention	Security Council negotiations
Left-wing sovereigntists	SDGs	Right to development	National ownership
	HRC	Rights must respond to peoples' will	Capacity-building
	PoC	State sovereignty as the cardinal principle	C34 negotiations

ideologies and repertoires of practices structuring the political dynamics of global governance.

In the macropolitics of global governance, globalists basically differ from sovereigntists in that they are more supportive of widening and deepening global governance. Globalists value the rise of interdependence, while sovereigntists argue that national independence is the strongest

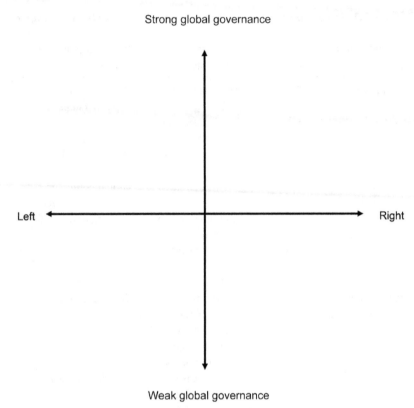

Figure 7.1 The macropolitics of global governance

guarantor of stability within the world order. Globalists are also more inclined to promote the principle of supranationalism, while sovereigntists defend that of intergovernmentalism. In today's context, globalists and sovereigntists each recognize the need for some multilevel governance mechanisms, but their respective approaches differ significantly, with globalists being more likely to support upward subsidiarity (top-down), and sovereigntists advocating downward subsidiarity (bottom-up).

For globalists, the common good ought to be conceived on a planetary scale. They see the expansion of international rules and norms as a way of promoting the predictability of international relations. In terms of practices, globalists prefer to invest their resources in global fora that dilute power relations and generate universal agreements. As a result, they have more confidence in multilateral institutions such as the UN and its related agencies. And as advocates of more inclusive global governance, they are generally more attracted to multistakeholderism and partnerships of all kinds. Following this pluralist logic, globalists actively participate in global conferences where states, civil society, and the business community come together to form networks.

For their part, sovereigntists want to slow down the forces pushing for global governance. Considering the state as the political unit that best delimits the boundaries of the demos, sovereigntists orient their external behavior so as to respond, above all, to domestic priorities. In general, they believe that delegation of power beyond the nation-state leads to ineffective or undemocratic results. In their practices, sovereigntists maintain a selective approach to the groupings in which they participate. They are thus more likely to use unilateral, bilateral, or minilateral channels to promote their interests. They often prefer club diplomacy and ad hoc forms of cooperation such as "issue-, place-, and time-contingent coalitions."[8] Finally, as their worldview remains territorially based, sovereigntists place less importance on the role that transnational actors can play in political decision making.

Beyond their points of convergence, globalists and sovereigntists are divided, respectively, into a Right and a Left wing. In fact, when it comes to substantive politics, the Left–Right cleavage is often more significant than the divide between globalists and sovereigntists. Consider the following distinctions. Globalists of the Right believe that moves to strengthen global governance are justified by the need to promote global order and prosperity. For them, social objectives are subordinated to security and economic ones. They thus advocate rules that would ensure the stability of the international system, the further opening of markets, and the free trade of goods and services. While they support the idea of special responsibilities for great powers, Right-wing globalists often show a degree of indifference with respect to the public or private nature of global governance. In their view, the decisive criterion of good governance is efficiency, defined in terms of cost-effectiveness.

Globalists of the Left, for their part, believe that strengthened global governance is a precondition for the promotion of global justice. They support the creation of institutions and norms that would lead to a

---

[8] Keukeleire and Schunz 2015, 70.

more egalitarian and democratic international system. Their main battlegrounds concern the promotion of development, the rebalancing of the human rights regime, the democratization of international organizations, the establishment of environmental rules, and the reduction of military expenditures. Skeptical of markets, Left-wing globalists believe that the strengthening of global governance must be done through public rather than private institutions, since the former are the only ones with enough legitimacy to define the common good.

Like globalists, sovereigntists are divided between their Right and Left wings. Driven by the two ideals of nationalism and economic growth, Right-wing sovereigntists tend to espouse isolationism and protectionism. That said, their reservations toward global governance can occasionally be overcome when they believe that a multilateral approach would protect national security or employment. On the other hand, sovereigntists of the Right remain wary of the social objectives of global governance, which they fear could endanger national cultures and ways of life. In recent decades, this hostility has been particularly visible in the areas of human rights, immigration, and environmental policy.

Like Left-wing globalists, Left-wing sovereigntists defend the values of solidarity and equality, but they argue that social justice begins at home. Distrustful of the benefits of globalization, sovereigntists of the Left display mixed views vis-à-vis global governance. For them, social multilateralism is clearly more compatible with the national interest than is economic multilateralism. As such, they are more inclined to accept the strengthening of global governance in areas such as peace promotion, health, or the environment. On the other hand, Left-wing sovereigntists denounce the dogma of free trade, and feel that international economic institutions like the IMF and the WTO are instruments that enable the domination of markets over peoples.

In this mapping of the politics of global governance, alliances can take a wide variety of forms. The two most common coalitions are those that bring together globalists and sovereigntists of the Right, on the one hand, and globalists and sovereigntists of the Left, on the other. Given their common interest in order and economic growth, there are certain affinities between the conservative wings of the globalist and sovereigntist camps when it comes to the use of force or the promotion of global trade. And although they differ in terms of their openness to nonstate actors, globalists and sovereigntists of the Right share the same favorable attitude toward the private sector. More broadly, they also share a top-down approach to global governance in line with the rules of procedural democracy.

In contrast, progressive globalists and sovereigntists are more appreciative of social institutions that focus on the welfare of communities, the promotion of human rights, and the protection of the environment. Despite their different views on the diversification of international actors, both groups tend to favor greater participation on the part of civil society and NGOs in political life. Finally, globalists and sovereigntists of the Left take a more bottom-up approach to global governance. This has been illustrated, for example, in many popular demonstrations against "neoliberal globalization" in which the two groups have united.

This admittedly impressionistic overview of the basic political cleavages characterizing global governance is by no means definitive. Yet, it has the advantage of showing how global policymaking, far from floating in a political void, is in fact embedded in a broader fabric of social conflict. In addition, it offers a cogent narrative to help make sense of recent debates about world ordering. While globalists of the Right have maintained the upper hand since the end of the Cold War, the nature of global contestation is arguably undergoing a process of transformation. Until the 2000s, resistance came mainly from globalists of the Left linked to civil society and the international public service. More recently, however, the simultaneous rise of emerging countries and populist movements has given unprecedented vigor to sovereigntists of the Right. This realignment of forces, we surmise, goes a long way toward explaining the current crisis of global policymaking and global governance more broadly.

Final Thoughts: Toward Critical Problem-Solving?

This book has argued that global governance is best understood as a patchwork. Far from following a rational blueprint, the bricolage of global governance and global policymaking evolves in a haphazard and combinatorial manner. The materials that give shape to this process are both normative and practical. More specifically, global governance can be seen as the outcome of universal value clashes and more or less exclusionary policymaking practices. This approach is fruitful in that it provides a more holistic account of the political struggles over the objectives and solutions debated at the global level, as well as the social dynamics that structure global governance. At the macrolevel, a patchwork perspective helps show how global governance is shaped by the values and practices of four social groups that hold distinct views about the reach and the object of global policymaking. We labeled these groups Left-wing globalist, Right-wing globalist, Left-wing sovereigntist, and Right-wing sovereigntist. As they change over time, the power relations between these groups shape the collective aspirations and practices that enable humanity to muddle through global politics.

Conceiving global governance as a patchwork also has implications at the metatheoretical level. We find it useful to return to Cox's classic distinction between critical and problem-solving theory that was evoked in the introduction of this book.[9] In a nutshell, we suggest that studying the politics of global governance as a patchwork of competing values and practices opens up an intellectual space that straddles critical and problem-solving approaches. On the one hand, global policymaking and global governance clearly refer to the collective search for concrete solutions to pressing needs. Not only global governors but also scholars find themselves concerned with improving the fate of humanity. On the other hand, by showing that global governance is a process rife with exclusion, struggle, and inequality, we move closer to critical theory, with an interest in alternative worlds and emancipation. Marginalized actors, sidelined proposals, and roads not taken – the consequences, in other words, of the politics of policymaking – offer a useful reminder that the world as it currently is could indeed have been otherwise.

These observations lead us to revisit Cox's distinction, away from epistemology and toward empirics. For Cox, one distinctive trait of critical theory is reflexivity, or the urge "to become clearly aware of the perspective which gives rise to theorising."[10] As a result, critical theory should aim at "creating an alternative world."[11] Yet, important as reflexivity may be in good scholarship, it is unclear how such a move can, in and of itself, capture – let alone reshape – the politics of global governance. Instead, we advocate a brand of critical problem-solving theory that asks how things could have been otherwise, not by generating a master plan crafted by scholars but, as Cox suggested, by reconstructing the alternative political projects put forward by global actors.

---

[9] Cox 1981.   [10] Ibid., 128.   [11] Ibid.

Because of their failure to materialize, these roads not taken exclude competing values from the political landscape, as well as alternative modes of action and governance. Yet, their political significance should not be underestimated – empirically, in assessing the direction of history, and normatively, in imagining the future of global politics.

Put differently, in order to straddle critical and problem-solving theory, we propose focusing on how global actors, as opposed to scholars, think that global governance could and should work. Empirically thick, this approach requires highlighting how things could have been otherwise – that is, investigating the alternative models left behind, the voices muted, and the experiences of the losing side in the political fight. It also rests on historicization, which involves the unpacking of political debates and the policymaking processes leading to exclusionary dynamics.

Overall, critical problem-solving as we construe it focuses on the concrete practices by which some viewpoints get sidelined and others triumph. The goal, as Cox nicely put it, should be "to clarify [the] range of possible alternatives"[12] – although not as a set of academic "utopias," to borrow his term, but as actual templates for action that have been relegated to the political margins by the machinery of global governance. Here, scholarship and policymaking essentially meet halfway, in terms of both emphasizing that things need not necessarily be so and pointing to how they could in fact be(come) different.

---

[12] Ibid., 130.

References

Abbott, Kenneth W. and Benjamin Faude. 2021. Choosing Low-Cost Institutions in Global Governance. *International Theory* 13(3): 397–426.

Abbott, Kenneth W., Philipp Genschel, Duncan Snidal and Bernhard Zangl, eds. 2015. *International Organizations as Orchestrators*. Cambridge: Cambridge University Press.

Abbott, Kenneth W., Jessica F. Green and Robert O. Keohane. 2016. Organizational Ecology and Institutional Change in Global Governance. *International Organization* 70(2): 247–77.

Abbott, Kenneth W., Robert O. Keohane, Andrew Moravcsik, Anne-Marie Slaughter and Duncan Snidal. 2000. The Concept of Legalization. *International Organization* 54(3): 401–19.

Abbott, Kenneth W. and Duncan Snidal. 2000. Hard and Soft Law in International Governance. *International Organization* 54(3): 421–56.

2009. The Governance Triangle: Regulatory Standards Institutions and the Shadow of the State. In *The Politics of Global Regulation*, edited by Walter Mattli and Ngaire Woods, 44–88. Princeton, NJ: Princeton University Press.

2010. International Regulation without International Government: Improving IO Performance through Orchestration. *The Review of International Organizations* 5(3): 315–44.

Abraham, Meghna. 2007. Building the New Human Rights Council: Outcome and Analysis of the Institution-Building Year. Dialogue on Globalization: Occasional Papers 33. Geneva: Friedrich Ebert Stiftung. Available from http://library.fes.de/pdf-files/bueros/genf/04769.pdf.

Acharya, Amitav. 2018. *Constructing Global Order: Agency and Change in World Politics*. Cambridge: Cambridge University Press.

Adamczyk, Sarah. 2019. Twenty Years of Protection of Civilians at the UN Security Council. Policy Brief 74 (May): 1–13. London: Humanitarian Policy Group, Overseas Development Institute.

Adams, Barbara, Roberto Bissio and Karen Judd. 2016. Measuring Accountability: The Politics of Indicators. In *Spotlight on Sustainable*

Development, edited by Reflection Group on the 2030 Agenda for Sustainable Development, 141–7. New York: Coordinated by the Global Policy Forum.

Adler, Emanuel. 1998. Seeds of Peaceful Change: The OSCE's Security Community-Building Model. In *Security Communities*, edited by Emanuel Adler and Michael Barnett, 119–60. Cambridge: Cambridge University Press.

2019. *World Ordering: A Social Theory of Cognitive Evolution.* Cambridge: Cambridge University Press.

Adler, Emanuel and Vincent Pouliot. 2011. International Practices. *International Theory* 3(1): 1–36.

Adler-Nissen, Rebecca. 2014. *Opting Out of the European Union: Diplomacy, Sovereignty and European Integration.* Cambridge: Cambridge University Press.

2016. Towards a Practice Turn in EU Studies: The Everyday of European Integration. *Journal of Common Market Studies* 54(1): 87–103.

Adler-Nissen, Rebecca and Alena Drieschova. 2019. Track-Change Diplomacy: Technology, Affordances, and the Practice of International Negotiations. *International Studies Quarterly* 63(3): 531–45.

Alden, Chris, Sally Morphet and Marco Antonio Vieira. 2010. *The South in World Politics.* Basingstoke: Palgrave Macmillan.

Alter, Karen J. and Sophie Meunier. 2009. The Politics of International Regime Complexity. *Perspectives on Politics* 7(1): 13–24.

Alter, Karen J. and Kal Raustiala. 2018. The Rise of International Regime Complexity. *Annual Review of Law and Social Science* 14(1): 329–49.

Ambrosetti, Massimo. 2012. Power and Influence: Ideational and Material Factors in the International Posture of China Rising as a Great Power. D.L.S., Georgetown University, Washington, DC. Available from http://hdl.handle.net/10822/557678.

Amnesty International. 2005. Meeting the Challenge: Transforming the Commission on Human Rights in to a Human Rights Council. April. Available from www.amnesty.org/download/Documents/84000/ior400082005en.pdf.

2015. UN Summit for the Adoption of the Post-2015 Development Agenda. Speech delivered by Secretary General Salil Shetty at the Opening Plenary Meeting, New York, September 25.

Anderl, Felix, Priska Daphi and Nicole Deitelhoff. 2021. Keeping Your Enemies Close? The Variety of Social Movements' Reactions to International Organizations' Opening Up. *International Studies Review* 23(4): 1273–99.

Andonova, Liliana B. 2010. Public–Private Partnerships for the Earth: Politics and Patterns of Hybrid Authority in the Multilateral System. *Global Environmental Politics* 10(2): 25–53.

2017. *Governance Entrepreneurs: International Organizations and the Rise of Global Public–Private Partnerships.* Cambridge: Cambridge University Press.

Anthony, Gordon, Jean-Bernard Auby, John Morison and Tom Zwart, eds. 2011. *Values in Global Administrative Law.* Oxford: Hart Publishing.

Anyangwe, Eliza. 2015. Glee, Relief and Regret: Addis Ababa Outcome Receives Mixed Reception. *The Guardian*, July 16. Available from www.theguardian.com/global-development/2015/jul/16/outcome-docu ment-addis-ababa-ffd3-financing-for-development.

Australia. 2015. Opening Statement by Kushla Munro, Assistant Secretary, Department of Foreign Affairs and Trade: 2nd Session of the Intergovernmental Negotiations, General Statements, New York, 19 January. Available from https://sustainabledevelopment.un.org/con tent/documents/12495150119%20Opening%20Session%20-% 20Australia%20statement%20-%20As%20delivered.pdf.

Australia, Netherlands and United Kingdom. 2013. Guiding Principles for the Post-2015 Development Agenda: 1st Session of the OWG, March 15. Available from https://sustainabledevelopment.un.org/con tent/documents/3484130315%20Team%20Australia-Netherlands-UK%20SDGs%20Guiding%20Principles.pdf.

Autesserre, Séverine. 2014. *Peaceland: Conflict Resolution and the Everyday Politics of International Intervention.* Cambridge: Cambridge University Press.

Avant, Deborah D. 2016. Pragmatic Networks and Transnational Governance of Private Military and Security Services. *International Studies Quarterly* 60(2): 330–42.

Avant, Deborah D., Martha Finnemore and Susan K. Sell. 2010a. Who Governs the Globe? In *Who Governs the Globe?* edited by Deborah D. Avant, Martha Finnemore and Susan K. Sell, 1–32. Cambridge: Cambridge University Press.

eds. 2010b. *Who Governs the Globe?* Cambridge: Cambridge University Press.

Avant, Deborah and Oliver Westerwinter. 2016. Introduction: Networks and Transnational Security Governance. In *The New Power Politics*, edited by Deborah D. Avant and Oliver Westerwinter, 1–18. New York: Oxford University Press.

Ba, Alice D. and Matthew J. Hoffmann, eds. 2005. *Contending Perspectives on Global Governance: Coherence, Contestation and World Order.* London: Routledge.

Bäckstrand, Karin and Jonathan W. Kuyper. 2017. The Democratic Legitimacy of Orchestration: The UNFCCC, Non-state Actors, and Transnational Climate Governance. *Environmental Politics* 26(4): 764–88.

Baele, Stephane J., Thierry Balzacq and Philippe Bourbeau. 2018. Numbers in Global Security Governance. *European Journal of International Security* 3(1): 22–44.

Baker, Ted and Reed E. Nelson. 2005. Creating Something from Nothing: Resource Construction through Entrepreneurial Bricolage. *Administrative Science Quarterly* 50(3): 329–66.

Ball, Stephen J. 1998. Big Policies/Small World: An Introduction to International Perspectives in Education Policy. *Comparative Education* 34(2): 119–30.

Bangladesh. 2015. *Statement by Md. Mustafizur Rahman, Deputy Permanent Representative of Bangladesh to the UN*. 6th Session of the OWG, Human Rights, Right to Development and Global Governance, New York. December 12. Available from https://sustainabledevelopment.un.org/content/documents/5008bangladesh3.pdf.

Bargués, Pol. 2020. Peacebuilding without Peace? On How Pragmatism Complicates the Practice of International Intervention. *Review of International Studies* 46(2): 237–55.

Barnett, Michael N. 2018. Human Rights, Humanitarianism, and the Practices of Humanity. *International Theory* 10(3): 314–49.

Barnett, Michael N. and Raymond Duvall, eds. 2005. *Power in Global Governance*. Cambridge: Cambridge University Press.

Barnett, Michael N. and Martha Finnemore. 2004. *Rules for the World: International Organizations in Global Politics*. Ithaca, NY: Cornell University Press.

Barnett, Michael N., Jon Pevehouse and Kal Raustiala. 2022a. Introduction: Modes of Global Governance. In *Global Governance in a World of Change*, edited by Michael Barnett, Jon Pevehouse and Kal Raustiala, 1–47. Cambridge: Cambridge University Press.

eds. 2022b. *Global Governance in a World of Change*. Cambridge: Cambridge University Press.

Barrett, Scott. 2007. *Why Cooperate? The Incentive to Supply Global Public Goods*. Oxford: Oxford University Press.

Bartelson, Jens. 2009. *Visions of World Community*. Cambridge: Cambridge University Press.

Beitz, Charles R. 1979. *Political Theory and International Relations*. Princeton, NJ: Princeton University Press.

2009. *The Idea of Human Rights*. Oxford: Oxford University Press.

Béland, Daniel and Mitchell A. Orenstein. 2013. International Organizations as Policy Actors: An Ideational Approach. *Global Social Policy* 13(2): 125–43.

Benin. 2015. *Statement by H.E. Mr. Jean-Francis R. Zinsou, Ambassador Permanent Representative of Benin to the United Nations, Chair of the Global Coordination Bureau of LDCs.* Informal Meetings of the Plenary on Stocktaking in the Process of Intergovernmental Negotiations on the Post-2015 Development Agenda, 69th Session of UNGA, New York. 20 January. Available from https://sustainabledevelopment.un.org/content/documents/12418benin.pdf.

Bennett, Colin J. 1991. What Is Policy Convergence and What Causes It? *British Journal of Political Science* 21(2): 215–33.

Bernstein, Steven. 2001. *The Compromise of Liberal Environmentalism.* New York: Columbia University Press.

2011. Legitimacy in Intergovernmental and Non-State Global Governance. *Review of International Political Economy* 18(1): 17–51.

Bernstein, Steven and Hamish van der Ven. 2017. Best Practices in Global Governance. *Review of International Studies* 43(3): 534–56.

Best, Jacqueline. 2005. *The Limits of Transparency: Ambiguity and the History of International Finance.* Ithaca, NY: Cornell University Press.

2014. *Governing Failure: Provisional Expertise and the Transformation of Global Development Finance.* Cambridge: Cambridge University Press.

Best, Jacqueline and Alexandra Gheciu. 2014a. Theorizing the Public as Practices: Transformations of the Public in Historical Context. In *The Return of the Public in Global Governance*, edited by Jacqueline Best and Alexandra Gheciu, 15–44. Cambridge: Cambridge University Press.

eds. 2014b. *The Return of the Public in Global Governance.* Cambridge: Cambridge University Press.

Bexell, Magdalena. 2014. Global Governance, Legitimacy and (De) Legitimation. *Globalizations* 11(3): 289–99.

Bexell, Magadalena and Ulrika Mörth. 2010. Introduction: Partnerships, Democracy, and Governance. In *Democracy and Public-Private Partnerships in Global Governance*, edited by Magadalena Bexell and Ulrika Mörth, 3–23. Basingstoke: Palgrave Macmillan.

Bexell, Magdalena and Kristina Jönsson. 2021. *The Politics of the Sustainable Development Goals: Legitimacy, Responsibility, and Accountability.* New York: Routledge.

Beyond 2015. 2013. *Just Governance for the World We Need: A Critical Cornerstone for an Equitable and Human Rights-Centered Sustainable Development Agenda Post-2015.* Global Thematic Consultation on Governance and the Post-2015 Development Framework. Available from www.cesr.org/sites/default/files/Beyond%202015_Governance_position_paper.pdf.

Bhutan, Thailand and Vietnam. 2014. *Intervention by Vietnam on General Comments and Focus Area 1 (Poverty Eradication).* 11th session of the OWG. Available from https://sustainabledevelopment.un.org/content/documents/8962vietnam.pdf.

Bicchi, Federica. 2011. The EU as a Community of Practice: Foreign Policy Communications in the COREU Network. *Journal of European Public Policy* 18(8): 1115–32.

Billaud, Julie. 2015. Keepers of the Truth: Producing "Transparent" Documents for the Universal Periodic Review. In *Human Rights and the Universal Periodic Review: Rituals and Ritualism,* edited by Hilary Charlesworth and Emma Larking, 63–84. Cambridge: Cambridge University Press.

Bjola, Corneliu and Markus Kornprobst, eds. 2013. *Understanding International Diplomacy: Theory, Practice and Ethics.* London: Routledge.

Blavoukos, Spyros and Dimitris Bourantonis. 2011. *Chairing Multilateral Negotiations: The Case of the United Nations.* London: Routledge.

Blyth, Mark. 2002. *Great Transformations: Economic Ideas and Institutional Change in the Twentieth Century.* Cambridge: Cambridge University Press.

Bob, Clifford. 2010. Packing Heat: Pro-gun Groups and the Governance of Small Arms. In *Who Governs the Globe?* edited by Deborah D. Avant, Martha Finnemore and Susan K. Sell, 183–201. Cambridge: Cambridge University Press.

2012. *The Global Right Wing and the Clash of World Politics.* Cambridge: Cambridge University Press.

Bobbio, Norberto. 1996. *Left and Right: The Significance of a Political Distinction.* Chicago, IL: University of Chicago Press.

Bodansky, Daniel. 2012. What's in a Concept? Global Public Goods, International Law, and Legitimacy. *European Journal of International Law* 23(3): 651–68.

Bode, Ingvild and John Karlsrud. 2019. Implementation in Practice: The Use of Force to Protect Civilians in United Nations Peacekeeping. *European Journal of International Relations* 25(2): 458–85.

Boli, John and George M. Thomas, eds. 1999. *Constructing World Culture: International Nongovernmental Organizations since 1875.* Stanford, CA: Stanford University Press.

Bourantonis, Dimitris. 2005. *The History and Politics of UN Security Council Reform.* London: Routledge.

Bourbeau, Philippe. 2017. The Practice Approach in Global Politics. *Journal of Global Security Studies* 2(2): 170–82.

Brand, Ulrich. 2005. Order and Regulation: Global Governance as a Hegemonic Discourse of International Politics? *Review of International Political Economy* 12(1): 155–76.

Brassett, James and Eleni Tsingou. 2011. The Politics of Legitimate Global Governance. *Review of International Political Economy* 18(1): 1–16.

Brazil. 2015a. *Comments on the Post-2015 Agenda Declaration Discussion Draft Paper.* 2nd Session of the Intergovernmental Negotiations, New York. February 20. Available from https://sustainabledevelopment.un .org/content/documents/13055brazil2.pdf.

2015b. *Intervention of Brazil: General Comments and Political Declaration.* 6th Session of Intergovernmental Negotiations on the Post-2015 Development Agenda. June 22. Available from https:// sustainabledevelopment.un.org/content/documents/15568brazil.pdf.

Brazil and Nicaragua. 2014. *Statement by H.E. Ambassador Antonio de Aguiar Patriota Permanent Representative of Brazil to the United Nations.* 8th session of the OWG, Conflict Prevention, Post-Conflict Peacebuilding and the Promotion of Durable Peace, Rule of Law and Governance, New York. Available from https://sustainabledevelopment .un.org/content/documents/6520brazil.pdf.

Bremberg, Niklas. 2015. The European Union as Security Community-Building Institution: Venues, Networks and Co-operative Security Practices. *Journal of Common Market Studies* 53(3): 674–92.

Broome, André and Joel Quirk. 2015. Governing the World at a Distance: The Practice of Global Benchmarking. *Review of International Studies* 41(5): 819–41.

Broome, André and Leonard Seabrooke. 2012. Seeing like an International Organisation. *New Political Economy* 17(1): 1–16.

Brown, Garrett W., Gavin Yamey and Sarah Wamala, eds. 2014. *The Handbook of Global Health Policy.* Oxford: Wiley-Blackwell.

Browne, Stephen. 2017. *Sustainable Development Goals and UN Goal-Setting.* London: Routledge.

Buchanan, Allen and Robert O. Keohane. 2006. The Legitimacy of Global Governance Institutions. *Ethics & International Affairs* 20(4): 405–37.

Bueger, Christian. 2015. Making Things Known: Epistemic Practices, the United Nations, and the Translation of Piracy. *International Political Sociology* 9(1): 1–18.

Bueger, Christian and Frank Gadinger. 2014. *International Practice Theory.* 1st ed. Cham, Switzerland: Palgrave Macmillan.

Bull, Hedley. 1977. *The Anarchical Society: A Study of Order in World Politics.* London: Macmillan.

Bull, Hedley and Adam Watson, eds. 1984. *The Expansion of International Society*. Oxford: Clarendon Press.

Burkina Faso. 2012. *Discours de son excellence M. Blaise Compaoré, Président du Faso, à la Conférence des Nations Unies sur le Développement Durable (CNUDD): Rio+20*. Speech delivered by the Minister of Environment and Sustainable Development at the High-Level Round Table, Rio de Janeiro. June 20. Available from https://sustainabledevelopment.un.org/content/documents/16837burkinafaso.pdf.

Business and Industry Major Group. 2013. *Remarks by Dr. Louise Kantrow, Permanent Representative of the International Chamber of Commerce to the UN on behalf of the Global Business Alliance (GBA) for Post-2015*. 9th Session of the OWG Meeting with Major Groups and other Stakeholders, New York. March 5. Available from https://sdgs.un.org/sites/default/files/statements/7267GBA_Statement_NinthOWG_Annex.pdf.

Búzás, Zoltán I. and Erin R. Graham. 2020. Emergent Flexibility in Institutional Development: How International Rules Really Change. *International Studies Quarterly* 64(4): 821–33.

Caballero, Paula. 2019. The SDGs: Changing How Development Is Understood. *Global Policy* 10(S1): 138–40.

Campbell, John L. 2004. *Institutional Change and Globalization*. Princeton, NJ: Princeton University Press.

Canada. 2005. *Human Rights Peer Review Mechanism*. Non-paper version #2. July 6.

2008. *Standing Senate Committee on Human Rights. Canada and the United Nations Human Rights Council: A Time for Serious Re-evaluation*. 39th Parliament – 2nd Session, Ottawa. June. Available from https://publications.gc.ca/collections/collection_2011/sen/yc32–0/YC32–0-392-13-eng.pdf.

2015. *Statements for the Stocktaking Session*. 1st Session of the Intergovernmental Negotiations. 21 January. Available from https://sustainabledevelopment.un.org/content/documents/12412canada3.pdf.

Carayannis, Tatiana and Thomas G. Weiss. 2021. *The "Third" United Nations: How a Knowledge Ecology Helps the UN Think*. Oxford: Oxford University Press.

Carbone, Maurizio. 2007. Supporting or Resisting Global Public Goods? The Policy Dimension of a Contested Concept. *Global Governance* 13 (2): 179–98.

CARICOM. 2015a. *Statement by H.E. Mrs. Janine Coye-Felson, Amabassador, Deputy Permanent Representative of Belize to the UN on behalf of CARICOM*. Informal Meeting of the Plenary on the Process of Intergovernmental Negotiations on the Post-2015

Development Agenda, Pursuant to Resolution 69/244 and Decisions 69/ 550 and 69/555. February 17. Available from https:// sustainabledevelopment.un.org/content/documents/12857caricom.pdf.

2015b. *Statement by H.E. Mrs. Janine Coye Felson, Ambassador, Deputy Permanent Representative of Belize to the UN: "Integrating SDGs into the Post-2015 Development Agenda."* Informal Meeting of the Plenary on stocktaking in the process of intergovernmental negotiations on the post-2015 development agenda, pursuant to resolution 69/ 244 and decision 69/550. 20 January. Available from https://sustainable development.un.org/content/documents/12346Caricom%20Internvention %20on%20Integrating%20SDGs%20into%20the%20post-2015% 20development%20agenda.pdf.

Carpenter, R. Charli. 2010. Governing the Global Agenda: "Gatekeepers" and "Issue Adoption" in Transnational Advocacy Networks. In *Who Governs the Globe?*, edited by Deborah D. Avant, Martha Finnemore and Susan K. Sell, 202–37. Cambridge: Cambridge University Press.

Carstensen, Martin B. 2011. Paradigm Man vs. the Bricoleur: Bricolage as an Alternative Vision of Agency in Ideational Change. *European Political Science Review* 3(1): 147–67.

2016. Bricolage as an Analytical Lens in New Institutionalist Theory. In *Conceptualising Comparative Politics*, edited by Anthony Petros Spanakos and Francisco Panizza, 46–67. London: Routledge.

Center for Civilians in Conflict. 2019. *Joint Statement: 22 NGOs Call for Action to Strengthen the Protection of Civilians in Armed Conflict.* May. Available from https://civiliansinconflict.org/wp-content/uploads/ 2019/05/Joint-NGO-Statement-May-2019.pdf.

Center for U.N. Reform Education. 2005. Reform Forum Report – The Proposed Human Rights Council: Prospects and Obstacles. *U.N. Reform Watch* 3: September 22. New York: Center for U.N. Reform Education. Available from https://archive.globalpolicy.org/images/pdfs/ 0922panel.pdf.

Cerny, Philip G. 2010. *Rethinking World Politics: A Theory of Transnational Neopluralism.* New York: Oxford University Press.

Charlesworth, Hilary and Emma Larking. 2015. Introduction: The Regulatory Power of the Universal Periodic Review. In *Human Rights and the Universal Periodic Review: Rituals and Ritualism*, edited by Hilary Charlesworth and Emma Larking, 1–22. Cambridge: Cambridge University Press.

Chasek, Pamela S., Lynn M. Wagner, Faye Leone, Ana-Maria Lebada and Nathalie Risse. 2016. Getting to 2030: Negotiating the Post-2015 Sustainable Development Agenda. *Review of European, Comparative & International Environmental Law* 25(1): 5–14.

Chidyausiku, Boniface. 2006. *Will the Human Rights Council Do Better – Interview with Ambassador Boniface Chidyausiku*. By Someshwar Singh. New York: Global Policy Forum. Available from https://archive .globalpolicy.org/reform/topics/hrc/2006/0215better.htm.

Child Rights International Network. 2006. NGO Participation in HRC Intersessional Working Group Meetings. Available from https:// archive.crin.org/en/library/news-archive/ngo-participation-hrc-interses sional-working-group-meetings.html.

China. 2006. *Statement by H.E. Mr Yang Jiechi, Vice Minister of Foreign Affairs: Work in Cooperation for a New Chapter in the Cause of International Human Rights*. At the inaugural session of the U.N. Human Rights Council, Geneva. June 20. Available from www.fmprc .gov.cn/ce/cegv/eng/rqrd/thsm/t258933.htm.

2012. *Work Together to Write a New Chapter in Promoting Sustainable Development for Mankind: Statement by H.E. Wen Jiabao, Premier of the State Council of the People's Republic of China*. United Nations Conference on Sustainable Development, Rio+20, 1st Plenary Meeting, Rio de Janeiro. June 20. Available from https://sustainabledevelopment .un.org/content/documents/16694china.pdf.

2015. *Reflections on the Human Rights Council: The Way Forward*. By H.E. Ambassador Wu Hailong, Permanent Representative of China to the UN Office at Geneva. Universal Rights Group. July 22. Available from www.universal-rights.org/blog/reflections-on-the-human-rights-council-the-way-forward/.

2021. *Remarks by Ambassador Zhang Jun at Security Council VTC Open Debate on Protection of Civilians in Armed Conflict*. New York: Permanent Mission of the People's Republic of China to the UN. 25 May. Available from http://chnun.chinamission.org.cn/eng/hyyfy/ t1879241.htm.

China, Indonesia and Kazakhstan. 2013. *Statement by Mr. Akan Rakhmetullin Deputy Representative of the Republic of Kazakhstan*. 6th Session of the OWG, Needs of Countries in Special Situations, New York. December 9–13. Available from https://sustainabledevelopment .un.org/content/documents/4838kazakhstan2.pdf.

2014a. *Statement by Dr. Endah Murniningtyas, Deputy Minister for Natural Resources and Environment of the National Development Planning Agency of the Republic of Indonesia, on behalf of China, Indonesia and Kazakhstan*. 8th Meeting of the Open-Working Group on Sustainable Development Goals Promoting Equality, Including Social Equity, Gender Equality and Women's Empowerment, New York. February 3–7. Available from https://sustainabledevelopment.un .org/content/documents/6335indonesia2.pdf.

2014b. *Statement on Focus Area 15: "Means of Implementation/Global Partnership for Sustainable Development" and Focus Area 16: "Peaceful and Inclusive Societies, Rule of Law, and Capable Institutions."* 11th Session of the OWG, New York. 5–9 May. Available from https://sdgs.un .org/sites/default/files/statements/10057china5.pdf.

Chomsky, Noam. 2011. Future Global Hegemony and the US. New York: Global Policy Forum. August 26. Available from https://archive.global policy.org/challenges-to-the-us-empire/general-analysis-on-challenges-to-the-us-empire/50643-future-global-hegemony-and-the-us.html.

Christensen, Johan and Kutsal Yesilkagit. 2019. International Public Administrations: A Critique. *Journal of European Public Policy* 26(6): 946–61.

Civil Society Statement on the Protection of Civilians in Armed Conflict. 2021. Available from www.unocha.org/sites/unocha/files/Joint%20Civil %20Society%20Statement%20on%20POC_May%202021_Final.pdf.

Clark, Ian and Christian Reus-Smit. 2013. Liberal Internationalism, the Practice of Special Responsibilities and Evolving Politics of the Security Council. *International Politics* 50(1): 38–56.

Claude, Inis L. 1964. *Swords into Plowshares: The Problems and Progress of International Organization.* 3rd ed. New York: Random House.

Cleaver, Frances. 2012. *Development through Bricolage: Rethinking Institutions for Natural Resource Management.* London: Routledge.

Coate, Roger A. and Donald J. Puchala. 1990. Global Policies and the United Nations System: A Current Assessment. *Journal of Peace Research* 27(2): 127–40.

Coleman, William D. 2012. Governance and Global Public Policy. In *The Oxford Handbook of Governance*, edited by David Levi-Faur, 673–85. Oxford: Oxford University Press.

2019. Scales and Network Societies: The Expansion of Global Public Policy. In *The Oxford Handbook of Global Policy and Transnational Administration*, edited by Diane Stone and Kim Moloney, 223–39. Oxford: Oxford University Press.

Coleman, William D. and Anthony Perl. 1999. Internationalized Policy Environments and Policy Network Analysis. *Political Studies* 47(4): 691–709.

Commission on Global Governance. 1995. *Our Global Neighbourhood: The Report of the Commission on Global Governance.* Oxford: Oxford University Press.

Constantin, François. 2002. *Les biens publics mondiaux: un mythe légitimateur pour l'action collective?* Paris: L'Harmattan.

Cooley, Alexander. 2010. Outsourcing Authority: How Project Contracts Transform Global Governance Networks. In *Who Governs the Globe?*, edited by Deborah D. Avant, Martha Finnemore and Susan K. Sell, 238–65. Cambridge: Cambridge University Press.

Cooley, Alexander and Jack L. Snyder, eds. 2015. *Ranking the World: Grading States as a Tool of Global Governance.* Cambridge: Cambridge University Press.

Cooper, Andrew F. and John English. 2005. International Commissions and the Mind of Global Governance. In *International Commissions and the Power of Ideas*, edited by Ramesh Thakur, Andrew F. Cooper and John English, 1–26. New York: United Nations University Press.

Cooper, Andrew F. and Vincent Pouliot. 2015. How Much Is Global Governance Changing? The G20 as International Practice. *Cooperation and Conflict* 50(3): 334–50.

Cornut, Jérémie. 2015. To Be a Diplomat Abroad: Diplomatic Practice at Embassies. *Cooperation and Conflict* 50(3): 385–401.

2017. Diplomacy, Agency, and the Logic of Improvisation and Virtuosity in Practice. *European Journal of International Relations* 24(3): 712–36.

Cornut, Jérémie and Nicolas de Zamaróczy. 2021. How Can Documents Speak about Practices? Practice Tracing, the Wikileaks Cables, and Diplomatic Culture. *Cooperation and Conflict* 56(3): 328–45.

Costa-Buranelli, Filippo. 2015. "Do you Know What I Mean?" "Not exactly": English School, Global International Society and the Polysemy of Institutions. *Global Discourse* 5(3): 499–514.

Council Monitor. 2006. International Service for Human Rights. *Human Rights Council: Working Group to Develop the Modalities of the Universal Periodic Review (UPR).* Geneva. November 20–24. Available from http://olddoc.ishr.ch/hrm/council/wg/wg_reports/wg_upr_nov_2006.pdf.

Coussy, Jean. 2005. The Adventures of a Concept: Is Neo-Classical Theory Suitable for Defining Global Public Goods? *Review of International Political Economy* 12(1): 177–94.

Cowan, Jane K. 2013. Before Audit Culture: A Genealogy of International Oversight of Rights. In *The Gloss of Harmony: The Politics of Policy-Making in Multilateral Organisations*, edited by Birgit Müller, 103–33. London: Pluto Press.

2015. The Universal Periodic Review as a Public Audit Ritual: An Anthropological Perspective on Emerging Practices in the Global Governance of Human Rights. In *Human Rights and the Universal Periodic Review: Rituals and Ritualism*, edited by Hilary Charlesworth and Emma Larking, 42–62. Cambridge: Cambridge University Press.

Cowan, Jane K. and Julie Billaud. 2015. Between Learning and Schooling: The Politics of Human Rights Monitoring at the Universal Periodic Review. *Third World Quarterly* 36(6): 1175–90.

Cox, Robert W. 1981. Social Forces, States, and World Orders: Beyond International Relations Theory. *Millennium* 10(2): 126–55.

    1983. Gramsci, Hegemony and International Relations: An Essay in Method. *Millennium* 12(2): 162–75.

    1992. Multilateralism and World Order. *Review of International Studies* 18(2): 161–80.

    1997. Introduction. In *The New Realism: Perspectives on Multilateralism and World Order*, edited by Robert W. Cox, xv–xxx. Basingstoke: Macmillan Press.

Cox, Robert W. and Michael G. Schechter. 2002. *The Political Economy of a Plural World: Critical Reflections on Power, Morals and Civilization*. London: Routledge.

Cox, Robert W. and Timothy J. Sinclair. 1996. *Approaches to World Order*. Cambridge: Cambridge University Press.

Croatia. 2012. *Statement by H.E. Mr. Neven Mimica, Deputy Prime Minister for Home, Foreign and European Affairs, of the Republic of Croatia*. United Nations Conference on Sustainable Development, Rio +20, High-Level Round Table, Rio de Janeiro. June 22. Available from https://sustainabledevelopment.un.org/content/documents/16885croatia.pdf.

Cronin, Bruce and Ian Hurd, eds. 2008. *The UN Security Council and the Politics of International Authority*. London: Routledge.

De Burca, Grainne, Robert O. Keohane and Charles Sabel. 2012. New Modes of Pluralist Global Governance. *New York University Journal of International Law and Politics* 45: 723–86.

De Frouville, Olivier. 2011. Building a Universal System for the Protection of Human Rights. In *New Challenges for the UN Human Rights Machinery: What Future for the UN Treaty Body System and the Human Rights Council Procedures?*, edited by M. Cherif Bassiouni and William Schabas. Cambridge: Intersentia.

de la Vega, Constance and Tamara N. Lewis. 2011. Peer Review in the Mix: How the UPR Transforms Human Rights Discourse. In *New Challenges for the UN Human Rights Machinery: What Future for the UN Treaty Body System and the Human Rights Council Procedures?*, edited by M. Cherif Bassiouni and William A. Schabas, 353–86. Cambridge: Intersentia.

Deacon, Bob. 2007. *Global Social Policy and Governance*. London: Sage.

Death, Carl. 2015. Disrupting Global Governance: Protest at Environmental Conferences from 1972 to 2012. *Global Governance* 21(4): 579–98.

Deitelhoff, Nicole and Lisbeth Zimmermann. 2018. Things We Lost in the Fire: How Different Types of Contestation Affect the Robustness of International Norms. *International Studies Review* 22(1): 51–76.

della Porta, Donatella, Massimiliano Andretta, Lorenzo Mosca and Herbert Reiter. 2006. *Globalization from Below: Transnational Activists and Protest Networks.* Minneapolis, MN: University of Minnesota Press.

Denmark, Ireland and Norway. 2013. *Intervention on behalf of Denmark, Norway and Ireland by Ambassador Ib Petersen, Permanent Representative of Denmark to the UN.* 6th Session of the Open Working Group on Sustainable Development Goals Meeting on Human Rights, the Right to Development, Global Governance, New York. December 13. Available from https://sustainabledevelopment.un.org/content/documents/5333denmark.pdf.

Devin, Guillaume. 2013. *La gouvernance mondiale: Une perspective de sciences politiques.* Centre de droit comparé du travail et de la sécurité sociale, Université Montesquieu Bordeaux IV, Working Paper 2013/4.

Diehl, Paul F., ed. 2005. *The Politics of Global Governance: International Organizations in an Interdependent World.* 3rd ed. Boulder, CO: Lynne Rienner.

Dingwerth, Klaus. 2005. The Democratic Legitimacy of Public-Private Rule Making: What Can We Learn from the World Commission on Dams? *Global Governance* 11(1): 65–83.

Dingwerth, Klaus and Philipp Pattberg. 2006. Global Governance as a Perspective on World Politics. *Global Governance* 12(2): 185–203.

Dingwerth, Klaus, Henning Schmidtke and Tobias Weise. 2020. The Rise of Democratic Legitimation: Why International Organizations Speak the Language of Democracy. *European Journal of International Relations* 26(3): 714–41.

Dingwerth, Klaus, Antonia Witt, Ina Lehmann, Ellen Reichel and Tobias Weise. 2019a. International Organizations under Pressure: Introduction. In *International Organizations under Pressure: Legitimating Global Governance in Challenging Times,* edited by Klaus Dingwerth, Antonia Witt, Ina Lehmann, Ellen Reichel and Tobias Weise, 1–28. Oxford: Oxford University Press.

2019b. *International Organizations under Pressure: Legitimating Global Governance in Challenging Times.* Oxford: Oxford University Press.

Dobbin, Frank, Beth Simmons and Geoffrey Garrett. 2007. The Global Diffusion of Public Policies: Social Construction, Coercion, Competition, or Learning? *Annual Review of Sociology* 33(1): 449–72.

Dodds, Felix, David Donoghue and Jimena Leiva Roesch. 2016. *Negotiating the Sustainable Development Goals.* London: Routledge.

Doern, G. Bruce, Leslie A. Pal and Brian W. Tomlin. 1996. The Internationalization of Canadian Public Policy. In *Border Crossings: The Internationalization of Canadian Public Policy,* edited by G.

Bruce Doern, Leslie A. Pal and Brian W. Tomlin, 1–26. Oxford: Oxford University Press.

Donnelly, Jack. 1990. Global Policy Studies: A Skeptical View. *Journal of Peace Research* 27(2): 221–30.

dos Santos Cruz, Carlos Alberto, William R. Phillips and Salvator Cusimano. 2017. *Improving Security of United Nations Peacekeepers: We Need to Change the Way We Are Doing Business*. New York: United Nations. Available from https://peacekeeping.un.org/sites/default/files/improving_security_of_united_nations_peacekeepers_report.pdf.

Doyle, Michael W. 2012. Dialectics of a Global Constitution: The Struggle over the UN Charter. *European Journal of International Relations* 18 (4): 601–24.

Drezner, Daniel W., Henry Farrell and Abraham Newman, eds. 2021. *The Uses and Abuses of Weaponized Interdependence*. Washington, DC: Brookings Institution Press.

Duffield, Mark R. 2007. *Development, Security and Unending War: Governing the World of Peoples*. Cambridge: Polity.

Dunne, Timothy and Christian Reus-Smit, eds. 2017. *The Globalization of International Society*. Oxford: Oxford University Press.

Dutkiewicz, Piotr, Tom Casier and Jan Aart Scholte, eds. 2021. *Hegemony and World Order: Reimagining Power in Global Politics*. London: Routledge.

Dye, Thomas R. 1998. *Understanding Public Policy*. 9th ed. Upper Saddle River, NJ: Prentice Hall.

Eagleton-Pierce, Matthew. 2013. *Symbolic Power in the World Trade Organization*. Oxford: Oxford University Press.

Eccleston, Charles H. and Frederic March, eds. 2014. *Global Environmental Policy: Concepts, Principles, and Practice*. Boca Raton, FL: CRC Press.

Egypt. 2012. *Statement of the Delegation of Egypt before the General Debate of the General Assembly on Agenda Item 64: "Report of the Human Rights Council."* November 14.

  2015. *Statement*. 2nd Session of the Intergovernmental Negotiations, Comments on the Discussion Document for Declaration. Available from https://sustainabledevelopment.un.org/content/documents/13115egypt.pdf.

Eilstrup-Sangiovanni, Mette and Oliver Westerwinter. 2022. The Global Governance Complexity Cube: Varieties of Institutional Complexity in Global Governance. *The Review of International Organizations* 17(2): 233–62.

Elder, Mark and Simon Høiberg Olsen. 2019. The Design of Environmental Priorities in the SDGs. *Global Policy* 10(S1): 70–82.

Elster, Jon. 1998. Deliberation and Constitution Making. In *Deliberative Democracy*, edited by Jon Elster, 97–122. Cambridge: Cambridge University Press.

European Commission. 2014. *A Decent Life for All: From Vision to Collective Action*. COM(2014)335, Brussels. February 6. Available from https:// eur-lex.europa.eu/resource.html?uri=cellar:441ba0c0-eb02–11e3–8cd4–01 aa75ed71a1.0001.02/DOC_1&format=PDF.

European Union. 2007. *Council. Human Rights Council: Declaration by the Presidency on behalf of the EU on the Outcome of the Institution Building Process*. 11074/07 (Presse 147), Brussels. June 21. Available from https://ec.europa.eu/commission/presscorner/detail/en/PESC_07_49.

   2015a. *Statement*. 6th Session of the Intergovernmental Negotiations. June 22. Available from https://sustainabledevelopment .un.org/content/documents/14920eu.pdf.

   2015b. *Statement*. 2nd Session of the Intergovernmental Negotiations, General Statements. 19 January. Available from https://sustainabledevelop ment.un.org/content/documents/12414Commissioner%20Mimica%20-% 20EU%20intervention%20-%20Post2015%20Stocktaking%20Session %20-%201.pdf.

   2015c. *Statement Delivered by Mr. Gaspar Frontini, DG DEVCO – European Commission*. 7th Session of the Intergovernmental Negotiations, Session on the Declaration, New York. July 20. Available from https://sustainabledevelopment.un.org/content/docu ments/15748eu2.pdf.

Evans, Gareth. 2005. *Reforming the 60 Year Old*. Address by the President of the International Crisis Group to the UN Association of Sweden Dag Hammarskjold Centenary Conference, UN and Global Security, Stockholm, February 8. Available from www.gevans.org/speeches/ speech116.html.

   2013. Commission Diplomacy. In *The Oxford Handbook of Modern Diplomacy*, edited by Andrew F. Cooper, Jorge Heine and Ramesh Thakur, 278–302. Oxford: Oxford University Press.

Evans, Mark. 2019. International Policy Transfer: Between the Global and Sovereign and between the Global and Local. In *The Oxford Handbook of Global Policy and Transnational Administration*, edited by Diane Stone and Kim Moloney, 94–110. Oxford: Oxford University Press.

Falk, Richard A., Samuel S. Kim and Saul H. Mendlovitz, eds. 1991. *The United Nations and a Just World Order*. Boulder, CO: Westview Press.

Farias, Déborah B. L. 2019. Outlook for the "Developing Country" Category: A Paradox of Demise and Continuity. *Third World Quarterly* 40(4): 668–87.

Farrell, Henry and Abraham Newman. 2014. Domestic Institutions beyond the Nation-State: Charting the New Interdependence Approach. *World Politics* 66(2): 331–63.

2016. The New Interdependence Approach: Theoretical Development and Empirical Demonstration. *Review of International Political Economy* 23(5): 713–36.

Faude, Benjamin and Felix Große-Kreul. 2020. Let's Justify! How Regime Complexes Enhance the Normative Legitimacy of Global Governance. *International Studies Quarterly* 64(2): 431–39.

Fearon, James D. 1998. Deliberation as Discussion. In *Deliberative Democracy*, edited by Jon Elster, 44–68. Cambridge: Cambridge University Press.

Fehl, Caroline and Katja Freistein. 2020. Organising Global Stratification: How International Organisations (Re)Produce Inequalities in International Society. *Global Society* 34(3): 285–303.

Ferguson, James. 1990. *The Anti-politics Machine: "Development," Depoliticization, and Bureaucratic Power in Lesotho*. Cambridge: Cambridge University Press.

Ferroni, Marco and Ashoka Mody, eds. 2002. *International Public Goods: Incentives, Measurement, and Financing*. New York: Springer US.

Fieldhouse, D. K. 1999. *The West and the Third World: Trade, Colonialism, Dependence, and Development*. Oxford: Blackwell Publishers.

Finkelstein, Lawrence S. 1995. What Is Global Governance? *Global Governance* 1(3): 367–72.

Finnemore, Martha and Michelle Jurkovich. 2014. Getting a Seat at the Table: The Origins of Universal Participation and Modern Multilateral Conferences. *Global Governance* 20(3): 361–73.

Fioretos, Orfeo. 2022. Conclusion: Global Governance and Institutional Diversity. In *Global Governance in a World of Change*, edited by Michael Barnett, Jon Pevehouse and Kal Raustiala, 338–66. Cambridge: Cambridge University Press.

Fischer, Frank. 2003. *Reframing Public Policy: Discursive Politics and Deliberative Practices*. Oxford: Oxford University Press.

Fischer, Frank, Douglas Torgerson, Anna Durnová and Michael Orsini. 2015a. Introduction to Critical Policy Studies. In *Handbook of Critical Policy Studies*, edited by Frank Fischer, Douglas Torgerson, Anna Durnová and Michael Orsini, 1–24. Cheltenham: Edward Elgar.

eds. 2015b. *Handbook of Critical Policy Studies*. Cheltenham: Edward Elgar.

Fligstein, Neil and Doug McAdam. 2012. *A Theory of Fields*. New York: Oxford University Press.

Foley, Conor. 2017. *UN Peacekeeping Operations and the Protection of Civilians: Saving Succeeding Generations*. Cambridge: Cambridge University Press.

Forsythe, David P. 2017. *Human Rights in International Relations*. 4th ed. Cambridge: Cambridge University Press.

France, Germany and Switzerland. 2014. *Common Statement on Sustainable Consumption and Production, Including Chemicals and Waste in the Post-2015 Agenda*. 7th Session of the OWG, New York. 6–10 January. Available from https://sustainabledevelopment.un.org/content/docu ments/6555france2.pdf.

Freedman, Rosa. 2013. *The United Nations Human Rights Council: A Critique and Early Assessment*. New York: Routledge.

Freeman, Richard, Steven Griggs and Annette Boaz. 2011. The Practice of Policy Making. *Evidence & Policy* 7(2): 127–36.

Fukuda-Parr, Sakiko. 2014. Global Goals as a Policy Tool: Intended and Unintended Consequences. *Journal of Human Development and Capabilities* 15(2–3): 118–31.

2019. Keeping out Extreme Inequality from the SDG Agenda: The Politics of Indicators. *Global Policy* 10(S1): 61–69.

ed. 2017. *Millennium Development Goals: Ideas, Interests and Influence*. London: Routledge.

Fukuda-Parr, Sakiko and Desmond McNeill. 2019. Knowledge and Politics in Setting and Measuring the SDGs: Introduction to Special Issue. *Global Policy* 10(S1): 5–15.

Fukuda-Parr, Sakiko and Bhumika Muchhala. 2020. The Southern Origins of Sustainable Development Goals: Ideas, Actors, Aspirations. *World Development* 126: 1–11.

Fukuda-Parr, Sakiko, Alicia Ely Yamin and Joshua Greenstein. 2014. The Power of Numbers: A Critical Review of Millennium Development Goal Targets for Human Development and Human Rights. *Journal of Human Development and Capabilities* 15(2–3): 105–17.

G77 and China. 2013. *Statement by H.E. Mr. Peter Thomson, Ambassador, Permanent Representative of Fiji to the United Nations, Chairman of the G77*. 1st Session of the OWG, Opening Statements, New York. March 14. Available from https://sustainabledevelopment.un.org/con tent/documents/3426g77second.pdf.

2015a. *Statement by H.E. Ambassador Kingsley Mamabolo, Permanent Representative of the Republic of South Africa to the UN and Chairman of the G77*. 1st Session of the Intergovernmental Negotiations, General Statements. 20 January. Available from https://sustainabledevelopment .un.org/content/documents/123762group77.pdf.

2015b. *Statement by Mr. Thembela Ngculu, Counsellor for Sustainable Development, on the Relationship between the FfD and Post-2015 Processes (Global Partnership and Possible Key Deliverables).* 4th Session of the Intergovernmental Negotiations, New York. April 23. Available from https://sustainabledevelopment.un.org/content/docu ments/13946g77.pdf.

Gabel, Matthew and Simon Hix. 2002. Defining the EU Political Space: An Empirical Study of the European Elections Manifestos, 1979–1999. *Comparative Political Studies* 35(8): 934–64.

Gaer, Felice D. 2007. A Voice Not an Echo: Universal Periodic Review and the UN Treaty Body System. *Human Rights Law Review* 7(1): 109–39.

Gaus, Alexander. 2019. Transnational Policy Communities and Regulatory Networks as Global Administration. In *The Oxford Handbook of Global Policy and Transnational Administration*, edited by Diane Stone and Kim Moloney, 471–90. Oxford: Oxford University Press.

Gehring, Thomas and Thomas Dörfler. 2019. Constitutive Mechanisms of UN Security Council Practices: Precedent Pressure, Ratchet Effect, and Council Action Regarding Intrastate Conflicts. *Review of International Studies* 45(1): 120–40.

Germany. 2013. *Statement by H.E. Ambassador Dr. Petter Wittig, Permanent Representative of Germany to the United Nations.* 1st Session of the OWG, General Discussion. March 14. Available from https:// sustainabledevelopment.un.org/content/documents/3450germany.pdf.

2015a. *Statement. 2nd Session of the Intergovernmental Negotiations, Comments on the Elements Paper for Declaration Discussion*, New York. Available from https://sustainabledevelopment.un.org/content/ documents/12788germany.pdf.

2015b. *Statement on Preamble and Declaration by Dr. Ingolf Dietrich, Deputy Director General Post-2015, Federal Ministry of Economic Cooperation and Development.* 6th Session of the Intergovernmental Negotiations, New York. June 22–25. Available from https://sustaina bledevelopment.un.org/content/documents/14875germany2.pdf.

Gerrard, Christopher D., Marco A. Ferroni and Ashoka Mody, eds. 2001. *Global Public Policies and Programs: Implications for Financing and Evaluation. Proceedings from a World Bank Workshop.* Washington, DC: World Bank.

Ghanea, Nazila. 2008. From UN Commission on Human Rights to UN Human Rights Council: One Step Forwards or Two Steps Sideways? *International and Comparative Law Quarterly* 55(3): 695–705.

Gharekhan, Chinmaya R. 2007. *The Horseshoe Table: An Inside View of the UN Security Council.* New Delhi: Pearson Longman.

Gilardi, Fabrizio and Fabio Wasserfallen. 2019. The Politics of Policy Diffusion. *European Journal of Political Research* 58(4): 1245–56.

Gill, Stephen, ed. 1993. *Gramsci, Historical Materialism and International Relations*. Cambridge: Cambridge University Press.

Giossi Caverzasio, Sylvie. 2001. *Strengthening Protection in War: A Search for Professional Standards*. Geneva: International Committee of the Red Cross.

Glas, Aarie. 2017. Habits of Peace: Long-term Regional Cooperation in Southeast Asia. *European Journal of International Relations* 23(4): 833–56.

Goodin, Robert E., Martin Rein and Michael Moran. 2008. The Public and Its Policies. In *The Oxford Handbook of Public Policy*, edited by Robert E. Goodin, Michael Moran and Martin Rein, 3–36. Oxford: Oxford University Press.

Gordenker, Leon and Thomas G. Weiss. 1995. NGO Participation in the International Policy Process. *Third World Quarterly* 16(3): 543–56.

Gowan, Richard. 2019. The Security Council and the Protection of Civilians. In *Evolution of the Protection of Civilians in UN Peacekeeping*, edited by Lisa Sharland, 7–10: Australian Strategic Policy Institute.

Græger, Nina. 2016. European Security as Practice: EU–NATO Communities of Practice in the Making? *European Security* 25(4): 478–501.

Gray, Julia and Alex Baturo. 2021. Delegating Diplomacy: Rhetoric across Agents in the United Nations General Assembly. *International Review of Administrative Sciences* 87(4): 718–36.

Green, Jessica F. 2014. *Rethinking Private Authority: Agents and Entrepreneurs in Global Environmental Governance*. Princeton, NJ: Princeton University Press.

Greenhill, Brian and Yonatan Lupu. 2017. Clubs of Clubs: Fragmentation in the Network of Intergovernmental Organizations. *International Studies Quarterly* 61(1): 181–95.

Grigorescu, Alexandru. 2020. *The Ebb and Flow of Global Governance: Intergovernmentalism Versus Nongovernmentalism in World Politics*. Cambridge: Cambridge University Press.

Hajer, Maarten. 2003. Policy without Polity? Policy Analysis and the Institutional Void. *Policy Sciences* 36(2): 175–95.

Hale, Thomas, David Held and Kevin Young. 2013. *Gridlock: Why Global Cooperation Is Failing When We Need It Most*. Cambridge: Polity Press.

Hale, Thomas and David Held et al. 2017. *Beyond Gridlock*. Cambridge: Polity Press.

Hanrieder, Tine. 2014. Gradual Change in International Organisations: Agency Theory and Historical Institutionalism. *Politics* 34(4): 324–33.

2015a. *International Organization in Time: Fragmentation and Reform.* Oxford: Oxford University Press.

2015b. WHO Orchestrates? In *International Organizations as Orchestrators*, edited by Kenneth W. Abbott, Philipp Genschel, Duncan Snidal and Bernhard Zangl, 191–213. Cambridge: Cambridge University Press.

Hansen, Lene. 2006. *Security as Practice: Discourse Analysis and the Bosnian War.* London: Routledge.

Hanson, Kobena, Korbla P. Puplampu and Timothy M. Shaw, eds. 2017. *From Millennium Development Goals to Sustainable Development Goals: Rethinking African Development.* London: Routledge.

Haq, Mahbub ul. 1995. *Reflections on Human Development.* New York: Oxford University Press.

Haugevik, Kristin M. 2018. *Special Relationships in World Politics: Inter-State Friendship and Diplomacy after the Second World War.* London: Routledge.

Hazra, Somnath and Anindya Bhukta, eds. 2020. *Sustainable Development Goals: An Indian Perspective.* Cham: Springer.

Held, David. 1995. *Democracy and the Global Order: From the Modern State to Cosmopolitan Governance.* Stanford, CA: Stanford University Press.

Henke, Marina E. 2017. The Politics of Diplomacy: How the United States Builds Multilateral Military Coalitions. *International Studies Quarterly* 61(2): 410–24.

Hestermeyer, Holger. 2008. *Human Rights and the WTO: The Case of Patents and Access to Medicines.* Oxford: Oxford University Press.

Hewson, Martin and Timothy J. Sinclair, eds. 1999. *Approaches to Global Governance Theory.* Albany, NY: State University of New York Press.

Hickmann, Thomas, Oscar Widerberg, Markus Lederer and Philipp Pattberg. 2021. The United Nations Framework Convention on Climate Change Secretariat as an Orchestrator in Global Climate Policymaking. *International Review of Administrative Sciences* 87(1): 21–38.

High-level Independent Panel on United Nations Peace Operations. 2015. *Uniting our Strengths for Peace: Politics, Partnership and People.* June 16. Available from www.refworld.org/docid/558bb0134.html.

High-Level Panel of Eminent Persons on the Post-2015 Development Agenda. 2013. *A New Global Partnership: Eradicate Poverty and Transform Economies through Sustainable Development.* New York.

Available from www.post2015hlp.org/wp-content/uploads/2013/05/UN-Report.pdf.

Hofferberth, Matthias. 2015. Mapping the Meanings of Global Governance: A Conceptual Reconstruction of a Floating Signifier. *Millennium* 43(2): 598–617.

Hofferberth, Matthias and Daniel Lambach. 2020. "It's the End of the World as We Know It": World Politics in a Postgovernance World. *Global Governance* 26(4): 553–76.

Hoffmann, Matthew J. 2011. *Climate Governance at the Crossroads: Experimenting with a Global Response after Kyoto.* Oxford: Oxford University Press.

Hoffmann, Matthew and Alice D. Ba. 2005. Introduction: Coherence and Contestation. In *Contending Perspectives on Global Governance: Coherence, Contestation, and World Order,* edited by Matthew Hoffmann and Alice D. Ba, 1–12. London: Routledge.

Hofius, Maren. 2016. Community at the Border or the Boundaries of Community? The Case of EU Field Diplomats. *Review of International Studies* 42(5): 939–67.

Holt, Victoria, Glyn Taylor and Max Kelly. 2009. *Protecting Civilians in the Context of UN Peacekeeping Operations: Successes, Setbacks and Remaining Challenges.* New York: United Nations. Available from www.unocha.org/sites/dms/Documents/Protecting%20Civilians%20in%20the%20Context%20of%20UN%20Peacekeeping%20Operations.pdf.

Holthaus, Leonie and Jens Steffek. 2020. Ideologies of International Organisation: Exploring the Trading Zones between Theory and Practice. In *Theory as Ideology in International Relations: The Politics of Knowledge,* edited by Benjamin Martill and Sebastian Schindler, 187–208. London: Routledge.

Hooghe, Liesbet, Gary Marks and Carole J. Wilson. 2002. Does Left/Right Structure Party Positions on European Integration? *Comparative Political Studies* 35(8): 965–89.

Hopf, Ted. 2010. The Logic of Habit in International Relations. *European Journal of International Relations* 16(4): 539–61.

2018. Change in International Practices. *European Journal of International Relations* 24(3): 687–711.

Horner, Rory. 2020. Towards a New Paradigm of Global Development? Beyond the Limits of International Development. *Progress in Human Geography* 44(3): 415–36.

Howlett, Michael and M. Ramesh. 2002. The Policy Effects of Internationalization: A Subsystem Adjustment Analysis of Policy Change. *Journal of Comparative Policy Analysis* 4(1): 31–50.

Hulme, David. 2009. *The Millennium Development Goals (MDGs): A Short History of the World's Biggest Promise. Brooks World Poverty Institute (BWPI) Working Paper 100*. Manchester: University of Manchester.

Human Rights Watch. 2004. *UN: Credibility at Stake for Rights Commission*. New York: Global Policy Forum. March 10. Available from https://archive.globalpolicy.org/component/content/article/157-un/26893.html.

2006. 160 NGOs Identify Essential Elements of a U.N. Human Rights Council. 18 January. Available from www.hrw.org/news/2006/01/18/160-ngos-identify-essential-elements-un-human-rights-council.

2009. NGOs Urge Latin American and Caribbean States to Hold Competitive Elections for UN Rights Council. Human Rights Watch. March 25. Available from www.hrw.org/news/2009/03/25/ngos-urge-latin-american-and-caribbean-states-hold-competitive-elections-un-rights.

2010. *Curing the Selectivity Syndrome: The 2011 Review of the Human Rights Council*. June. Available from www.hrw.org/sites/default/files/reports/hrc0610webwcover.pdf.

Hurd, Ian. 1999. Legitimacy and Authority in International Politics. *International Organization* 53(2): 379–408.

2002. Legitimacy, Power, and the Symbolic Life of the UN Security Council. *Global Governance* 8: 35–51.

2019. Legitimacy and Contestation in Global Governance: Revisiting the Folk Theory of International Institutions. *The Review of International Organizations* 14(4): 717–29.

2020. The Case against International Cooperation. International Theory: 1–22.

Hurrell, Andrew. 2007. *On Global Order: Power, Values, and the Constitution of International Society*. Oxford: Oxford University Press.

Hurrell, Andrew and Sandeep Sengupta. 2012. Emerging Powers, North–South Relations and Global Climate Politics. *International Affairs* 88 (3): 463–84.

Ikenberry, G. John. 2001. *After Victory: Institutions, Strategic Restraint, and the Rebuilding of Order After Major Wars*. Princeton, NJ: Princeton University Press.

2018. The End of Liberal International Order? *International Affairs* 94(1): 7–23.

Independent Expert Advisory Group on a Data Revolution for Sustainable Development. 2014. *A World That Counts: Mobilising the Data Revolution for Sustainable Development*. New York: United Nations. November. Available from www.undatarevolution.org/wp-content/uploads/2014/11/A-World-That-Counts.pdf.

India. 2014. *Remarks by Ambassador Asoke K. Mukerji, Permanent Representative of India to the UN.* 10th Session of the OWG. March 31. Available from https://sustainabledevelopment.un.org/con tent/documents/7767india.pdf.

2015a. *Intervention by Mr. Amit Narang, Counsellor, Permanent Mission of India on Common but Differentiated Responsibilities.* 6th Session of Intergovernmental Negotiations on Post-2015 Development Agenda. June 23. Available from https://sustainabledevelopment.un .org/content/documents/15040india2.pdf.

2015b. *Intervention by Mr. Amit Narang, Counsellor, Permanent Mission of India on Global Partnership and North-South Divide.* 4th session of the Intergovernmental Negotiations, Relationship between FfD and Post-2015 Processes. April 23. Available from https:// sustainabledevelopment.un.org/content/documents/14024india3.pdf.

2016. *Statement by H.E. Mr. Ajit Kumar.* Ambassador and Permanent Representative of India to UN and other International Organizations on Behalf of LMG Countries at Human Rights Council 31st session, General Debate: Agenda Item 10 (Technical Assistance and Capacity Building). February 29–March 24.

India, Pakistan and Sri Lanka. 2014. *Remarks by H.E. Mr. Bhagwant Bishnoi, Deputy Permanent Representative of India to the United Nations on Behalf of India-Pakistan-Sri Lanka.* 7th Session of the OWG, Sustainable Consumption and Production and Climate Change, New York. 8 January. Available from https://sustainabledevelopment.un .org/content/documents/5768india2.pdf.

Inter-Agency Technical Support Team for the UNGA OWG. 2014. TST Issues Briefs. New York. October. Available from https:// sustainabledevelopment.un.org/content/documents/1554TST_compen dium_issues_briefs_rev1610.pdf.

International Chamber of Commerce. 2015. *Business Charter for Sustainable Development - Business Contributions to the UN Sustainable Development Goals.* Paris. September. Available from https://iccwbo.org/content/uploads/sites/3/2015/09/ICC-Business-Charter-for-Sustainable-Development-Business-contributions-to-the-UN-Sustainable-Development-Goals.pdf.

International Civil Aviation Organization (ICAO). 2006. *Convention on International Civil Aviation.* 7300/9. 9th ed. Available from www.icao .int/publications/pages/doc7300.aspx.

International Committee of the Red Cross (ICRC). 2005. *United Nations as Peacekeepers and Nation-Builder: Continuity and Change - What Lies ahead?*, Hiroshima. March 29. Available from www.icrc.org/en/doc/ resources/documents/statement/6bnadg.htm.

2010. *Peacekeeping Operations: ICRC Statement to the United Nations.* UNGA 65th session, Fourth Committee, New York. October 25. Available from www.icrc.org/en/doc/resources/documents/statement/united-nations-multinational-forces-statement-2010-10-26.htm.

2011. *Protection of Civilians: ICRC Statement to the UN Security Council – 2011.* New York. November 9. Available from www.icrc.org/en/doc/resources/documents/statement/2011-11-09-civilans-un-security-council.htm.

International Federation of Red Cross and Red Crescent Societies. 2013. *Feedback on the Report by the High-Level Panel of Eminent Persons on the Post-2015 Development Agenda.* Joint CSO Letter to the UN Secretary-General. July 22. Available from www.ifrc.org/PageFiles/126914/Joint%20CSO%20letter%20to%20UN%20Secretary-General.pdf.

International Institute for Sustainable Development. 2015. Summary of the UN Sustainable Development Summit: September 25–27, 2015. *Earth Negotiations Bulletin* 32(24): 1–18.

International Labour Organization (ILO). 1919. *ILO Constitution.* Available from www.ilo.org/dyn/normlex/en/f?p=1000:62:0::NO:62:P62_LIST_ENTRIE_ID:2453907:NO.

International Task Force on Global Public Goods (ITFGPG). 2006. *Meeting Global Challenges: International Cooperation in the National Interest.* Final report. Stockholm.

Italy. 2015. *Statement for General Discussion. Informal Meeting of the Plenary on the Process of Intergovernmental Negotiation in the post-2015 Development Agenda,* New York. February 17. Available from https://sustainabledevelopment.un.org/content/documents/12866italy.pdf.

Jabko, Nicolas. 2006. *Playing the Market: A Political Strategy for Uniting Europe, 1985–2005.* Ithaca, NY: Cornell University Press.

Jabko, Nicolas and Adam Sheingate. 2018. Practices of Dynamic Order. *Perspectives on Politics* 16(2): 312–27.

Jacobson, Harold K. 1979. *Networks of Interdependence: International Organizations and the Global Political System.* New York: Knopf.

Jaeger, Hans-Martin. 2010. UN Reform, Biopolitics, and Global Governmentality. *International Theory* 2(1): 50–86.

James, Paul and Céline Nahory. 2005. Theses Toward a Democratic Reform of the UN Security Council. New York: Global Policy Forum. July 13.

Japan. 2015. *Statement.* 7th Session of the Intergovernmental Negotiations, Statements on Declaration. July 20. Available from https://sustainabledevelopment.un.org/content/documents/15751Japan.pdf.

Jessop, Bob. 2010. Cultural Political Economy and Critical Policy Studies. *Critical Policy Studies* 3(3–4): 336–56.

Johnson, Tana. 2014. *Organizational Progeny: Why Governments Are Losing Control over the Proliferating Structures of Global Governance.* Oxford: Oxford University Press.

Johnstone, Ian. 2003. Security Council Deliberations: The Power of the Better Argument. *European Journal of International Law* 14(3): 437–80.

Joint Letter on the UN Human Rights Council. 2005. New York: Global Policy Forum.

Jolly, Richard. 2004. Global Development Goals: The United Nations Experience. *Journal of Human Development* 5(1): 69–95.

Jolly, Richard, Louis Emmerij and Thomas G. Weiss. 2009. *UN Ideas That Changed the World.* Bloomington, IN: Indiana University Press.

Jones, Debra. 2015. *Statement on "All Social and Economic Groups." Delivered on Behalf of Multiple NGOs at the 8th Session of the Intergovernmental Negotiations*, New York. July 28. Available from https://sustainabledevelopment.un.org/content/documents/16522Amendm ent%20by%20Debra%20Jones%20on%20behalf%20of%20multiple% 20NGOs%20of%20-%20all%20social%20and%20economic%20grou ps%20-.pdf.

Joseph, Sarah. 2013. *Blame It on the WTO: A Human Rights Critique.* Oxford: Oxford University Press.

Kalyanpur, Nikhil and Abraham Newman. 2017. Form over Function in Finance: International Institutional Design by Bricolage. *Review of International Political Economy* 24(3): 363–92.

Kamau, Macharia, Pamela S. Chasek and David O'Connor. 2018. *Transforming Multilateral Diplomacy: The Inside Story of the Sustainable Development Goals.* New York: Routledge.

Kanie, Norichika, Steven Bernstein, Frank Biermann and Peter M. Haas. 2017. Introduction: Global Governance through Goal Setting. In *Governing through Goals: Sustainable Development Goals as Governance Innovation*, edited by Norichika Kanie and Frank Biermann, 1–27. Cambridge, MA: The MIT Press.

Kanie, Norichika and Frank Biermann, eds. 2017. *Governing through Goals: Sustainable Development Goals as Governance Innovation.* Cambridge, MA: The MIT Press.

Kapto, Serge. 2019. Layers of Politics and Power Struggles in the SDG Indicators Process. *Global Policy* 10(S1): 134–6.

Kaul, Inge. 2019. Conceptualizing Global Public Policy: A Global Public Good Perspective. In *The Oxford Handbook of Global Policy and*

Transnational Administration, edited by Diane Stone and Kim Moloney, 257–73. Oxford: Oxford University Press.

Kaul, Inge, Pedro Conceição, Katell Le Goulven and Ronald U. Mendoza. 2003a. How to Improve the Provision of Global Public Goods. In *Providing Global Public Goods: Managing Globalization*, edited by Inge Kaul, Pedro Conceição, Katell Le Goulven and Ronald U. Mendoza, 21–58. Oxford: Oxford University Press.

2003b. Why Do Global Public Goods Matter Today? In *Providing Global Public Goods: Managing Globalization*, edited by Inge Kaul, Pedro Conceição, Katell Le Goulven and Ronald U. Mendoza, 2–20. Oxford: Oxford University Press.

eds. 2003c. *Providing Global Public Goods: Managing Globalization*. Oxford: Oxford University Press.

Kaul, Inge, Isabelle Grunberg and Marc Stern, eds. 1999. *Global Public Goods: International Cooperation in the 21st Century*. Oxford: Oxford University Press.

Kaul, Inge and Ronald U. Mendoza. 2003. Advancing the Concept of Public Goods. In *Providing Global Public Goods: Managing Globalization*, edited by Inge Kaul, Pedro Conceição, Katell Le Goulven and Ronald U. Mendoza, 78–111. Oxford: Oxford University Press.

Kauppi, Niilo and Mikael R. Madsen. 2014. Fields of Global Governance: How Transnational Power Elites Can Make Global Governance Intelligible. *International Political Sociology* 8(3): 324–30.

Keck, Margaret E. and Kathryn Sikkink. 1998. *Activists beyond Borders: Advocacy Networks in International Politics*. Ithaca, NY: Cornell University Press.

Kelley, Judith G. and Beth A. Simmons. 2015. Politics by Number: Indicators as Social Pressure in International Relations. *American Journal of Political Science* 59(1): 55–70.

Kennedy, David. 2008. The Mystery of Global Governance. *Ohio Northern University Law Review* 34(3): 827–60.

Kennedy, Paul M. 2006. *The Parliament of Man: The Past, Present, and Future of the United Nations*. New York: Random House.

Keohane, Robert O. 1984. *After Hegemony: Cooperation and Discord in the World Political Economy*. Princeton, NJ: Princeton University Press.

Keohane, Robert O. and Helen V. Milner, eds. 1996. *Internationalization and Domestic Politics*. Cambridge: Cambridge University Press.

Keohane, Robert O. and Joseph S. Nye. 1977. *Power and Interdependence: World Politics in Transition*. Boston, MA: Little, Brown.

1989. *Power and Interdependence*. 2nd ed. Glenview, IL: Scott, Foresman and Company.

Keohane, Robert O. and David G. Victor. 2011. The Regime Complex for Climate Change. *Perspectives on Politics* 9(1): 7–23.

Keukeleire, Stephan and Simon Schunz. 2015. Analysing Foreign Policy in a Context of Global Governance. In *Theorizing Foreign Policy in a Globalized World*, edited by Gunther Hellmann and Knud Erik Jørgensen, 58–80. Basingstoke: Palgrave Macmillan.

Kim, Jim Yong. 2015. *Ending Extreme Poverty by 2030: The Final Push*. Speech by World Bank Group President at the Center for Strategic and International Studies, Washington, DC. April 7. Available from https://openknowledge.worldbank.org/handle/10986/24307.

Kim, Rakhyun E. 2019. Is Global Governance Fragmented, Polycentric, or Complex? The State of the Art of the Network Approach. *International Studies Review* 22(4): 903–31.

Kimber, Leah Rachel. 2020. The Architecture of Exclusion at the United Nations: Analyzing the Inclusion of the Women's Group in the Negotiations of the Sendai Framework for Disaster Risk Reduction. PhD Dissertation, Université de Genève, Geneva. Available from https://archive-ouverte.unige.ch/unige:143590.

Kincheloe, Joe L. 2001. Describing the Bricolage: Conceptualizing a New Rigor in Qualitative Research. *Qualitative Inquiry* 7(6): 679–92.

Kingsbury, Benedict, Nico Krisch and Richard B. Stewart. 2005. The Emergence of Global Administrative Law. *Law and Contemporary Problems* 68(3–4): 15–61.

Klasen, Andreas, ed. 2020. *The Handbook of Global Trade Policy*. Oxford: Wiley-Blackwell.

Klassen, Thomas R., Denita Cepiku and T. J. Lah, eds. 2017. *The Routledge Handbook of Global Public Policy and Administration*. London: Routledge.

Knappe, Henrike. 2021. Representation as Practice: Agency and Relationality in Transnational Civil Society. *Journal of International Relations and Development* 24(2): 430–54.

Knight, W. Andy. 2013. US Hegemony. In *International Organization and Global Governance*, edited by Thomas G. Weiss and Rorden Wilkinson, 292–303. London: Routledge.

Knill, Christoph and Michael W. Bauer, eds. 2017. *Governance by International Public Administrations: Bureaucratic Influence and Global Public Policies*. London: Routledge.

Koenig-Archibugi, Mathias and Michael Zürn, eds. 2006. *New Modes of Governance in the Global System: Exploring Publicness, Delegation and Inclusiveness*. Basingstoke: Palgrave Macmillan.

Koinova, Maria, Maryam Zarnegar Deloffre, Frank Gadinger, Zeynep Sahin Mencutek, Jan Aart Scholte and Jens Steffek. 2021. It's Ordered Chaos:

What Really Makes Polycentrism Work. *International Studies Review* 23(4): 1988–2018.

König-Reis, Saionara. 2017. A Human Rights-Based Approach to the SDGs. *Dianova International*, August 22. Available from www.dianova.org/opinion/a-human-rights-based-approach-to-the-sdgs/.

Koppell, Jonathan G. S. 2010. *World Rule: Accountability, Legitimacy, and the Design of Global Governance*. Chicago, IL: University of Chicago Press.

Krebs, Ronald R. and Patrick Thaddeus Jackson. 2007. Twisting Tongues and Twisting Arms: The Power of Political Rhetoric. *European Journal of International Relations* 13(1): 35–66.

Kreuder-Sonnen, Christian. 2020. *Emergency Powers of International Organizations: Between Normalization and Containment*. Oxford: Oxford University Press.

Krisch, Nico. 2017. Liquid Authority in Global Governance. *International Theory* 9(2): 237–60.

Krisch, Nico and Benedict Kingsbury. 2006. Introduction: Global Governance and Global Administrative Law in the International Legal Order. *European Journal of International Law* 17(1): 1–13.

Kuo, Ming-Sung. 2019. Law-Space Nexus, Global Governance, and Global Administrative Law. In *The Oxford Handbook of Global Policy and Transnational Administration*, edited by Diane Stone and Kim Moloney, 328–45. Oxford: Oxford University Press.

Kupchan, Charles A. 2012. *No One's World: The West, the Rising Rest, and the Coming Global Turn*. New York: Oxford University Press.

Laatikainen, Katie V. 2017. Conceptualizing Groups in UN Multilateralism: The Diplomatic Practice of Group Politics. *The Hague Journal of Diplomacy* 12(2–3): 113–37.

Lake, David A. 2021. The Organizational Ecology of Global Governance. *European Journal of International Relations* 27(2): 345–68.

Lasswell, Harold. 1968. Policy Sciences. In *International Encyclopedia of the Social Sciences* edited by David L. Sills and Robert K. Merton. 1st ed. Vol. 12, 181–9. New York: Macmillan.

Lasswell, Harold D. and Abraham Kaplan. 1950. *Power and Society: A Framework for Political Inquiry*. New Haven, CT: Yale University Press.

Lauren, Paul G. 2007. "To Preserve and Build on Its Achievements and to Redress Its Shortcomings": The Journey from the Commission on Human Rights to the Human Rights Council. *Human Rights Quarterly* 29(2): 307–45.

Laurence, Marion. 2019. An "Impartial" Force? Normative Ambiguity and Practice Change in UN Peace Operations. *International Peacekeeping* 26(3): 256–80.

Laws, David and Maarten Hajer. 2006. Policy in Practice. In *The Oxford Handbook of Public Policy*, edited by Robert E. Goodin, Michael Moran and Martin Rein, 409–24. Oxford: Oxford University Press.

Leander, Anna. 2010. Practices (Re)producing Orders: Understanding the Role of Business in Global Security Governance. In *Business and Global Governance*, edited by Morten Ougaard and Anna Leander, 57–77. London: Routledge.

Leander, Anna and Tanja Aalberts. 2013. Introduction: The Co-Constitution of Legal Expertise and International Security. *Leiden Journal of International Law* 26(4): 783–92.

Lechner, Silviya and Mervyn Frost. 2018. *Practice Theory and International Relations*. Cambridge: Cambridge University Press.

Lederer, Markus and Philipp S. Müller, eds. 2005. *Criticizing Global Governance*. Basingstoke: Palgrave Macmillan.

Lerner, Patricia. 2012. *Sustainable Development Goals: New Global Goals to Be Agreed at Rio+20*. Amsterdam: Greenpeace International.

Lévi-Strauss, Claude. 1966 [1962]. *The Savage Mind*. London: Weidenfeld and Nicolson.

Lindblom, Charles E. 1959. The Science of "Muddling Through." *Public Administration Review* 19(2): 79–88.

    1980. *The Policy-Making Process*. 2nd ed. Englewood Cliffs, NJ: Prentice-Hall.

Lipsky, Michael. 1980. *Street-Level Bureaucracy: The Dilemmas of the Individual in Public Service*. New York: Russell Sage.

Littoz-Monnet, Annabelle, ed. 2017. *The Politics of Expertise in International Organizations: How International Bureaucracies Produce and Mobilize Knowledge*. London: Routledge.

Loconte, Joseph. 2005. *Reforming the Human Rights Agenda of the United Nations*. Washington, DC: The Heritage Foundation. Available from www.heritage.org/global-politics/report/reforming-the-human-rights-agenda-the-united-nations.

Long, David and Frances Woolley. 2009. Global Public Goods: Critique of a UN Discourse. *Global Governance* 15(1): 107–22.

Louis, Marieke and Lucile Maertens. 2021. *Why International Organizations Hate Politics: Depoliticizing the World*. London: Routledge.

Lu, Catherine. 2017. *Justice and Reconciliation in World Politics*. Cambridge: Cambridge University Press.

Lundgren, Magnus, Theresa Squatrito and Jonas Tallberg. 2018. Stability and Change in International Policy-Making: A Punctuated Equilibrium Approach. *Review of International Organizations* 13(4): 547–72.

Lynch, Colum. 2006. US Deflects Criticism of Commitment to UN: Priority of New Rights Council Questioned. New York: Global Policy Forum. 16 January. Available from https://archive.globalpolicy.org/reform/topics/hrc/2006/0116criticism.htm.

MacFarlane, S. Neil and Yuen Foong Khong. 2006. *Human Security and the UN: A Critical History*. Bloomington, IN: Indiana University Press.

Mahbubani, Kishore. 2013. *The Great Convergence: Asia, the West, and the Logic of One World*. New York: Public Affairs.

Malan, Mark and Charles T. Hunt. 2014. Between a Rock and a Hard Place: The UN and the Protection of Civilians in South Soudan. *ISS Paper* 275 (November): 1–23. Institute for Security Studies.

Malone, David, ed. 2004. *The UN Security Council: From the Cold War to the 21st Century*. Boulder, CO: Lynne Rienner.

Malone, David M. and Lotta Hagman. 2002. The North-South Divide at the United Nations: Fading at Last? *Security Dialogue* 33(4): 399–414.

March, James G. and Johan P. Olsen. 1998. The Institutional Dynamics of International Political Orders. *International Organization* 52(4): 943–69.

Margulis, Matias E. 2021. Intervention by International Organizations in Regime Complexes. *The Review of International Organizations* 16: 871–902.

Marks, Gary and Marco R. Steenbergen, eds. 2004. *European Integration and Political Conflict*. Cambridge: Cambridge University Press.

Marsh, David and J. C. Sharman. 2009. Policy Diffusion and Policy Transfer. *Policy Studies* 30(3): 269–88.

Martens, Kerstin. 2005. *NGOs and the United Nations: Institutionalization, Professionalization and Adaptation*. Basingstoke: Palgrave Macmillan.

Martin, Mary and Taylor Owen, eds. 2014. *Routledge Handbook of Human Security*. London: Routledge.

Maskus, Keith E. and Jerome H. Reichman, eds. 2005. *International Public Goods and Transfer of Technology under a Globalized Intellectual Property Regime*. Cambridge: Cambridge University Press.

Mattli, Walter and Ngaire Woods, eds. 2009. *The Politics of Global Regulation*. Princeton, NJ: Princeton University Press.

Mazower, Mark. 2009. *No Enchanted Palace: The End of Empire and the Ideological Origins of the United Nations*. Princeton, NJ: Princeton University Press.

2012. *Governing the World: The History of an Idea.* New York: The Penguin Press.

2014. Response. *International Studies Quarterly* 58(1): 219–20.

McNamara, Kathleen R. 1998. *The Currency of Ideas: Monetary Politics in the European Union.* Ithaca, NY: Cornell University Press.

2015. *The Politics of Everyday Europe: Constructing Authority in the European Union.* Oxford: Oxford University Press.

McNeill, Desmond. 2019. The Contested Discourse of Sustainable Agriculture. *Global Policy* 10(S1): 16–27.

Médecins Sans Frontières. 2016. *MSF International President to UN Security Council: "This Failure Reflects a Lack of Political Will."* Speech delivered by Dr Joanne Liu, International President. September 28. Available from www.msf.org/msf-international-president-un-security-council-failure-reflects-lack-political-will.

Mérand, Frédéric. 2008. *European Defence Policy: Beyond the Nation State.* Oxford: Oxford University Press.

Meuleman, Louis. 2019. *Metagovernance for Sustainability: A Framework for Implementing the Sustainable Development Goals.* New York: Routledge.

Miller, Sarah D. 2014. Lessons from the Global Public Policy Literature for the Study of Global Refugee Policy. *Journal of Refugee Studies* 27(4): 495–513.

Mitzen, Jennifer. 2013. *Power in Concert: The Nineteenth-century Origins of Global Governance.* Chicago, IL: The University of Chicago Press.

Moloney, Kim and Diane Stone. 2019. Beyond the State: Global Policy and Transnational Administration. *International Review of Public Policy* 1 (1): 104–18.

Moon, Suerie, John-Arne Røttingen and Julio Frenk. 2017. Global Public Goods for Health: Weaknesses and Opportunities in the Global Health System. *Health Economics, Policy and Law* 12(2): 195–205.

Morse, Julia C. and Robert O. Keohane. 2014. Contested Multilateralism. *The Review of International Organizations* 9(4): 385–412.

Moyn, Samuel. 2018. *Not Enough: Human Rights in an Unequal World.* Cambridge, MA: Harvard University Press.

Muchhala, Bhumika and Mitu Sengupta. 2014. A Déjà Vu Agenda or a Development Agenda? *Economic and Political Weekly* 49(46): 28–30.

Müller, Birgit, ed. 2013. *The Gloss of Harmony: The Politics of Policy Making in Multilateral Organisations.* London: Pluto.

Mundy, Karen. 2010. "Education for All" and the Global Governors. In *Who Governs the Globe?* edited by Deborah D. Avant, Martha Finnemore and Susan K. Sell, 333–55. Cambridge: Cambridge University Press.

Murdie, Amanda and David R. Davis. 2012. Looking in the Mirror: Comparing INGO Networks across Issue Areas. *Review of International Organizations* 7(2): 177–202.

Murphy, Craig N. 1994. *International Organization and Industrial Change: Global Governance since 1850*. Oxford: Oxford University Press.

2000. Global Governance: Poorly Done and Poorly Understood. *International Affairs* 76(4): 789–803.

Nagel, Stuart S., ed. 1991. *Global Policy Studies: International Interaction toward Improving Public Policy*. New York: St. Martin's Press.

Nair, Deepak. 2019. Saving Face in Diplomacy: A Political Sociology of Face-to-Face Interactions in the Association of Southeast Asian Nations. *European Journal of International Relations* 25(3): 672–97.

Nay, Olivier. 2012. How Do Policy Ideas Spread among International Administrations? Policy Entrepreneurs and Bureaucratic Influence in the UN Response to AIDS. *Journal of Public Policy* 32(1): 53–76.

2014. International Organisations and the Production of Hegemonic Knowledge: How the World Bank and the OECD Helped Invent the Fragile State Concept. *Third World Quarterly* 35(2): 210–31.

Nedeva, Gergana. 2006. The New Human Rights Council: Will the UN's Best Effort Be Good Enough? An Interview with Lawrence Moss. Center for UN Reform Education. Available from https://centerforunreform .org/2006/03/16/the-new-human-rights-council-will-the-uns-best-effort-be-good-enough-an-interview-with-lawrence-moss/.

NGO Committee on Financing for Development. 2013. *Statement by Celine Paramunda, Representative of Medical Mission Sisters, on behalf of the NGO Committee on Financing for Development – Finance and Trade Cluster*. 6th Session of the OWG, New York. December 13. Available from https://sustainabledevelopment.un.org/content/docu ments/4962ngocommittee.pdf.

NGO Major Group. 2013. *Statement*. 2nd Session of the OWG, New York. April 18. Available from https://sdgs.un.org/sites/default/files/state ments/3553ngo1.pdf.

2015. *Statement by Stefano Prato, Society for International Development: Talking Points for the May 20 Interactive Dialogue with Major Groups*. 5th Session of the Intergovernmental Negotiations, Major Groups. Available from https://sustainabledevelopment.un.org/content/docu ments/14440Society%20for%20International%20Development%20 (Major%20Group%20for%20NGOs).pdf.

Niederberger, Aurel. 2020. Independent Experts with Political Mandates: "Role Distance" in the Production of Political Knowledge. *European Journal of International Security* 5(3): 350–71.

Niemann, Holger. 2018. *The Justification of Responsibility in the UN Security Council: Practices of Normative Ordering in International Relations*. London: Routledge.

Noël, Alain and Jean-Philippe Thérien. 2023. Left and Right: The Significance of a Political Distinction. In *The Routledge Handbook of Ideology and International Relations*, edited by Jonathan L. Maynard and Mark L. Haas, 249-66. New York: Routledge.

2008. *Left and Right in Global Politics*. Cambridge: Cambridge University Press.

Nollkaemper, André. 2012. International Adjudication of Global Public Goods: The Intersection of Substance and Procedure. *European Journal of International Law* 23(3): 769–91.

Nonviolent Peaceforce. Unarmed Civilian Protection (UCP). Available from www.nonviolentpeaceforce.org/index.php?option=com_content& view=article&id=297&Itemid=522.

Normand, Roger and Sarah Zaidi. 2008. *Human Rights at the UN: The Political History of Universal Justice*. Bloomington, IN: Indiana University Press.

Nuñez-Mietz, Fernando G. 2016. Lawyering Compliance with International Law: Legal Advisers in the "War on Terror." *European Journal of International Security* 1(2): 215–38.

2018. *The Use of Force under International Law: Lawyerized States in a Legalized World*. London: Routledge.

O'Brien, Robert, Anne Marie Goetz, Jan Aart Scholte and Marc Williams. 2000. *Contesting Global Governance: Multilateral Economic Institutions and Global Social Movements*. Cambridge: Cambridge University Press.

O'Neill, Ryan. 2015. Blurred Lines, Shrunken Space? Offensive Peacekeepers, Networked Humanitarians and the Performance of Principle in the Democratic Republic of the Congo. In *The New Humanitarians in International Practice: Emerging Actors and Contested Principles*, edited by Zeynep Sezgin and Dennis Dijkzeul, 105–25. London: Routledge.

Oguz Gok, Gonca and Hakan Mehmetcik, eds. 2022. *The Crises of Legitimacy in Global Governance*. London: Routledge.

Ohanyan, Anna. 2015. On Networks, International Organizations, and Institutional Hegemony. *Journal of International Organizations Studies* 6(1): 4–27.

Open Letter to Member States of the Human Rights Council. 2009. June 11. Available from www.alhaq.org/advocacy/7204.html.

Orford, Anne. 2011. *International Authority and the Responsibility to Protect*. Cambridge: Cambridge University Press.

Orsini, Amandine, Philippe Le Prestre, Peter M. Haas, Malte Brosig, Philipp Pattberg, Oscar Widerberg, Laura Gomez-Mera, Jean-Frédéric Morin, Neil E. Harrison, Robert Geyer and David Chandler. 2019. Forum: Complex Systems and International Governance. *International Studies Review* 22(4): 1008–38.

Ottaway, Marina. 2001. Corporatism Goes Global: International Organizations, Nongovernmental Organization Networks, and Transnational Business. *Global Governance* 7(3): 265–92.

Ougaard, Morten and Anna Leander, eds. 2010. *Business and Global Governance*. London: Routledge.

Oxfam. 2011. UNSC's Efforts to Protect Civilians in Armed Conflict Inconsistent and at Times Biased. Available from www.oxfam.org/en/press-releases/unscs-efforts-protect-civilians-armed-conflict-inconsistent-and-times-biased.

    2014a. Conflict Transformation: Transforming Cultures of Violence to Overcome Injustice and Poverty. *Oxfam Humanitarian Policy Note*. Oxford. February. Available from https://oxfamilibrary.openrepository.com/bitstream/handle/10546/313320/hpn-conflict-transformation-240214-en.pdf;jsessionid=573A8368345A89C805D8FC2E512A8921?sequence=1.

    2014b. Making it Happen: Oxfam's Proposals for the Post-2015 Framework. *Oxfam Briefing Paper*, June 17. Available from https://oi-files-d8-prod.s3.eu-west-2.amazonaws.com/s3fs-public/file_attachments/bp187-making-happen-proposals-post-2015-framework-170614-en.pdf.

Pagani, Fabricio. 2002. Peer Review as a Tool for Co-Operation and Change: An Analysis of an OECD Working Method. *African Security Review* 11(4): 15–24.

Pahuja, Sundhya. 2011. *Decolonising International Law: Development, Economic Growth and the Politics of Universality*. Cambridge: Cambridge University Press.

Pakistan. 2017a. Permanent Mission to the UN and other IOs. *33 HRC Session, Human Rights, Item 10*. March 28.

    2017b. *Statement by H.E. Ms. Tehmina Janjua*. Permanent Representative to the United Nations Office at Geneva, United Nations Human Rights Office of the High Commissioner.

Pattberg, Philipp H. 2007. *Private Institutions and Global Governance: The New Politics of Environmental Sustainability*. Cheltenham: Edward Elgar.

Pauwelyn, Joost, Ramses A. Wessel and Jan Wouters. 2012. An Introduction to Informal International Lawmaking. In *Informal International Lawmaking*, edited by Joost Pauwelyn, Ramses Wessel and Jan Wouters, 1–10. Oxford: Oxford University Press.

Payne, Anthony. 2005. *The Global Politics of Unequal Development*. Basingstoke: Palgrave Macmillan.

Pedersen, Susan. 2015. *The Guardians: The League of Nations and the Crisis of Empire*. Oxford: Oxford University Press.

Peter, Mateja. 2019. UN Peace Operations: Adapting to a New Global Order? In *United Nations Peace Operations in a Changing Global Order*, edited by Cedric De Coning and Mateja Peter, 1–22. Cham: Palgrave MacMillan.

Petiteville, Franck. 2018. International Organizations beyond Depoliticized Governance. *Globalizations* 15(3): 301–13.

Petiteville, Franck and Andy Smith. 2006. Analyser les politiques publiques internationales. *Revue française de science politique* 56(3): 357–66.

Pillay, Navi. 2013. *Looking Back at History: Building the Post-2015 Agenda on the Foundation of Human Rights*. Keynote Remarks by United Nations High Commissioner for Human Rights at the 6th session of the Open Working Group on Sustainable Development Goals on "Human rights, the Right to Development, Global Governance," New York. December 13. Available from https://sustainabledevelopment.un.org/content/documents/4974Speech%20ASG%20for%20HC.pdf.

Pingeot, Lou. 2018. United Nations Peace Operations as International Practices: Revisiting the UN Mission's Armed Raids against Gangs in Haiti. *European Journal of International Security* 3(3): 364–81.

Poland and Romania. 2013. *Poverty Eradication: Talking Points. 2nd Session of the Open Working Group, Poverty Eradication*, New York. Available from https://sustainabledevelopment.un.org/content/documents/5870poland4.pdf.

Porto de Oliveira, Osmany. 2022. Global Public Policy Studies. *Policy & Politics* 50(1): 59–77.

Pouliot, Vincent. 2007. "Sobjectivism": Toward a Constructivist Methodology. *International Studies Quarterly* 51(2): 359–84.

2008. The Logic of Practicality: A Theory of Practice of Security Communities. *International Organization* 62(2): 257–88.

2013. Methodology: Putting Practice Theory into Practice. In *Bourdieu in International Relations: Rethinking Key Concepts in IR*, edited by Rebecca Adler-Nissen, 45–58. London: Routledge.

2014. Practice Tracing. In *Process Tracing: From Metaphor to Analytic Tool*, edited by Andrew Bennett and Jeffrey T. Checkel, 237–59. Cambridge: Cambridge University Press.

2016. *International Pecking Orders: The Politics and Practice of Multilateral Diplomacy*. Cambridge: Cambridge University Press.

2020. Historical Institutionalism Meets Practice Theory: Renewing the Selection Process of the United Nations Secretary-General. *International Organization* 74(4): 742–72.

2021. The Gray Area of Institutional Change: How the Security Council Transforms its Practices on the Fly. *Journal of Global Security Studies* 6 (3) ogaa043.

Pouliot, Vincent and Jean-Philippe Thérien. 2015. The Politics of Inclusion: Changing Patterns in the Global Governance of International Security. *Review of International Studies* 41(2): 211–37.

2018a. Global Governance in Practice. *Global Policy* 9(2): 163–72.

2018b. Global Governance: A Struggle over Universal Values. *International Studies Review* 20(1): 55–73.

Power, Samantha. 2014. *Remarks by Ambassador Samantha Power: Reforming Peacekeeping in a Time of Conflict*. Delivered at AEI on November 7. Available from www.aei.org/research-products/speech/remarks-ambassador-samantha-power-reforming-peacekeeping-time-conflict/.

Prantl, Jochen. 2006. *The UN Security Council and Informal Groups of States: Complementing or Competing for Governance?* Oxford: Oxford University Press.

Puchala, Donald J. 2005. World Hegemony and the United Nations. *International Studies Review* 7(4): 571–84.

Ramcharan, Bertrand G. 2011. *The UN Human Rights Council*. New York: Routledge.

2015. *The Law, Policy and Politics of the UN Human Rights Council*. Leiden: Brill Nijhoff.

2020. *A History of the UN Human Rights Programme and Secretariat*. Leiden: Brill Nijhoff.

Raustiala, Kal and David G. Victor. 2004. The Regime Complex for Plant Genetic Resources. *International Organization* 58(2): 277–309.

Raymond, Mark and Laura DeNardis. 2015. Multistakeholderism: Anatomy of an Inchoate Global Institution. *International Theory* 7(3): 572–616.

Recchia, Stefano. 2020. Overcoming Opposition at the UNSC: Regional Multilateralism as a Form of Collective Pressure. *Journal of Global Security Studies* 5(2): 265–81.

Reflection Group on the 2030 Agenda for Sustainable Development. 2016. *Spotlight on Sustainable Development*. New York: Coordinated by Global Policy Forum. Available from www.reflectiongroup.org/sites/default/files/contentpix/spotlight/pdfs/Agenda2030_engl_160708_WEB.pdf.

Reinalda, Bob and Bertjan Verbeek, eds. 2004. *Decision Making within International Organizations*. London: Routledge.

Reinicke, Wolfgang H. 1998. *Global Public Policy: Governing without Government?*. Washington, DC: Brookings Institution Press.

Reinicke, Wolfgang H., Francis Deng, Jan M. Witte, Thorsten Benner, Beth Whitaker and John Gershman. 2000. *Critical Choices: The United Nations, Networks, and the Future of Global Governance*. Ottawa: International Development Research Centre.

Reus-Smit, Christian. 1999. *The Moral Purpose of the State: Culture, Social Identity, and Institutional Rationality in International Relations*. Princeton, NJ: Princeton University Press.

2013. *Individual Rights and the Making of the International System*. Cambridge: Cambridge University Press.

2018. *On Cultural Diversity: International Theory in a World of Difference*. Cambridge: Cambridge University Press.

Rhoads, Emily Paddon and Jennifer Welsh. 2019. Close Cousins in Protection: The Evolution of Two Norms. *International Affairs* 95(3): 597–617.

Rizvi, Haider. 2005. UN: NGOs Seek Louder Voice in. July 29. New York: Global Policy Forum. Available from https://archive.globalpolicy.org/component/content/article/228-topics/32464.html.

Roger, Charles B. 2020. *The Origins of Informality: Why the Legal Foundations of Global Governance Are Shifting, and Why It Matters*. New York: Oxford University Press.

Ronit, Karsten. 2019. Organized Business and Global Public Policy: Administration, Participation, and Regulation. In *The Oxford Handbook of Global Policy and Transnational Administration*, edited by Diane Stone and Kim Moloney, 565–82. Oxford: Oxford University Press.

Rosenau, James N. 1995. Governance in the Twenty-First Century. *Global Governance* 1(1): 13–43.

1999. Toward an Ontology for Global Governance. In *Approaches to Global Governance Theory*, edited by Martin Hewson and Timothy J. Sinclair, 287–301. Albany, NY: State University of New York Press.

Rosenau, James N. and Ernst-Otto Czempiel, eds. 1992. *Governance without Government: Order and Change in World Politics*. Cambridge: Cambridge University Press.

Rotmann, Philipp, Gerrit Kurtz and Sarah Brockmeier. 2014. Major Powers and the Contested Evolution of a Responsibility to Protect. *Conflict, Security & Development* 14(4): 355–77.

Ruggie, John Gerard. 1982. International Regimes, Transactions, and Change: Embedded Liberalism in the Postwar Economic Order. *International Organization* 36(2): 379–415.

1998. What Makes the World Hang Together? Neo-Utilitarianism and the Social Constructivist Challenge. *International Organization* 52(4): 855–85.

2004. Reconstituting the Global Public Domain: Issues, Actors, and Practices. *European Journal of International Relations* 10(4): 499–531.

2010. Foreword. In *Global Governance and the UN: An Unfinished Journey*, edited by Thomas G. Weiss and Ramesh Thakur, xv–xx. Bloomington, IN: Indiana University Press.

Ruhlman, Molly A. 2015. *Who Participates in Global Governance: States, Bureaucracies, and NGOs in the United Nations*. London: Routledge.

Russett, Bruce M. and John R. Oneal. 2001. *Triangulating Peace: Democracy, Interdependence, and International Organizations*. New York: W.W. Norton & Company.

Sachs, Jeffrey. 2015. *The Age of Sustainable Development*. New York: Columbia University Press.

Sampson, Gary P. 2000. *Trade, Environment, and the WTO: The Post-Seattle Agenda*. Washington, DC: Overseas Development Council.

Satterthwaite, Margaret L. and Sukti Dhital. 2019. Measuring Access to Justice: Transformation and Technicality in SDG 16.3. *Global Policy* 10(S1): 96–109.

Save the Children. 2012. *Ending Poverty in Our Generation: Save the Children's Vision for a Post-2015 Framework*. London. Available from https://sustainabledevelopment.un.org/content/documents/777children .pdf.

Schaefer, Brett. 2006. The U.N. Human Rights Council Is not Enough: Time for a New Approach to Human Rights. The Heritage Foundation. Available from www.heritage.org/report/the-un-human-rights-council-not-enough-time-newapproach-human-rights.

Schia, Niels N. 2013. Being Part of the Parade: "Going Native" in the United Nations Security Council. PoLAR: *Political and Legal Anthropology Review* 36(1): 138–56.

Schimmelfennig, Frank. 2001. The Community Trap: Liberal Norms, Rhetorical Action, and the Eastern Enlargement of the European Union. *International Organization* 55(1): 47–80.

Schmidt, Vivien A. 2008. Discursive Institutionalism: The Explanatory Power of Ideas and Discourse. *Annual Review of Political Science* 11 (1): 303–26.

Schmidtke, Henning. 2019. Elite Legitimation and Delegitimation of International Organizations in the Media: Patterns and Explanations. *The Review of International Organizations* 14(4): 633–59.

Scholte, Jan Aart. 2002. Civil Society and Democracy in Global Governance. *Global Governance* 8(3): 281–304.

2005. *Globalization: A Critical Introduction.* 2nd ed. New York: Palgrave Macmillan.

2011a. Introduction. In *Building Global Democracy? Civil Society and Accountable Global Governance*, edited by Jan Aart Scholte, 1–7. Cambridge: Cambridge University Press.

ed. 2011b. *Building Global Democracy? Civil Society and Accountable Global Governance.* Cambridge: Cambridge University Press.

Scholte, Jan Aart and Fredrik Söderbaum. 2017. A Changing Global Development Agenda? *Forum for Development Studies* 44(1): 1–12.

Seabrooke, Leonard. 2006. *The Social Sources of Financial Power: Domestic Legitimacy and International Financial Orders.* Ithaca, NY: Cornell University Press.

2014. Identity Switching and Transnational Professionals. *International Political Sociology* 8(3): 335–7.

Seabrooke, Leonard and Ole Jacob Sending. 2020. Contracting Development: Managerialism and Consultants in Intergovernmental Organizations. *Review of International Political Economy* 27(4): 802–27.

Security Council Report. 2020. UN Security Council Working Methods: Arria-Formula Meetings. Available from www.securitycouncilreport .org/un-security-council-working-methods/arria-formula-meetings.php.

Sending, Ole Jacob. 2015. *The Politics of Expertise: Competing for Authority in Global Governance.* Ann Arbor, MI: University of Michigan Press.

Sending, Ole Jacob and Iver B. Neumann. 2006. Governance to Governmentality: Analyzing NGOs, States, and Power. *International Studies Quarterly* 50(3): 651–72.

2011. Banking on Power: How Some Practices in an International Organization Anchor Others. In *International Practices*, edited by Emanuel Adler and Vincent Pouliot, 231–54. Cambridge: Cambridge University Press.

Sending, Ole Jacob, Vincent Pouliot and Iver B. Neumann, eds. 2015. *Diplomacy and the Making of World Politics.* Cambridge: Cambridge University Press.

Sénit, Carole-Anne. 2020. Leaving No One behind? The Influence of Civil Society Participation on the Sustainable Development Goals. *Environment and Planning C: Politics and Space* 38(4): 693–712.

Shapiro, Martin. 2001. Administrative Law Unbounded: Reflections on Government and Governance. *Indiana Journal of Global Legal Studies* 8(2): 369–78.

Sharland, Lisa. 2018. How Peacekeeping Policy Gets Made: Navigating Intergovernmental Processes at the UN. *Providing for Peacekeeping* No. 18 (May). New York: International Peace Institute.

2019. Protection of Civilians in UN Peacekeeping: A Decade of Seeking Consensus. In *Special Report: Evolution of the Protection of Civilians in UN Peacekeeping*, edited by Lisa Sharland, 34–41. Barton: Australian Strategic Policy Institute.

Shore, Cris, Susan Wright and Davide Però, eds. 2011. *Policy Worlds: Anthropology and the Analysis of Contemporary Power*. New York: Berghahn Books.

Sievers, Loraine and Sam Daws. 2015. *The Procedure of the UN Security Council*. 4th ed. Oxford: Oxford University Press.

Sikkink, Kathryn. 2017. *Evidence for Hope: Making Human Rights Work in the 21st Century*. Princeton, NJ: Princeton University Press.

Sinclair, Timothy J. 2012. *Global Governance*. Cambridge: Polity Press.

Singh, J. P. 2017. *Sweet Talk: Paternalism and Collective Action in North-South Trade Relations*. Stanford, CA: Stanford University Press.

Slaughter, Anne-Marie. 1997. The Real New World Order. *Foreign Affairs* 76(5): 183–97.

2004. *A New World Order*. Princeton, NJ: Princeton University Press.

Smouts, Marie-Claude. 1998. The Proper Use of Governance in International Relations. *International Social Science Journal* 50(155): 81–9.

Soederberg, Susanne. 2006. *Global Governance in Question: Empire, Class, and the New Common Sense in Managing North-South Relations*. London: Pluto Press.

Sondarjee, Maïka. 2021a. Change and Stability at the World Bank: Inclusive Practices and Neoliberal Technocratic Rationality. *Third World Quarterly* 42(2): 348–65.

2021b. Collective Learning at the Boundaries of Communities of Practice: Inclusive Policymaking at the World Bank. *Global Society* 35(3): 307–26.

Soroos, Marvin S. 1986. *Beyond Sovereignty: The Challenge of Global Policy*. Columbia, SC: University of South Carolina Press.

1990. A Theoretical Framework for Global Policy Studies. *International Political Science Review* 11(3): 309–22.

Sri Lanka. 2013. *Statement by H.E. Dr. Palita Kohona, Permanent Representative of Sri Lanka to the United Nations*. 1st Meeting of the OWG, General Discussion, New York. March 15. Available from https://sustainabledevelopment.un.org/content/documents/3456sri%20lanka.pdf.

Srivastava, Swati. 2013. Assembling International Organizations. *Journal of International Organizations Studies* 4(Special Issue): 72–83.

Steffek, Jens. 2003. The Legitimation of International Governance: A Discourse Approach. *European Journal of International Relations* 9 (2): 249–75.

2006. *Embedded Liberalism and Its Critics: Justifying Global Governance in the American Century*. New York: Palgrave Macmillan.

2010. Public Accountability and the Public Sphere of International Governance. *Ethics & International Affairs* 24(1): 45–67.

2015. The Output Legitimacy of International Organizations and the Global Public Interest. *International Theory* 7(2): 263–93.

2021. *International Organization as Technocratic Utopia*. Oxford: Oxford University Press.

Steffek, Jens and Leonie Holthaus. 2018. The Social-Democratic Roots of Global Governance: Welfare Internationalism from the 19th Century to the United Nations. *European Journal of International Relations* 24(1): 106–29.

Steffek, Jens, Claudia Kissling and Patrizia Nanz, eds. 2008. *Civil Society Participation in European and Global Governance: A Cure for the Democratic Deficit?* Basingstoke: Palgrave Macmillan.

Steger, Manfred B. 2009. *Globalisms: The Great Ideological Struggle of the Twenty-First Century*. 3rd ed. Lanham, MD: Rowman & Littlefield.

Stone, Deborah A. 2012. *Policy Paradox: The Art of Political Decision Making*. 3rd ed. New York: W.W. Norton.

Stone, Diane. 2008. Global Public Policy, Transnational Policy Communities, and Their Networks. *Policy Studies Journal* 36(1): 19–38.

2019. Global Policy and Transnational Administration: Intellectual Currents in World Making. In *The Oxford Handbook of Global Policy and Transnational Administration*, edited by Diane Stone and Kim Moloney, 364–82. Oxford: Oxford University Press.

2020. *Making Global Policy*. Cambridge: Cambridge University Press.

Stone, Diane and Stella Ladi. 2015. Global Public Policy and Transnational Administration. *Public Administration* 93(4): 839–55.

Stone, Diane and Kim Moloney. 2019. The Rise of Global Policy and Transnational Administration. In *The Oxford Handbook of Global Policy and Transnational Administration*, edited by Diane Stone and Kim Moloney, 3–22. Oxford: Oxford University Press.

Stone, Randall W. 2011. *Controlling Institutions: International Organizations and the Global Economy*. Cambridge: Cambridge University Press.

Strange, Susan. 1987. The Persistent Myth of Lost Hegemony. *International Organization* 41(4): 551–74.

Stuenkel, Oliver. 2016. *Post-Western World: How Emerging Powers Are Remaking Global Order.* Cambridge: Polity Press.

Sustainable Development Solutions Network. 2013. *An Action Agenda for Sustainable Development: Report for the UN Secretary-General.* New York. June 6. Available from https://unstats.un.org/unsd/broaderpro gress/pdf/130613-SDSN-An-Action-Agenda-for-Sustainable-Development-FINAL.pdf.

Swidler, Ann. 2001. What Anchors Cultural Practices. In *The Practice Turn in Contemporary Theory*, edited by Karin Knorr-Cetina, Theodore R. Schatzki and Eike von Savigny, 83–101. London: Routledge.

Switzerland. 2006a. Federal Department of Foreign Affairs. *Switzerland Has Held a Seminar in Lausanne on the New UN Human Rights Council.* Berne. 15 May. Available from www.admin.ch/gov/en/start/documenta tion/media-releases.msg-id-5114.html.

2006b. Federal Department of Foreign Affairs. *Switzerland Organises a Third Seminar in Lausanne on the UN Human Rights Council.* Berne. August 28. Available from www.admin.ch/gov/en/start/documen tation/media-releases.msg-id-6842.html.

Tallberg, Jonas, Karin Backstrand and Jan Aart Scholte, eds. 2018. *Legitimacy in Global Governance: Sources, Processes, and Consequences.* Oxford: Oxford University Press.

Tallberg, Jonas, Thomas Sommerer, Theresa Squatrito and Christer Jönsson. 2013. *The Opening Up of International Organizations: Transnational Access in Global Governance.* Cambridge: Cambridge University Press.

Tallberg, Jonas and Michael Zürn. 2019. The Legitimacy and Legitimation of International Organizations: Introduction and Framework. *The Review of International Organizations* 14(4): 581–606.

Tao, Jill L. 2019. Transnational Administration from the Beginning: The Importance of Charisma in Shaping International Organizational Norms. In *The Oxford Handbook of Global Policy and Transnational Administration*, edited by Diane Stone and Kim Moloney, 419–36. Oxford: Oxford University Press.

Terlingen, Yvonne. 2007. The Human Rights Council: A New Era in UN Human Rights Work? *Ethics & International Affairs* 21(2): 167–78.

Thakur, Ramesh and Thomas G. Weiss. 2009. United Nations "Policy": An Argument with Three Illustrations. *International Studies Perspectives* 10(1): 18–35.

Thérien, Jean-Philippe. 1999. Beyond the North-South Divide: The Two Tales of World Poverty. *Third World Quarterly* 20(4): 723–42.

2012a. Human Security: The Making of a UN Ideology. *Global Society* 26 (2): 191–213.

2012b. The United Nations and Human Development: From Ideology to Global Policies. *Global Policy* 3(1): 1–12.

2015. The United Nations Ideology: From Ideas to Global Policies. *Journal of Political Ideologies* 20(3): 221–43.

Thérien, Jean-Philippe and Philippe Joly. 2014. "All Human Rights for All": The United Nations and Human Rights in the Post-Cold War Era. *Human Rights Quarterly* 36(2): 373–96.

Timossi, Adriano José. 2019. *Developing Country Coalitions in Multilateral Negotiations: Addressing Key Issues and Priorities of the Global South Agenda*. Research Paper 98, September. Geneva: South Centre.

Tistounet, Eric. 2020. *The UN Human Rights Council: A Practical Anatomy*. Cheltenham: Edward Elgar.

Towns, Ann E. 2012. Norms and Social Hierarchies: Understanding International Policy Diffusion "From Below." *International Organization* 66(2): 179–209.

UN Department of Economic and Social Affairs. 2010. *UN System Task Team on the Post-2015 UN Development Agenda: Membership*. New York: United Nations. Available from www.un.org/en/development/desa/policy/untaskteam_undf/untt_members.pdf.

2015. Statistics Division. *First Meeting of the Inter-Agency and Expert Group on the Sustainable Development Goal Indicators*. ESA/ST/AC.300/L3, New York: United Nations. June 24. Available from https://unstats.un.org/sdgs/files/First%20meeting%20IAEG-SDGs%20-%20June%202015%20-%20Meeting%20report%20-%2024%20June%202015.pdf.

2021. Statistics Division. *SDG Indicators: Global Indicator Framework for the Sustainable Development Goals and Targets of the 2030 Agenda for Sustainable Development*. New York: United Nations. Available from https://unstats.un.org/sdgs/indicators/indicators-list.

UN Department of Peace Operations. 2019. *Policy: The Protection of Civilians in United Nations Peacekeeping*. 2019.17, New York: United Nations. November 1. Available from https://peacekeeping.un.org/sites/default/files/poc_policy_2019_.pdf.

2020. *The Protection of Civilians in United Nations Peacekeeping: Handbook*. 2020.09, New York: United Nations. 1 May. Available from https://peacekeeping.un.org/sites/default/files/dpo_poc_handbook_final_as_printed.pdf.

UN Department of Peacekeeping Operations. 2002. *Guidelines for the Development of Rules of Engagement (ROE) for United Nations Peacekeeping Operations. MD/FGS/0220.001*, New York: United

Nations. May. Available from www.aaptc.asia/images/resourcess/9_RULES_OF_ENGAGEMENTS/120_ROE_Guidelines.pdf.

2010a. *DPKO/DFS Lessons Learned Note on the Protection of Civilians in UN Peacekeeping Operations: Dilemmas, Emerging Practices and Lessons.* New York: United Nations. Available from http://biblioteca.f59.com.br/documentos/100129%20%20DPKO-DFS%20POC%20Lessons%20Learned%20Note.pdf.

2010b. *Draft DPKO/DFS Operational Concept on the Protection of Civilians in United Nations Peacekeeping Operations.* New York: United Nations. Available from www.peacekeeping.org.uk/wp-content/uploads/2013/02/100129-DPKO-DFS-POC-Operational-Concept.pdf.

2015. *DPKO/DFS Policy: The Protection of Civilians in United Nations Peacekeeping.* 2015.07, New York: United Nations. April 1. Available from http://civilianprotection.rw/wp-content/uploads/2015/05/2015-07-Policy-on-PoC-in-Peacekeeping-Operations.pdf.

UN Economic and Social Council. 2017. Statistical Commission. *Report of the Inter-Agency and Expert Group on Sustainable Development Goal Indicators: Note by the Secretary-General.* E/CN.3/2017/2, New York: United Nations. March. Available from www.un.org/en/ga/search/view_doc.asp?symbol=E/CN.3/2017/2.

UN General Assembly. 1993. *Question of Equitable Representation on and Increase in the Membership of the Security Council: Report of the Secretary-General.* A/48/264, New York: United Nations. July 20. Available from https://digitallibrary.un.org/record/170875?ln=fr.

2000a. *Report of the Panel on United Nations Peace Operations.* A/55/305, New York: United Nations. August 21.

2000b. *United Nations Millennium Declaration.* A/RES/55/2, New York: United Nations. September 18.

2004. *A More Secure World: Our Shared Responsibility – Report of the High-level Panel on Threats, Challenges and Change.* A/59/565, New York: United Nations. December 2. Available from https://digitallibrary.un.org/record/536113?ln=fr.

2005a. *2005 World Summit Outcome.* A/RES/60/1, New York: United Nations. October 24. Available from https://digitallibrary.un.org/record/556636?ln=fr.

2005b. Special Committee on Peacekeeping Operations. *As Special Committee Concludes Debate, Troop Contributors Say Peacekeeping Burden Falls Disproportionately on Developing Countries.* GA/PK/184, New York: United Nations. February 1. Available from www.un.org/press/en/2005/gapk184.doc.htm.

2005c. *Human Rights Council: Explanatory Note by the Secretary-General.* A/59/2005/Add.1, New York: United Nations. May 23. Available from https://digitallibrary.un.org/record/550204.

2005d. *In Larger Freedom: Towards Development, Security and Human Rights for All - Report of the Secretary-General.* A/59/2005, New York: United Nations. March 21. Available from https://undocs.org/A/59/2005.

2005e. *Plan of Action Submitted by the United Nations High Commissioner for Human Rights, Louise Arbour.* A/59/2005/Add.3, New York: United Nations. May 26. Available from https://digitallibrary.un.org/record/551384?ln=fr.

2005f. *Security Council Reform.* A/59/L.64, New York: United Nations. July 6. Available from https://digitallibrary.un.org/record/552665?ln=fr.

2006a. *General Assembly Establishes New Human Rights Council by Vote of 170 in Favour to 4 Against, with 3 Abstentions.* GA/10449, New York: United Nations. March 15. Available from www.un.org/press/en/2006/ga10449.doc.htm.

2006b. *Human Rights Council.* A/RES/60/251, New York: United Nations. April 3. Available from https://digitallibrary.un.org/record/571575?ln=fr.

2007. *Although Different in Name, Human Rights Commission, Council the Same, Third Committee Told.* GA/SHC/3901, New York: United Nations. November 6. Available from www.un.org/press/en/2007/gashc3901.doc.htm.

2010a. *General Assembly Considers Annual Report of Human Rights Council.* GA/11018, New York: United Nations. November 3. Available from www.un.org/press/en/2010/ga11018.doc.htm.

2010b. *Keeping the Promise: United to Achieve the Millennium Development Goals.* A/RES/65/1, New York: United Nations. September 22. Available from www.un.org/ga/search/view_doc.asp?symbol=A%2FRES%2F65%2F1&Submit=Search&Lang=E.

2011a. *Establishment of the Office of the President of the Human Rights Council.* A/HRC/DEC/17/118, New York: United Nations. July 15. Available from https://digitallibrary.un.org/record/707201?ln=fr.

2011b. *Review of the Human Rights Council.* A/RES/65/281, New York: United Nations. July 20. Available from https://digitallibrary.un.org/record/707633?ln=fr.

2011c. *Review of the Work and Functioning of the Human Rights Council.* A/HRC/RES/16/21, New York: United Nations. April 12. Available from https://digitallibrary.un.org/record/702161?ln=fr.

2012. *The Future We Want*. A/RES/66/288, New York: United Nations. July 27. Available from www.un.org/ga/search/view_doc.asp?symbol= A%2FRES%2F66%2F288&Submit=Search&Lang=E.

2013a. *Cooperation with the United Nations, Its Representatives and Mechanisms in the Field of Human Rights*. A/HRC/RES/24/24, New York: United Nations. October 9. Available from https://digitallibrary .un.org/record/765469?ln=fr.

2013b. *Outcome Document of the Special Event to Follow Up Efforts Made towards Achieving the Millennium Development Goals*. A/68/ L.4, New York: United Nations. October 1. Available from https:// documents-dds-ny.un.org/doc/UNDOC/LTD/N13/490/97/pdf/ N1349097.pdf?OpenElement.

2014a. *Report of the Office of Internal Oversight Services: Evaluation of the Implementation and Results of Protection of Civilians Mandates in United Nations Peacekeeping Operations*. A/68/787, New York: United Nations. March 7.

2014b. *Report of the Open Working Group of the General Assembly on Sustainable Development Goals*. A/68/970, New York: United Nations. August 12. Available from www.un.org/ga/search/view_doc.asp? symbol=A%2F68%2F970&Submit=Search&Lang=E.

2015. *Transforming Our World: The 2030 Agenda for Sustainable Development*. A/RES/70/1, New York: United Nations, September 25. Available from www.un.org/ga/search/view_doc.asp?symbol=A% 2FRES%2F70%2F1&Submit=Search&Lang=E.

2016. Special Committee on Peacekeeping Operations. *Delegates Express Concern over Safety of Peacekeepers, Civilians amid Rising Targeted Attacks, as Special Committee Concludes General Debate*. GA/PK/225, New York: United Nations. February 17.

2018a. Special Committee on Peacekeeping Operations. *Peacekeeping Missions Need More Flexible Approach, Resources to Better Foresee, Tackle New Threats, Speakers Say as Special Committee Concludes General Debate*. GA/PK/232, New York: United Nations. February 13. Available from www.un.org/press/en/2018/gapk232.doc .htm.

2018b. *Report of the Special Committee on Peacekeeping Operations*. A/ 72/19, New York: United Nations. March 15.

2018c. *Statement by the President: Enhancing the Efficiency of the Human Rights Council, Including by Addressing Financial and Time Constraints*. A/HRC/PRST/OS/12/1, New York: United Nations. December 10. Available from https://undocs.org/A/HRC/PRST/OS/12/1.

2021. *Report of the Special Committee on Peacekeeping Operations*. A/ 75/19, New York: United Nations.

UN Human Rights Council. 2005. Draft text presented by the co-Chairs of the informal HRC negotiations: United Nations. December 19. Available from https://archive.globalpolicy.org/images/pdfs/1219text .pdf.

2006a. *Human Rights Council Concludes Third Session Largely Devoted to Organization of Future Work.* Geneva: United Nations. December 8. Available from https://reliefweb.int/report/lebanon/human-rights-coun cil-concludes-third-session-largely-devoted-organization-future-work.

2006b. *The Universal Periodic Review.* A/HRC/DEC/1/103, Geneva: United Nations. June 30.

2007a. *Human Rights Council Takes Up Situation of Human Rights in Cambodia, Haiti and Somalia.* New York: United Nations. June 12. Available from https://reliefweb.int/report/haiti/human-rights-council-takes-situation-human-rights-cambodia-haiti-and-somalia.

2007b. *Institution-building of the United Nations Human Rights Council.* A/HRC/RES/5/1, New York: United Nations. June 18 Available from www.refworld.org/docid/4ae9acbbd.html.

2008a. *Modalities and Practices for the Universal Periodic Review Process.* A/HRC/PRST/8/1, New York: United Nations. April 9. Available from https://ap.ohchr.org/documents/E/HRC/p_s/A_HRC_ PRST_8_1.pdf.

2008b. *Presidential Statement at the Opening of the Meeting for the Selection of the UPR Troikas.* A/HRC/OM/L.1, New York: United Nations. February 28. Available from www.upr-info.org/sites/default/ files/general-document/pdf/-a_hrc_om_l.1_president_statement_selec tion_of_troika_28.02.08.pdf.

2009. *Open-ended Intergovernmental Working Group on the Review of the Work and Functioning of the Human Rights Council.* A/HRC/RES/ 12/1, New York: United Nations. October 12. Available from https:// documents-dds-ny.un.org/doc/RESOLUTION/GEN/G09/165/22/PDF/ G0916522.pdf?OpenElement.

2011. *Report of the Open-ended Intergovernmental Working Group on the Review of the Work and Functioning of the Human Rights Council.* A/HRC/WG.8/2/1, New York: United Nations. May 4. Available from https://digitallibrary.un.org/record/707153?ln=fr.

2017. *Human Rights Council Concludes Debate on Human Rights Bodies and Mechanisms and Starts General Debate on Universal Periodic Review.* United Nations. September 22. Available from www.ohchr.org/EN/ NewsEvents/Pages/DisplayNews.aspx?NewsID=22141&LangID=E.

2021. *Human Rights Council Review: Informal Initiatives on the Council Review.* United Nations. July 12. Available from www.ohchr.org/EN/ HRBodies/HRC/Pages/InformalInitiatives.aspx.

UN Office for the Coordination of Humanitarian Affairs. 2011. *Framework for Drafting Comprehensive Protection of Civilians (POC): Strategies in UN Peacekeeping Operations.* New York: United Nations. Available from www.refworld.org/docid/523998464.html.

    2019. *Building a Culture of Protection: 20 Years of Security Council Engagement on the Protection of Civilians.* OCHA Policy and Studies Series 019: United Nations. May. Available from www.unocha.org/sites/unocha/files/Building%20a%20culture%20of%20protection.pdf.

UN Office of the High Commissioner for Human Rights. 2005a. *Commission on Human Rights Opens Sixty-First Session.* HR/CN/1107, Geneva: United Nations. March 14. Available from www.un.org/press/en/2005/hrcn1107.doc.htm.

    2005b. *Statement by Ms. Louise Arbour United Nations High Commissioner for Human Rights on the Closure of the 61st Session of the Commission on Human Rights.* Geneva: United Nations. April 22. Available from https://newsarchive.ohchr.org/EN/NewsEvents/Pages/DisplayNews.aspx?NewsID=5807&LangID=E.

    2006. *Statement by Louise Arbour: High Commissioner for Human Rights Urges Support for Human Rights Council.* Geneva: United Nations. February 23. Available from www2.ohchr.org/english/press/hrc/hrc-hc-english.pdf.

    2013a. *A Practical Guide for Civil Society: How to Follow Up on United Nations Human Rights Recommendations.* Geneva: United Nations. Available from www.ohchr.org/Documents/AboutUs/CivilSociety/HowtoFollowUNHRRecommendations.pdf.

    2013b. *Who Will Be Accountable? Human Rights and the Post-2015 Development Agenda: Summary.* HR/PUB/13/1/Add.1, Geneva: United Nations. Available from www.ohchr.org/Documents/Publications/WhoWillBeAccountable_summary_en.pdf.

    2014. *Addressing Inequalities in the SDGs: A Human Rights Imperative for Poverty Eradication. Statement by the High Commissioner Navanethem Pillay,* Geneva: United Nations. February 4. Available from www.ohchr.org/EN/NewsEvents/Pages/DisplayNews.aspx?NewsID=14529&LangID=E.

    2015. *Opening Statement to the 29th Session of the Human Rights Council by the High Commissioner for Human Rights.* Geneva: United Nations. June 15. Available from www.ohchr.org/EN/NewsEvents/Pages/DisplayNews.aspx?NewsID=16074&LangID=E.

    2017. *Human Rights Council Holds General Debate on Technical Assistance and Capacity Building.* Geneva. September 28. Available from www.ohchr.org/EN/NewsEvents/Pages/DisplayNews.aspx? NewsID=22177&LangID=E.

UN Open Working Group for Sustainable Development Goals. 2014a. *Focus Areas Documents*. New York: United Nations. Available from https://sustainabledevelopment.un.org/content/documents/ 3276focusareas.pdf

2014b. *Introduction to the Proposal of the Open Working Group for Sustainable Development Goals*. New York: United Nations. July 19. Available from https://sustainabledevelopment.un.org/content/docu ments/4518SDGs_FINAL_Proposal%20of%20OWG_19%20July% 20at%201320hrsver3.pdf.

UN Secretary-General. 2005. *Transcript of Press Conference by Secretary-General Kofi Annan at United Nations Headquarters*. SG/SM/9772, New York: United Nations. March 21. Available from www.un.org/ press/en/2005/sgsm9772.doc.htm.

2006. *Secretary-General Urges Human Rights Activists to "Fill Leadership Vacuum," Hold World Leaders to Account, in Address to International Day Event*. SG/SM/10788, New York: United Nations. December 8. Available from www.un.org/press/en/2006/sgsm10788.doc.htm.

2007. *Secretary-General Urges Human Rights Council to Take Responsibilities Seriously, Stresses Importance of Considering all Violations Equally*. SG/SM/11053-HRC/8, New York: United Nations. June 20. Available from www.un.org/press/en/2007/ sgsm11053.doc.htm.

2009. *Speech to the High-Level Segment of the 15th Non-Aligned Movement Summit*. Delivered by Secretary-General Ban Ki-moon, Sharm El Sheikh. July 15. Available from www.un.org/sg/en/content/ sg/speeches/2009-07-15/speech-high-level-segment-15th-non-aligned-movement-summit.

2012. *United Nations Secretary-General Announces New Sustainable Development Initiative*. United Nations Press Release, New York. August 9. Available from www.un.org/millenniumgoals/pdf/ SDSN%20FINAL%20release_9Aug.pdf.

2014. *The Road to Dignity by 2030: Ending Poverty, Transforming All Lives and Protecting the Planet*. Synthesis report of the Secretary-General on the post-2015 sustainable development agenda, A/69/700, New York: United Nations. December 4. Available from www.un.org/ ga/search/view_doc.asp?symbol=A/69/700&referer=/english/&Lang=E.

2016. *Secretary-General-designate António Guterres' Remarks to the General Assembly on Taking the Oath of Office*. December 12, New York: United Nations. Available from www.un.org/sg/en/content/sg/

speeches/2016-12-12/secretary-general-designate-ant%C3%B3nio-
guterres-oath-office-speech.

UN Security Council. 1998. *The Causes of Conflict and the Promotion of Durable Peace and Sustainable Development in Africa: Report of the United Nations Secretary-General to the Security Council.* S/1998/318, New York: United Nations. April 13.

1999a. *4046th Meeting of the UNSC.* S/PV.4046, New York: United Nations. September 16.

1999b. *Report of the Secretary-General to the Security Council on the Protection of Civilians in Armed Conflict.* S/1999/957, New York: United Nations. September 8.

1999c. *Resolution 1265.* S/RES/1265, New York: United Nations. September 17.

1999d. *Resolution 1270.* S/RES/1270, New York: United Nations. October 22.

1999e. *Statement by the President of the Security Council.* S/PRST/1999/6, New York: United Nations. February 12.

2000. *Resolution 1296.* S/RES/1296, New York: United Nations. April. 19

2002. *Statement by the President of the Security Council.* S/PRST/2002/6, New York: United Nations. March 15.

2005a. *5319th Meeting of the UNSC.* S/PV.5319(Resumption 1), New York: United Nations. December 9. Available from https://digitallibrary .un.org/record/562355?ln=en.

2005b. *Report of the Secretary-General to the Security Council on the Protection of Civilians in Armed Conflict.* S/2005/740, New York: United Nations. November 28. Available from https://digitallibrary.un .org/record/561816?ln=fr.

2006. *Resolution 1694.* S/RES/1694, New York: United Nations. July 13.

2008. *Resolution 1856.* S/RES/1856, New York: United Nations. December 22.

2009a. *6151st Meeting of the UNSC.* S/PV.6151, New York: United Nations. June 26.

2009b. *6216th Meeting of the UNSC.* S/PV.6216, New York: United Nations. November 11.

2009c. *Report of the Secretary-General on the Protection of Civilians in Armed Conflict.* S/2009/277, New York: United Nations. May 29.

2009d. *Resolution 1894.* S/RES/1894, New York: United Nations. November 11.

2010a. *6354th Meeting of the UNSC.* S/PV.6354, New York: United Nations. July 7.

2010b. *6427th Meeting of the UNSC.* S/PV.6427, New York: United Nations. November 22.

2011a. *6531st Meeting of the UNSC.* S/PV.6531, New York: United Nations. May 10.

2011b. *6650th Meeting of the UNSC.* S/PV.6650, New York: United Nations. November 9.

2012. *6790th Meeting of the UNSC.* S/PV.6790, New York: United Nations. June 25.

2013a. *6917th Meeting of the UNSC.* S/PV.6917, New York: United Nations. February 12.

2013b. *7019th Meeting of the UNSC.* S/PV.7019, New York: United Nations. August 19.

2013c. *Resolution 2098.* S/RES/2098, New York: United Nations. March 28.

2014a. *7109th Meeting of the UNSC.* S/PV.7109, New York: United Nations. February 12.

2014b. *Resolution 2155.* S/RES/2155, New York: United Nations. May 27.

2015a. *7374th Meeting of the UNSC.* S/PV.7374, New York: United Nations. January 30.

2015b. *Resolution 2222 of the UNSC.* New York: United Nations. May 27. Available from http://unscr.com/en/resolutions/doc/2222.

2015c. *Statement by the President of the Security Council.* S/PRST/2015/23, New York: United Nations. November 25.

2016a. *7606th Meeting of the UNSC.* S/PV.7606, New York: United Nations. January 19.

2016b. *7711th Meeting of the UNSC.* S/PV.7711, New York: United Nations. June 10.

2016c. *Resolution 2286 of the UNSC.* S/RES/2286, New York: United Nations. May 3. Available from https://digitallibrary.un.org/record/827916?ln=en.

2018a. *8264th Meeting of the UNSC.* S/PV.8264, New York: United Nations. May 22.

2018b. *8267th Meeting of the UNSC.* S/PV.8267, New York: United Nations. May 24.

2018c. *Resolution 2417 of the UNSC.* S/RES/2417, New York: United Nations. May 24. Available from https://digitallibrary.un.org/record/1627380?ln=en.

2018d. *Statement by the President of the Security Council.* S/PRST/2018/18, New York: United Nations. September 21.

2019a. *8534th Meeting of the UNSC.* S/PV.8534, New York: United Nations. May 23.

2019b. *Protection of Civilians in Armed Conflict: Report of the Secretary-General.* S/2019/373, New York: United Nations. May 7.

2019c. *Resolution 2475 of the UNSC.* S/RES/2475, New York: United Nations. June 20. Available from https://digitallibrary.un.org/record/3810148?ln=en.

2021. *Conflict-related Sexual Violence: Report of the Secretary-General.* S/2021/312, New York: United Nations. March 30. Available from https://undocs.org/en/S/2021/312.

UN Statistics Division. 2014. *Compendium of Statistical Notes for the Open Working Group on Sustainable Development Goals (OWG).* New York: United Nations. March. Available from https://sustainabledevelopment.un.org/content/documents/3647Compendium%20of%20statistical%20notes.pdf.

UN System Task Team on the Post-2015 UN Development Agenda. 2012. *Realizing the Future We Want for All: Report to the Secretary General.* New York: United Nations. June. Available from https://www.un.org/en/development/desa/policy/untaskteam_undf/untt_report.pdf.

2013a. *A Renewed Global Partnership for Development.* New York: United Nations. March. Available from www.un.org/en/development/desa/policy/untaskteam_undf/glob_dev_rep_2013.pdf.

2013b. *Statistics and Indicators for the Post-2015 Development Agenda.* New York: United Nations. March. Available from www.un.org/en/development/desa/policy/untaskteam_undf/UNTT_MonitoringReport_WEB.pdf.

Unger, Brigitte and Frans van Waarden, eds. 1995. *Convergence or Diversity? Internationalization and Economic Policy Response.* Aldershot: Avebury.

United Kingdom. 2015a. *Opening Statement and Declaration.* 2nd Session of the Intergovernmental Negotiations. Available from https://sustainabledevelopment.un.org/content/documents/14881uk.pdf.

2015b. *Statement.* 4th Session of the Intergovernmental Negotiations, Relationship between FfD and Post-2015 Outcomes, New York. Available from https://sustainabledevelopment.un.org/content/documents/13813uk.pdf.

United Nations. 2005a. *Commission on Human Rights Holds Informal Meeting on Secretary-General's Reform Proposals.* HR/CN/1110, New York. June 21. Available from www.un.org/press/en/2005/hrcn1110.doc.htm.

2005b. *Options Paper: Human Rights Council.* By Ambassadors Ricardo Alberto Arias and Dumisani S. Kumalo, co-chairs of the Informal Consultations of the Plenary on the Human Rights Council. November 3.

2006. *Daily Press Briefing by the Offices of the Spokesman for the Secretary-General and the Spokesperson for the General Assembly President.* New York. February 22. Available from www.un.org/press/en/2006/db060222.doc.htm.

2008. *Official List of MDG Indicators.* New York. January 15. Available from http://mdgs.un.org/unsd/mdg/Resources/Attach/Indicators/OfficialList2008.pdf.

2015a. *Addis Ababa Action Agenda of the Third International Conference on Financing for Development.* New York. July 13–16. Available from www.un.org/esa/ffd/wp-content/uploads/2015/08/AAAA_Outcome.pdf.

2015b. *Kigali Principles on the Protection of Civilians: Report of the High-Level International Conference on the Protection of Civilians.* May 28–29, Kigali.

2015c. *Terms of Reference for the High-level Group for Partnership, Coordination and Capacity-Building for Post-2015 Monitoring.* New York. Available from https://unstats.un.org/files/HLG%20-%20Terms%20of%20Reference%20(April%202015).pdf.

2017. *Cape Town Global Action Plan for Sustainable Development Data.* Prepared by the High-level Group for Partnership, Coordination and Capacity-Building for Statistics for the 2030 Agenda for Sustainable Development, Adopted by the UN Statistical Commission at its 48th Session, New York. March. Available from https://unstats.un.org/sdgs/hlg/Cape_Town_Global_Action_Plan_for_Sustainable_Development_Data.pdf.

United Nations Development Group (UNDG). 2013a. *The Global Conversation Begins: Emerging Views for a New Development Agenda.* New York: UNDG.

2013b. *A Million Voices: The World We Want.* New York: UNDG. Available from www.ohchr.org/Documents/Issues/MDGs/UNDGAMillionVoices.pdf.

United Nations Development Program (UNDP). 2013. *The Rise of the South: Human Progress in a Diverse World. Human Development Report.* New York: UNDP. Available from www.undp.org/publications/human-development-report-2013.

2014. *Building the Post-2015 Development Agenda.* New York: UNDP.

United States of America. 2006. Department of State. *Remarks on UN Reform, the Human Rights Council, and Other Issues.* By Ambassador John R. Bolton, U.S. permanent representative to the United Nations. Washington, DC. 25 January. Available from https://2001-2009.state.gov/p/io/rls/rm/59880.htm.

2011. Mission to the United Nations. *Explanation of Vote by John F. Sammis, Deputy Representative to the Economic and Social*

Council, in the General Assembly on the Human Rights Council Review. New York. June 17.

2012. Statement. United Nations Conference on Sustainable Development, Rio+20, High-Level Round Table, Rio de Janeiro. Available from https://sustainabledevelopment.un.org/content/docu ments/17521usa1.pdf.

2015. General/Political Declaration Statement. 7th Session of the Intergovernmental Negotiations. July 21. Available from https:// sustainabledevelopment.un.org/content/documents/16543usa5.pdf.

United States of America, Canada and Israel. 2013a. Remarks by Ambassador Elizabeth Cousens, US Representative to ECOSOC, for the US/Canada/Israel. 1st Session of the OWG, General Discussion, New York. March 15. Available from https://sustainabledevelopment .un.org/content/documents/7512us1.pdf.

2013b. Remarks by Ambassador Elizabeth Cousens, US Representative to ECOSOC, for the US/Canada/Israel Team. 2nd Session of the OWG, on a Proposal for SDGs, New York. April 17. Available from https:// sustainabledevelopment.un.org/content/documents/7522us3.pdf.

2013c. Remarks by Ambassador Elizabeth Cousens, US Representative to ECOSOC, for the US/Canada/Israel Team. 6th Session of the OWG on Human Rights, the Right to Development and Global Governance, New York. December 12. Available from https://sustainabledevelopment.un .org/content/documents/7557us10.pdf.

United States of America and Israel. 2014. Remarks by Ambassador David Roet, Israel Deputy Permanent Representative to the United Nations, for the US and Israel. 8th Session of the SDG Open Working Group on Promoting Equality, Including Social Equity, Gender Equality and Women's Empowerment, New York. February 6. Available from https://sustainabledevelopment.un.org/content/documents/7577us14 .pdf.

Universal Rights Group. 2019. Glion VI Human Rights Dialogue 2019: Towards 2026 –Perspectives on the Future of the Human Rights Council. Geneva: Universal Rights Group. Available from www.universal-rights .org/wp-content/uploads/2019/09/Glion-VI-page-by-page.pdf.

Unterhalter, Elaine. 2019. The Many Meanings of Quality Education: Politics of Targets and Indicators in SDG4. Global Policy 10(S1): 39–51.

Vabulas, Felicity and Duncan Snidal. 2013. Organization without Delegation: Informal Intergovernmental Organizations (IIGOs) and the Spectrum of Intergovernmental Arrangements. The Review of International Organizations 8(2): 193–220.

Verhaegen, Soetkin, Jan Aart Scholte and Jonas Tallberg. 2021. Explaining Elite Perceptions of Legitimacy in Global Governance. *European Journal of International Relations* 27(2): 622–50.

Viola, Lora Anne. 2020. *The Closure of the International System: How Institutions Create Political Equalities and Hierarchies.* Cambridge: Cambridge University Press.

Voeten, Erik. 2011. The Practice of Political Manipulation. In *International Practices*, edited by Emanuel Adler and Vincent Pouliot, 255–79. Cambridge: Cambridge University Press.

　2019. Making Sense of the Design of International Institutions. *Annual Review of Political Science* 22(1): 147–63.

　2021. *Ideology and International Institutions.* Princeton, NJ: Princeton University Press.

Volkmer, Ingrid. 2014. *The Global Public Sphere: Public Communication in the Age of Reflective Interdependence.* Cambridge: Polity.

von Einsiedel, Sebastian and David M. Malone. 2018. Security Council. In *The Oxford Handbook on the United Nations*, edited by Thomas G. Weiss and Sam Daws. 2nd ed., 140–61. Oxford: Oxford University Press.

Wallerstein, Immanuel Maurice. 1991. *Geopolitics and Geoculture: Essays on the Changing World-System.* Cambridge: Cambridge University Press.

Weaver, Catherine. 2008. *Hypocrisy Trap: The World Bank and the Poverty of Reform.* Princeton, NJ: Princeton University Press.

Weiss, Thomas G. 2000. Governance, Good Governance and Global Governance: Conceptual and Actual Challenges. *Third World Quarterly* 21(5): 795–814.

　2013. *Global Governance: What? Why? Whither?* Cambridge: Polity Press.

　2014. *Governing the World? Addressing "Problems without Passports."* London: Routledge.

　2018. *Would the World Be Better Without the UN?* Cambridge: Polity.

Weiss, Thomas G., Tatiana Carayannis and Richard Jolly. 2009. The "Third" United Nations. *Global Governance* 15(1): 123–42.

Weiss, Thomas G. and Sam Daws, eds. 2018. *The Oxford Handbook on the United Nations.* 2nd ed. Oxford: Oxford University Press.

Weiss, Thomas G. and Ramesh Thakur. 2010. *Global Governance and the UN: An Unfinished Journey.* Bloomington, IN: Indiana University Press.

Weiss, Thomas G. and Rorden Wilkinson. 2014. Rethinking Global Governance? Complexity, Authority, Power, Change. *International Studies Quarterly* 58(1): 207–15.

2018. The Globally Governed: Everyday Global Governance. *Global Governance* 24(2): 193–210.

2022. Making Sense of Global Governance Futures. In *Global Governance Futures*, edited by Thomas G. Weiss and Rorden Wilkinson, 1–19. London: Routledge.

Wessal, Arianne and Clay G. Wescott. 2019. Development Partnerships' Governance Structures, Accountability and Participation. In *The Oxford Handbook of Global Policy and Transnational Administration*, edited by Diane Stone and Kim Moloney, 529–46. Oxford: Oxford University Press.

Westerwinter, Oliver. 2021. Transnational Public-Private Governance Initiatives in World Politics: Introducing a New Dataset. *The Review of International Organizations* 16(1): 137–74.

Westerwinter, Oliver, Kenneth W. Abbott and Thomas Biersteker. 2021. Informal Governance in World Politics. *The Review of International Organizations* 16(1): 1–27.

Widerberg, Oscar and Philipp Pattberg. 2017. Accountability Challenges in the Transnational Regime Complex for Climate Change. *Review of Policy Research* 34(1): 68–87.

Widmaier, Wesley W. 2016. *Economic Ideas in Political Time: The Rise and Fall of Economic Orders from the Progressive Era to the Global Financial Crisis*. Cambridge: Cambridge University Press.

Wiener, Antje. 2014. *A Theory of Contestation*. New York: Springer.

Willetts, Peter. 2011. *Non-Governmental Organizations in World Politics: The Construction of Global Governance*. London: Routledge.

Willmot, Haidi, Ralph Mamiya, Scott Sheeran and Marc Weller, eds. 2016. *Protection of Civilians*. Oxford: Oxford University Press.

Willmot, Haidi and Scott Sheeran. 2013. The Protection of Civilians Mandate in UN Peacekeeping Operations: Reconciling Protection Concepts and Practices. *International Review of the Red Cross* 95 (891/892): 517–38.

Wiseman, Geoffrey. 2015. Diplomatic Practices at the United Nations. *Cooperation and Conflict* 50(3): 316–33.

Woods, Ngaire. 1999. Good Governance in International Organizations. *Global Governance* 5(1): 39–61.

World Bank. 2016. *Global Monitoring Report 2015/2016: Development Goals in an Era of Demographic Change*. Washington, DC.

World Peace Foundation. 2017. UNMISS Short Mission Brief. *African Politics, African Peace*: 1–14. Available from https://sites.tufts.edu/wpf/files/2017/07/South-Sudan-brief.pdf.

Wynn-Pope, Phoebe. 2013. *Evolution of Protection of Civilians in Armed Conflict: United Nations Security Council, Department of Peacekeeping*

Operations and the Humanitarian Community. Melbourne: Australian Civil Military Centre and Oxfam Australia.

Yamin, Alicia Ely. 2019. Power, Politics and Knowledge Claims: Sexual and Reproductive Health and Rights in the SDG Era. *Global Policy* 10(S1): 52–60.

Yanow, Dvora. 2015. Making Sense of Policy Practices: Interpretation and Meaning. In *Handbook of Critical Policy Studies*, edited by Frank Fischer, Douglas Torgerson, Anna Durnová and Michael Orsini, 401–21. Cheltenham: Edward Elgar.

Yates, JoAnne and Craig Murphy. 2019. *Engineering Rules: Global Standard Setting since 1880*. Baltimore, MA: Johns Hopkins University Press.

Yeates, Nicola, ed. 2014. *Understanding Global Social Policy*. 2nd ed. Bristol: Policy Press.

Yeates, Nicola and Chris Holden, eds. 2009. *The Global Social Policy Reader*. Bristol: Policy Press.

Yeboah, Nana. 2008. *The Establishment of the Human Rights Council. In Managing Change at the United Nations*, 79–95. New York: Center for UN Reform Education.

Young, Oran R. 2017. Conceptualization: Goal Setting as a Strategy for Earth System Governance. In *Governing through Goals: Sustainable Development Goals as Governance Innovation*, edited by Norichika Kanie and Frank Biermann, 31–51. Cambridge, MA: The MIT Press.

Zarakol, Ayşe, ed. 2017. *Hierarchies in World Politics*. Cambridge: Cambridge University Press.

Zürn, Michael. 2004. Global Governance and Legitimacy Problems. *Government and Opposition* 39(2): 260–87.

2012. Global Governance as Multi-Level Governance. In *The Oxford Handbook of Governance*, edited by David Levi-Faur, 730–44. Oxford: Oxford University Press.

2018. *A Theory of Global Governance: Authority, Legitimacy, and Contestation*. Oxford: Oxford University Press.

Zürn, Michael, Martin Binder and Matthias Ecker-Ehrhardt. 2012. International Authority and Its Politicization. *International Theory* 4 (1): 69–106.

Index

Note: Page references in **bold** denote tables.

Cambridge Studies in
International Relations